Women
and the
Use of Military Force

Women and the Use of Military Force

edited by

Ruth H. Howes
Michael R. Stevenson

Lynne Rienner Publishers • Boulder & London

Published in the United States of America in 1993 by
Lynne Rienner Publishers, Inc.
1800 30th Street, Boulder, Colorado 80301

and in the United Kingdom by
Lynne Rienner Publishers, Inc.
3 Henrietta Street, Covent Garden, London WC2E 8LU

Library of Congress Cataloging-in-Publication Data
Women and the use of military force / edited by Ruth H. Howes
    and Michael R. Stevenson
        p.   cm.
    Includes bibliographical references and index.
    ISBN 1-55587-329-4 (alk. paper)
    1. Women and the military. 2. Women and war. I. Howes, Ruth
(Ruth Hege) II. Stevenson, Michael R.
U21.75.W665   1993
355'.0082—dc20   92–46443
                                                                      CIP

British Cataloguing in Publication Data
A Cataloguing in Publication record for this book
is available from the British Library.

Printed and bound in the United States of America

The paper used in this publication meets the requirements
of the American National Standard for Permanence of
Paper for Printed Library Materials Z39.48–1984.

Contents

Acknowledgments

The editors wish to thank Dorothy Rudoni (Professor of Political Science, Emerita, Ball State University) for her role in initiating this project. The editors and the contributors are grateful for the support provided by Ball State University and the Midwest Consortium for International Security Studies (a program managed by the Midwest Center of the American Academy of Arts and Sciences and funded by the John D. and Catherine T. MacArthur Foundation). The editors wish to give special thanks to Marian Rice of the Academy for her role in this project.

The views, opinions, and findings contained in this book are those of the authors and do not necessarily reflect the views of the supporting organizations or the authors' employers or affiliations.

chapter 1

Overview

Michael R. Stevenson, Ruth H. Howes

No one who watched television coverage of the Gulf War can fail to be aware of the increasing role of women in the U.S. military. Although women are not formally permitted to be active in combat, they are contributing in almost every other capacity.

Some women have been punished for opposing the war. For example, Lisa Swanholm, who joined the army reserves when she was eighteen, came to question the morality of the war, refused to participate, and was sentenced to six months in prison for military desertion (Sisco, 1992). Swanholm's decision exemplifies a longstanding stereotype that women are inherently more peaceful (Tavris, 1991)—that they speak "in a different voice" that is more caring and connected to other people and the environment (Gilligan, 1982). If women and men are dramatically different in this respect, then increased participation of women in the military should lead to drastic changes in military policy and radical changes in the use of military force.

This volume grew from a series of workshops that were designed to bring together a multidisciplinary group of scholars representing diverse points of view to discuss the impact that women have or could have on the use of military force in the promotion of national security. Although initially focused on political theory and the extent to which women were represented in policymaking institutions, the project quickly expanded to include psychological and sociological perspectives on sex differences and social roles that provide a context for women's participation in the use of military force. In an attempt to predict the effects of increased participation of women, we document what is known about women and the use of force and their involvement in making and implementing national security policy.

The contributors to this volume represent a wide range of disciplines, including physics, psychology, sociology, philosophy, political science, and folklore. We write from diverse points of view based on such evidence as empirical research, interviews, and personal experience. We do not always agree on the answers to our questions. In fact, at times we disagree on how to frame the questions. However, we do agree that the impact of women on the use of military force can no longer be ignored.

The book is divided into three parts. The first provides a context, examining feminist perspectives, the gender gap in public opinion polls, women's impact in organizations, and the impact of stereotypical thinking on perceptions of women's use of force both in their homes and as part of their employment. Part 2 deals with data on the role women currently play in the use of force at a variety of levels, both as members of the military and as policymakers; and Part 3 offers a critical conclusion to the twelve central chapters.

Part 1

Scholarly views of the influence of women are strongly dependent on theoretical context. In Chapter 2, Carroll and Hall outline how feminist perspectives treat the question of women and the use of force and show that there is not one feminist or women's perspective. They describe a variety of feminist perspectives, including liberal feminism out of which the original question of women's impact on the use of military force grew. Some feminist perspectives see the use of force as legitimate, at least in some contexts; others do not. For example, radical feminism equates the use of military force with patriarchy, implying no legitimate role for armed struggle.

The strands of feminism that Carroll and Hall explore assume that gender is relevant, if not central, to discussions of military force. Other theoretical frameworks, outside of feminist theory, do not. For example, neorealism[1] is a perspective in international relations (Waltz, 1979) where issues of gender (as well as those of social structure, culture, and so on) are irrelevant to the use of force at the international level.

Waltz (1979) proposes a systemic theory of international politics, because he believes that the structure of the international system is the most important factor in explaining regularities over time. One could attempt to stretch Waltz's formulation and assert that issues of gender matter in that they affect the ability of a state to generate capabilities (e.g., the role of women in the work force). However, that would not be in keeping with the spirit of this theory, which strives to be completely concerned with the systemic level. Power (distribution of capabilities) is a system-level attribute. Gender is a unit-level attribute and is irrelevant for a neorealist. Gender is relevant at other levels of analysis, and this volume is an attempt to discuss contexts in which the concept of gender has value.

For example, Chapter 3 asks crucial questions concerning sex differences in attitudes toward the use of military force. Survey data from the political science literature indicate no gender difference in general approach to foreign policy but a widening gender gap in willingness to use military force to implement foreign policy. The evidence for this gap is compelling, even when race, party affiliation, or socioeconomic status is controlled. On the basis of existing research, it is clear that women are more reluctant than men to use force as an instrument of foreign policy and that this gap is beginning to influence views on such policy.

Although there is ample evidence that a gender gap exists, the causes are by no means clear. Theories of its origin include the presumption that women are more compassionate, the effect of the women's movement, the effects of socialization on women's attitudes, and the fact that women's attitudes are not well described on the survey instruments. Gallagher implies that the apparent sex differences may be attributable to a feminist-nonfeminist rather than a male-female dichotomy.

Carol Tavris's (1991) analysis provides further support for this position.

> One of the constructive impulses behind cultural feminism is the dream of a world that will be egalitarian, peaceful, and ecologically balanced. This dream, and visions of how to achieve it, rest on a belief in the most basic male-female dichotomy: that men are the warlike, dominating, planet-destroying sex, and women are the peacemaking, nonaggressive, planet-saving sex. . . . The trouble is that . . . there is no evidence that women are naturally more pacifistic, empathic, or earth-loving than men. They are just as likely to depersonalize enemies into vermin and beasts, to be carried away with patriotic fervor, and to justify brutality (pp. 97–98).

They also contribute to the construction of nuclear weapons (Chapter 8) and lead their countries into armed conflict (Chapter 11).

Tavris (1991), among others (e.g., Hunter, 1991), argues convincingly that stereotyped expectations about characteristic differences between men and women have no basis in individual biology. In contrast, Chapter 4 provides a structural perspective on the hypothesis that an influx of women into the U.S. military establishment might lead to political changes. The structural approach implies that women's attitudes about the use of force may differ from those of men because of their subordinate, less-powerful position in society, not because they are innately less aggressive or warlike.

In considering this viewpoint, Bystydzienski examines the influence of gender on small group and organizational behavior. Although small gender differences are apparent, women are typically found in low-level positions where they have little opportunity to direct others and to use force. The few who achieve high-level positions are likely to be selected for their counterstereotypical characteristics.

Using the experiences of women in Norway and Japan as examples, Bystydzienski discusses how women have changed politics and implies that commitment to a particular point of view may be more important than gender in successfully confronting the use of force. She argues that women as a group can make a significant difference in political agendas and governmental policies when they represent at least 15 percent of the total, have the support of well-organized women's groups that define pertinent issues, and bring those issues into the public realm. Under these conditions, female politicians are likely to support policies that are peaceful and oriented toward social human needs and that eschew the use of force.

In the past, weaponry of all sorts and guns in particular were primarily a male domain, but in the last five years, U.S. women have been purchasing guns in unprecedented numbers. The major gun manufacturers have begun targeting advertising toward women— advertising in which a handgun is treated as an elegant accessory or an essential tool in the service of motherhood and the protection of children! Chapter 5 examines the reasons American women are increasingly purchasing guns for use in defense of themselves and their homes. Although these data do not relate directly to military force, attitudes toward the use of handguns clearly relate to women's attitudes toward the use of the military in foreign policy.

Branscombe and Owen (Chapter 5) show that women who own a gun are seen as more masculine than women who do not and that women who do use force successfully are more likely to be penalized by observers than are women who do not do so. It is interesting to consider how women's increasing involvement in the military, as was the case in Desert Storm, may change some of these expectations.

It is also important to consider perceptions of women who use force as a part of their jobs. In Chapter 6, Carson defines force as the intent to cause pain or injury and argues that use of force is seen as legitimate in some contexts, as in policing. Indeed, women had been kept out of law enforcement because of the perception that they could not use force; their entrance into policing has frequently changed the way the organizations function (much as Bystydzienski implies in Chapter 4). However, women account for less than 10 percent of law enforcement officers in the United States. In comparison to men, they are less likely to use physical force and less likely to be cited for inappropriate behavior; although their strategies are different, they are equally effective. It is difficult to determine the extent to which the recent changes in policing organizations can be attributed to the influx of women.

Part 2

The second section of the book describes women's use of military force by documenting their role in the uniformed military, in the development of nuclear weapons, in the national security policy establishment, and in the peace movement. We examine the role recent female national leaders have played in the use of military force, as well as the role women have played in the Latin American guerrilla movements and the South African antiapartheid movement.

To introduce Part 2, Segal presents a summary of women's past and present participation in the U.S. military, including the roles they played in the Gulf conflict. In contrast to other authors, Segal does not expect that increased participation will change the way the military functions. She implies that the women and men who pursue military service are of like mind; this position is supported by a study comparing female and male West Point cadets (Adams, 1984). Chapter 7 also examines some current questions and some long-term issues raised by events in Grenada, Panama, and the Gulf. What will happen to women as military budgets shrink? Given that they were the last hired, will they be the first to be relieved of their duties? Do they perform their duties differently, as has been found of women in law enforcement (Chapter 6)?

In Chapter 8, Howes and Herzenberg document women's impact on weapons development by focusing on women's participation in the Manhattan Project (the effort that led to what was certainly the world's single most serious and devastating use of military force). Traditional accounts of the Manhattan Project imply that the development of nuclear weapons was conducted entirely by males and that women are inherently unable to deal with nuclear devices. History contradicts this perception. The roles of several women pursuing technical work are described in detail. Many joined to support the war effort, were recommended to the project by a faculty adviser, or followed a husband. It is evident from interviews with surviving participants (both male and female) and accounts left by those who have died that the women involved in the project made significant contributions to the development of atomic weaponry and were not unlike the men in their attitudes concerning the project. In contrast, empirical data on attitudes toward the threat of nuclear war show that women are more concerned about nuclear threat (Hamilton, Knox, Keilin, and Chavez, 1987).

In Chapter 9, Burwell and Reid Sarkees examine the role of women in formulating U.S. policy toward the use of military force. Initially the discussion centers on the process of foreign policy decisionmaking within the U.S. government by the Department of State and the Department of Defense. Data are presented on the numbers of women working in these departments and the positions they hold. Attitudes of women engaged in making defense policy are examined and found not to differ significantly from those of their male colleagues.

Clearly there are very few women engaged in formulating national security policy in the United States. The reasons for the absence of women at the highest levels of policymaking are discussed both in terms of traditional barriers to female advancement, such as the glass ceiling, and in terms of the difference between the use of force and other foreign policy decisions.

In contrast to the military establishment, women have traditionally figured prominently in peace movements. These movements have influenced government policy on a number of occasions—for example, during the negotiation of the Limited Test Ban Treaty in the early 1960s and the Nuclear Freeze Movement of the 1980s. Despite the prominence of female leaders in these movements, credit for the success of the movements has often gone to male leaders. Chapter 10 documents the leadership of women in the peace movement and their activity in the network of nongovernmental organizations that influence national security policy in the United States and elsewhere.

Although their numbers are limited, outside the United States several women, by virtue of their executive offices, have held the position of commander-in-chief of the armed forces of a nation. Chapter 11 documents the abilities and behavior of three of these women. Golda Meir served as prime minister of Israel during the

1973 Arab-Israeli war. The military decisions of Prime Minister Indira Gandhi of India during the war between West Pakistan and East Pakistan helped create the nation of Bangladesh. In Britain, Prime Minister Margaret Thatcher led her nation into war with Argentina during the Falklands crisis. The authors conclude that there are virtually no gender-related differences in military decisionmaking by chief executives.

Chapters 12 and 13 consider women and the use of force in Latin America and South Africa. Women in Latin America have fought in the revolutionary armies that overthrew the government of Nicaragua and engaged in armed conflict in El Salvador. Historically the roles of women in Latin American societies have been defined by cultures that cultivate machismo and idealize women as wives and mothers. Recent social changes have challenged this view. The roles of women in the revolutionary forces are motivated by this historical context and by the continuing struggle between a landed elite and the masses, as well as the forces of industrialization and urbanization. The strategies of the revolutionary movements in Latin America have made use of women's organizations along with the traditional female interest in social reform. Chapter 12 describes women's roles in revolutionary struggles and discusses what happens to women after they have used force.

In contrast, women have traditionally played a significant role in sociopolitical life throughout Africa. In the political realm, they have fought alongside men against colonialism and, in the case of South Africa, many have fought apartheid, repression, and oppression. Although their use of force has not been extensive, women in South Africa have occasionally resorted to force as an avenue of political protest. Chapter 13 traces the emergence of the use of force in the resistance movement in South Africa and the role women have played there. Morris suggests that violent and nonviolent protest are viewed differently, in that nonviolent protest is legitimate whereas violent protest is not, particularly for women. (It is interesting to consider the parallel between women's support of violent protest in South Africa and women's use of handguns to protect their homes, as described by Branscombe and Owen in Chapter 5. In both cases, women who step out of the stereotypical role get punished.)

Finally, in Chapter 14, we review what we have learned from this multidisciplinary and multiparadigmatic team of scholars. We find that in many ways there is a lack of consensus on whether the use of military force is legitimate and on the extent to which women's participation in the use of force has ethical ramifications. We agree that women are capable (probably just as capable) of using force when given the power and opportunity to do so, in spite of their somewhat less enthusiastic support for forceful solutions to threats to national security. Most important, however, we argue that an influx of women into the military establishment will have an impact only to the extent to which the women are in consensus on a particular point of view. In other words, if change in the system is deemed appropriate and advantageous, an individual's attitudes and political views may be more important than her or his gender.

Note

1. This analysis was provided by Stacy Bergstrom.

part 1
Theories, Concepts, and Attitudes

chapter 2

Feminist Perpsectives on Women and the Use of Force

Berenice Carroll, Barbara Welling Hall

All books on women, wrote Suzanne LaFollette, imply by their existence that women may be regarded as a class in society; that they have in common certain characteristics, conditions, or disabilities that, predominating over their individual variations, warrant grouping them on the basis of sex (LaFollette [1926], in Rossi, 1973, p. 542).

LaFollette's observation serves as a useful starting point to begin explorations on women and the use of force. The very title of this book—*Women and the Use of Military Force*—suggests that there is something distinct about women as a group that should inform our understanding of their collective relationship to the use of force. But the title reveals little else, because women still represent a great unknown (even to ourselves). That is, a reader in the socially constructed United States of the 1990s encountering a book titled *Men and the Use of Military Force* would "know" that that book examined how and why men use violence successfully or unsuccessfully to achieve personal, group, or national goals. The same reader encountering this book cannot know if the book is a defense of women using military force or an explanation for why women may not, cannot, or choose not to use it. The associations between gender and military force are prevalent, and yet full of confusion.

This uncertainty arises in part from the diversity of women's lives and of feminist perspectives. It is increasingly common to dispute LaFollette's formulation, that "women may be regarded as a class in society," and to emphasize instead differences by race, class, ethnicity, ability, sexual orientation, and sociohistorical context.

Moreover, the concept of "feminism" has always been elusive because of its unbounded scope. As a mass social movement with a long history and a complex political character, feminism through the centuries has engendered a host of responses compounding the problems of definition. As Sandra Harding (1991) points out:

> In some subcultures in the West and more extensively in the Second and Third Worlds, the term "feminist" is an epithet used against women who defend women's interests publicly or their own interests in more intimate settings. Sometimes it is used to place distance between the speaker and bourgeois, racist, Eurocentric, and heterosexist tendencies in feminism. And in the United States and elsewhere, one frequently finds women or men who insist that they are not feminists but who vigorously advocate agendas that are indistinguishable from those that have been advanced as specifically feminist. . . . Among feminists who claim the label, groups with varied and conflicting agendas compete to define what should be counted as feminism (p. 297).

Paradoxically, we also encounter today the phenomenon described by Susan Faludi in *Backlash* (1991, pp. 313–314, 319–321, 341) of women or men who insist that they *are* feminists while vigorously attacking feminism and advocating positions indistinguishable from those of declared antifeminists.

In this chapter we are dealing with *feminist* ideas, *not* all women's ideas on the issues. Though feminist perspectives would seem to be necessarily grounded in "women's experience," the relationships between "women's perspectives" or "female experience" and "feminist perspectives" are not simple (Harding, 1991, pp. 119–134, 298–299). As Carroll argues (1987), there is no inherent bond between "women" and "peace"; therefore, issues about gender and the use of force are based on ideology, theory, and political action, not on biologically determined or naturally immutable tendencies.

One way of dealing with these complexities has been to categorize varieties of feminism under ideological labels and to apply these labels to individual writers or groups—sometimes in ways that create opposition between them. This is not always salutary or illuminating, but it does convey a sense of the diversity of feminism while offering orderly "frameworks" to manage some of its complexities (see, for example, Jaggar and Rothenberg, 1984; Donovan, 1986; Tong, 1989).

The conventional categories of feminism usually include at least three main branches of the feminist movement: "mainstream" or liberal feminism, socialist and Marxist feminism, and radical feminism. Today we recognize many others, including African American or black feminism, Third World or "women of color" feminism, womanism, Jewish feminism, ecofeminism, anarchofeminism, cultural feminism, spiritualist feminism, lesbian feminism, pacifist feminism, postmodern feminism, and conservative feminism. Some of these terms are disputed and continue to be used either by choice or in the absence of a generally agreed-upon substitute (see, e.g., the discussion of "third world" in Mohanty, Torres and Russo, 1991, pp. ix–x, 5–7).

The complexities of and disputes about the principles of feminism are compounded by disputes about the nature and utility of *theory*. As Patricia Hill Collins notes, "most theories are characterized by internal instability, are contested, and are divided by competing emphases and interests" (1990, p. xiv). Feminist theory, now a major academic field, is certainly all of this, sometimes embraced with enthusiasm and sometimes viewed with suspicion by feminists.

The demand for theory may reflect an underlying assumption that women's lives and experience are not worthy of study in themselves (Carroll, 1976, pp. x–xi) or a diversion of energy from the "more pressing and interesting things to do," an intimidation and devaluing, a cooptation "into speaking a language . . . alien to and opposed to our needs and orientation" (Christian, 1988, p. 68). The charge has been made that feminist theory "addresses an audience of prestigious male academics and attempts to win its respect. . . . Mainly, feminist theorists excoriate their deviating sisters. . . . theory is a form of policing" (Baym, 1984, p. 45, quoted in Kramarae and Treichler, 1985, p. 448). The abstract, jargonistic language of theory "blocks communication, makes the general listener/reader feel bewildered and stupid" (Anzaldua, 1990, p. xxiii).

Yet theory is at the same time a strongly felt need in feminist practice (in and out of the academy) and an inescapable activity of the human mind. We have long felt the need for theory "as a guide to work in a field whose subject is full of paradoxes and does not conform to the patterns of [male] social experience with which historians [and other scholars] have mainly concerned themselves in the past" (Carroll, 1976, p. xii). Marilyn Frye argues that theory can provide us with a comprehensive vision of women's condition:

> Consider a birdcage. If you look closely at just one wire in the cage, you cannot see the other wires. If your conception of what is before you is determined by this myopic focus, you could look at that one wire, up and down the length of it, and be unable to see why a bird would not just fly around the wire any time it wanted to go somewhere (1983, pp. 4–5; also quoted in Kramarae and Treichler, 1985, p. 448).

It is theory, Frye suggests, that gives us a picture of "the whole cage."

Moreover, as Patricia Hill Collins emphasizes, "Theory and intellectual creativity are not the province of a select few but instead emanate from a range of people" (1990, p. xiii). Barbara Christian underscores the prevalence of theorizing in everyday life: "For people of color have always theorized—but in forms quite different from the Western form of abstract logic. . . . And women, at least the women I grew up around, continuously speculated about the nature of life through pithy language that unmasked the power relations of their world" (1988, p. 68). Drawing on both theory and everyday experience—as they indeed mesh with each other—Collins and others argue convincingly for the development and recognition of self-defined theoretical standpoints. "An articulated, self-defined, collective standpoint is key to Black women's survival" (Collins, 1990, p. 26). The authors of the DAWN document, prepared for the Nairobi World Conference for Women, have argued along similar lines:

> There is and must be a diversity of feminisms, responsive to the different needs and concerns of different women, and *defined by them for themselves.* . . . This heterogeneity gives feminism its dynamism and makes it the most potentially powerful challenge to the status quo. . . . Few contemporary social movements have the mass potential, the freshness of vision, the courage to experiment with new methods for action, and the respect for diversity and challenge of the women's movement. It is time for us to assert this with clarity, rigor, and passion (Sen and Grown, 1987, pp. 18–19, 22).

Gloria Anzaldua, too, tells us that theory "produces effects that change people and the way they perceive the world. . . . In our *mestizaje* theories we create new categories for those of us left out or pushed out of the existing ones. . . . If we have been gagged and disempowered by theories, we can also be loosened and empowered by theories" (1990, pp. xxv–xxvi).

Thus, for many feminist scholars today, comprehending "the whole cage" is acknowledged to encompass "the interlocking oppressions based on sex, gender, race, class, sexual preference, national origin, and ethnicity" (Kramarae and Treichler, 1985, p. 448). Nevertheless, in many widely used works on feminist theory, the concerns and intellectual contributions of African American and Latina women and other women of color have been neglected or silenced, producing theoretical distortions based on the false assumption of "a generic woman who is white and middle class" (Collins, 1990, p. 8).

This distortion is not easily overcome (see, e.g., the discussion by Alarcon in Anzaldua, 1990). Many feminist theorists in recent years have argued for critique of the gender-based, class-based, race-based, and historical standpoint of predominant theoretical paradigms that often parade as "universal," "neutral," "objective," or "scientific" (most recently, e.g., Collins, 1990; Goetz, 1991; Harding, 1991). These paradigms underlie a wide spectrum of feminist writings ranging from conservative to radical in political ideology, yet shaped by similar distortions emerging from the writers' common standpoint of race, class, culture, and historical context. Though the message is beginning to be heard, the problem remains pervasive.

In this context theory can offer grounding for a self-critical recognition of the standpoints represented in any given study. Chapters 12 and 13 in this book explore some aspects of the experience and agency of women engaged in revolution or resistance in Latin America and South Africa, but much work remains to be done to make books such as this one inclusive of the experience of women of color in this country and in other parts of the world.

In the field of feminist theory today, radical and socialist feminism, black and Third World feminism, lesbian feminism, ecofeminism, and others are strong voices contending for place and hearing. Indeed, the many important works by writers reflecting these perspectives are arguably the most incisive and provocative feminist analyses of issues concerning women, war, peace, and "security." (See, for example, Robinson and Hayden, 1970; Cook and Kirk, 1983; Hooks, 1984; French, 1985; Brock-Utne, 1985; Bunch, 1987; Russell, ed., 1989; Harris and King, eds., 1989; Eisler, 1987; Sen and Grown, 1987; Isaksson, 1988; Morgan, 1989; Diamond and Orenstein, eds., 1990; Enloe, 1983, 1990; Accad, 1990; Davis, 1990; Mohanty, Torres, and Russo, eds., 1991.)

Some of these works analyze the issues through the lens of race, others through the lens of class, others through the lens of sexual politics. Some express doubt about taking a fully pacifist or nonviolent stance, arguing that armed struggle in national liberation movements may be necessary and taking pride in women's participation as leaders or members of armed revolutionary groups. Some also address violence against women and the torture and enslavement of women in the international sex trade, linking issues of sexuality, violence, and war. But all are strongly critical of the military establishments and the monstrous weaponry of the United States and other Western nuclear powers, the drain of military expenditures and armed conflicts on the world's resources, and the damage done to the earth.

Some radical feminists have argued that the subjugation of

women under patriarchy is the oldest and most pervasive form of oppression and the model for all other systems of social hierarchy, oppression, and exploitation, including class society, the state, capitalism, racism, totalitarianism, and all forms of militarism (e.g., Redstockings Manifesto, in Morgan, 1970, p. 534). From this standpoint, war and all systematic violence (including rape, domestic violence, and other forms of violence usually seen as "private") are inherent in patriarchy as a social system. The implication is that war cannot be eliminated without eliminating patriarchy, and that there can be no true or lasting "peace" or "security" until the underlying patriarchal social structures and gender relations are transformed.

But in the public arenas of politics and policy in the United States, the prevailing forms of feminism in the "mainstream" are not those advocating extensive societal transformation, but rather various kinds of conservative and liberal feminism. This is evident in public debates on issues relating to women and the use of military force, such as women in military service, as well as in scholarship like this volume. Some further comments on the background and premises of these two branches of feminism may therefore prove useful.

The term "conservative feminism" might seem to be an oxymoron that would be rejected both by conservatives like Phyllis Schlafly whose trademark is to attack and deride feminism (e.g., Schlafly, 1991), and by feminists who find themselves attacked and derided by conservatives or whose political stance is strongly opposed to conservatism. In *Feminist Perspectives on Peace and Peace Education*, Birgit Brock-Utne suggests that the core of the conservative position on women's oppression rests on biological determinism, and she rejects the claim that the conservative position can be "feminist" on the ground that it fails to recognize the need and the possibilities for far-ranging educational, cultural, and political changes in society (1989, pp. 16–18).

Sandra Harding (1991) implies that a broad definition of feminism is most fair. Some would argue that naming the world is a basic political right and that we ought to accept the self-definition of all those who name themselves "feminist." There is also the problem of assigning the label to those who do not claim it, or even consciously disclaim it, on the ground that their position is in accord with some set of abstractly conceived criteria for what deserves to be called "feminist." This point is currently disputed by historians studying feminism, who often use the term for women or ideas preceding its actual appearance in European languages in the nineteenth century (Smith, 1982, pp. 4–9; Offen, 1988, 1989; DuBois, 1989).

While problematic, such a practice may be valid in clarifying connections that can be obscured by oppositional labeling. In some respects, for example, the term "conservative feminism" appears appropriate for people such as Jeane Kirkpatrick, who takes a conservative political stance but advocates increased political representation and participation of women (see Kirkpatrick, 1974). It may be less appropriate to apply the term to conservatives like Phyllis Schlafly who trade on antifeminism, even though their deeds do support "equal opportunity" and public political participation for women in the existing social structures. Schlafly vigorously opposes such policies as affirmative action (which she calls "reverse discrimination"), comparable worth, federally supported child care, and abortion rights. Yet, she claims to support "equal pay for equal work" and other policies that were once—not many decades ago—issues of feminist struggle (see, e.g., Schlafly, 1991).

The feminism (whether or not so named) of conservatives is generally not seen as contrary to the prevailing policies of conservative political parties and governments on the issues of war, peace, and security. Conservatives may advocate increased representation of women in existing structures of government, foreign services, corporations, political parties, and military institutions. But they draw the line at the draft or combat duty for women, equal rights for gays and lesbians, and compensatory programs to overcome effects of past discrimination. In general, they do not call for the entrance of women into high offices nor see it as implying any major changes in policy, institutional structures, or analysis of issues relating to war, peace, security, and the use of force.

In this respect and some others, liberal feminism has been closely related to conservative feminism. Many liberal feminists emphasize freedom of individual choice and trust in the competitive outcomes of those individual choices to provide the best outcomes for society. Thus, in *The Subjection of Women* (first published in 1868), J. S. Mill (1973) argues that "freedom of individual choice is now known to be the only thing which procures the adoption of the best processes" (p. 199). He continues, "Nobody thinks it necessary to make a law that only a strong-armed man shall be a blacksmith. Freedom and competition suffice to make blacksmiths strong-armed men, because the weak-armed can earn more by engaging in occupations for which they are more fit." Mill also argued that it was illogical to make laws that forbade women from engaging in activities contrary to an assumed female nature, because "that which is contrary to women's nature to do, they never will be made to do simply giving their nature free play" (p. 205).

Contemporary advocates of liberal feminism, such as the founders of the National Organization for Women (NOW), have built on the liberal values of individual choice and freedom of economic competition and the liberal rejection of essential differences between men and women in campaigning against discrimination based on sex in education and employment. The motivating goal of many liberal feminists—for the most part white and middle-class—has been to provide women with rights and opportunities *equal* to those available to men of their same class and race. Questions of personal and institutional transformation are not a necessary element of the liberal perspective. Women of color have pointed out repeatedly that white middle-class liberal feminists have traditionally been satisfied with making the opportunities and achievements of their male relatives accessible to themselves while otherwise protecting a racist and classist status quo.

However, liberal feminism today goes beyond ideas of "equal opportunity" and "equal rights" to call for policies (such as affirmative action) to correct the effects of past discrimination. It does not advocate the fundamental changes in our existing society that socialist and radical feminists envisage, but does recognize the need for significant alterations in policies and institutions to achieve "equality" between women and men and to overcome the inequalities based on race and ethnicity.

The liberal feminist position tends to assume that if women participate on an equal basis with men and are more fully represented in society's governing and military institutions, ameliorative changes will take place because of the "gender gap" between women and men on issues of peace and welfare. In general, this is seen not as a biologically determined difference but as a product of the long history of socialization of women to more peaceful and nurturant activities and their relative exclusion from aggressive, competitive, and combative pursuits (e.g. Boulding, 1977).

Concerned about the lack of educational and economic opportunity imposed by sex-based discrimination, the liberal feminist can take pleasure in the fact that the military offers some degree of economic equity to men and women (Moore, 1989). Liberal feminists have been vexed by the combat-exclusion law that has historically denied women the "plum" assignments that lead to the most prestigious jobs. The discussion of the combat-exclusion law in Chapter 7 of this book is reminiscent of Mill's assertion that the natural constraints of blacksmithing require no artificial reinforcements. The liberal feminist following Mill will note not only that weak men and women are equally unsuited to soldiering, but also that technological changes have transformed the profession of soldier just as blacksmithing as a profession has been rendered obsolete in the modern industrialized world.

In short, the liberal feminist perspective challenges sex-based discrimination based on the assumption that all men are suited to use force and all women are not. Researchers have accumulated data countering the conventional wisdom that men are naturally aggressive and women naturally passive. They have documented discrimination based on gender rather than on achieved characteristics. They offer evidence that women have been denied entry into public life based on fallacious assumptions about their nature.

This research is grounded in a liberal framework of academic theory or policy analysis with a basically ameliorative rather than revolutionary purpose. Yet, the liberal feminist stance can imply a broader transformation of society through significant challenges to existing institutions. Former Joint Chiefs of Staff Chairman John W. Vessey, Jr., lent unwitting support to these when he stated to a *Washington Post* reporter that "the influx of women has brought greater change to the U.S. military than the introduction of nuclear weapons" (quoted in Moore, 1989, p. A16). The kinds of changes Vessey means include responding (or not responding) to the needs of unmarried, pregnant soldiers; couples in dual-career marriages; and single fathers. These needs challenge a world we have created in which mothering is "inherently" a female activity and the work of soldiering makes "real men."

Among feminists, the argument that "the capacity to bear and nurture children gives women a special consciousness, a spiritual advantage rather than a disadvantage" (Barbara Deming, quoted in Snitow, 1989, p. 42) has had a varied fate. The argument has sometimes motivated social movements such as Another Mother for Peace and Women Strike for Peace. But for other people, the argument has been unpopular and labeled "essentialist" because it suggests a biological determinism repugnant to liberals. Social constructionists such as Sara Ruddick (1989) and Jean Bethke Elshtain (1987) have posed alternatives to the argument. Ruddick contrasts birthing labor and the often conflict-ridden work of mothering (preservative love, nurturing growth, and training) with the dehumanizing abstractions and psychologically violent methods of conflict management that make war possible. Elshtain sees disastrous consequences of the gender-training of boys and girls to become, respectively, "Just Warriors" or "Beautiful Souls." Paraphrasing Simone de Beauvoir (1968, p. 301), men and women are not born but are made. Few of us are taught how to become adults capable of negotiating competently, being passionately (but nonviolently) assertive. We all lose when we teach girls to tolerate needs unmet and boys to destroy others (figuratively more often than literally) in order to meet their own goals.

Ruddick (1989), quoting Simone Weil, defines force "as whatever 'turned a person into a thing' treating that person as if he [sic] counted for nothing" (p. 164). Force, for feminist social constructionists, is a more inclusive concept than the use of sanctioned violence in war. Force is coercion. Moreover, war is seen as more than the use of sanctioned violence by states in pursuit of the national interest. War and training for war are specifically designed to make men tough, to challenge that which is soft and feminine in them. Meanwhile, women applaud their own loss and humiliation in the name of patriotism. The use of sexual language, reinforcing the "thingness" of women, to dehumanize and to inspire military activity has been perceptively illustrated by Cohn (1989), Enloe (1990), and others. Filippo Marinetti observed a connection between militarism and misogyny in "The Founding and Manifesto of Futurism" (1991, p. 50, first published in 1909):

> We will glorify war—
> the world's only hygiene—
> militarism, patriotism,
> the destructive gesture of freedom-bringers
> beautiful ideas worth dying for,
> and scorn for woman.

When we talk about women and the use of force, then, we *are* digging at the roots of what simultaneously makes women feminine and men masculine. Not a biological determinism that makes males aggressive and females passive, but how we as human beings have constructed and continue to interpret the world.

What then would individuals who see gender as a social construct ask about women and the use of force? Where do they go when confronted by a pregnant soldier? Where do these intellectual journeys take us? Within this feminist framework, a human being might muse on these questions:

1. What purposes (social, psychological, economic, and political) are served by making/imagining warmaking as appropriate labor for men and childrearing as appropriate

labor for women?

2. How is the use of force/coercion related to a consciousness that insists on dividing the world into categories of Self and Other, whether by race, gender, or other characteristics?

3. What are the stories we tell ourselves and our children about the different lives of men and women, and the differences among men and among women?

4. What *are* the needs of and issues raised by a pregnant soldier? What kinds of labor are central to her identity? Are there contradictions implicit in these different labors? Are such contradictions resolvable?

These questions are not adequately addressed by poll data or traditional experiments in the social sciences. They are more often the stuff of philosophy, biography, psychoanalysis, and fiction. They may also be openings to theoretical understandings and transformational perspectives.

This chapter has attempted to introduce the reader to some of the issues of diversity and contentiousness in feminist understandings of women and the use of force. Some "mainstream" liberal feminists may find a discussion focused on women in the military and women using violence informative. Other feminists suspect that a focus on women and the use of (military) force may conceal as much as it reveals. There are still more feminist questions than feminist answers. At some level, each of the collective authors of this volume has asked from her or his own angle, "What do we want to know about what the use of force means for women?" or "What do we want to know about what the category 'woman' does to our understanding of the use of force?" One of the most exhilarating aspects of participating in this undertaking has been the recognition of the extent of our differences. One of the most exhilarating aspects of feminist undertakings is the sense that we are in the process of defining and redefining who we are and why we do what we do. Succeeding chapters in this volume plant some seeds for partial answers.

chapter 3

The Gender Gap in Popular Attitudes Toward the Use of Force

Nancy W. Gallagher

The perception that men and women have different ideas about the use of force in international relations is well rooted and widespread. As far back as early U.S. suffrage debates those proposing voting rights for women often claimed that there would be fewer wars if soldiers' mothers were consulted. Opponents countered that females had neither the mind nor the stomach for the brutal realities of international relations. For example, Carlos White (1870, pp. 155–163), an opponent of women's suffrage, maintained that women would have no relevant information about most public matters and that they could easily be led astray by shrewder male politicians who played on women's more sympathetic and emotional nature. Elizabeth Cady Stanton countered by arguing that women's natures and experiences as mothers suited them especially well to make life-and-death decisions:

> That great conservator of woman's love, if permitted to assert itself as it naturally would in freedom against oppression, violence, and war, would hold all these destructive forces in check, for woman knows the cost of life better than man does, and not with her consent would one drop of blood ever be shed, one life sacrificed in vain (1975, p. 64).

A more lighthearted supporter of votes for women answered the question, "Could women bear arms?" by saying:

> I do not see how anybody could ask that question after once seeing woman's success in getting into one of New York City's subways. . . . Anyway, most men would rather go to war than be left behind to do the hard work that women must do when taking the place of arms bearers (Allen, 1911, pp. 16–17).

Modern feminists emphasize the "gender gap" to publicize the view that women are a powerful voting block with distinct opinions on policy issues (Mueller, 1988). Meanwhile, contemporary conservatives use women's lack of combat experience to suggest that neither U.S. soldiers and citizens nor foreign leaders would expect a female president to be a skillful and decisive leader in a crisis. Comments made during the 1984 vice presidential debate between George Bush and Geraldine Ferraro illustrate this tactic (Tobias, 1990).

To make reliable predictions about whether the world would be safer, riskier, or unchanged if women had more influence on foreign policy, one must answer several key questions. Do significant differences actually exist between women's and men's attitudes toward the use of force in foreign policy? If so, what factors account for these differences? Would women's opinions change if more women joined the ranks of defense and foreign policy elite? Finally, does grassroots opinion affect policy enough that important changes would occur if more women voiced their ideas?

This chapter provides an introduction and overview of the political science literature addressing these questions. While suggestive research has been done, there are no consensual answers. Much of the confusion arises because some studies explore the public's general beliefs about international relations, while others investigate opinions about specific policy options. Although women's foreign policy belief systems have traditionally seemed to resemble men's, women have consistently shown less support for forceful means of pursuing foreign policy goals. This difference has persisted over time and remains even after controlling such factors as race, party affiliation, and socioeconomic status. Recent evidence shows that the use-of-force gap is widening and that splits are emerging in general attitudes about foreign policy. Less is known about the reasons for gender-related differences, although antiforce attitudes are more common among women (and men) with feminist consciousness than among people who uphold traditional feminine values. Correlations have been found between shifts in public attitudes and changes in policy, but little is certain about the direction of causation or the conditions under which popular opinion affects governmental choices.

The terms "gender" and "sex" often cause confusion. This chapter will use "sex" to refer to differences that are primarily biologically based, and "sex roles" or "gender" to refer to those that are largely the result of sociological or ideological factors. When reporting on others' research, however, I will use their terminology (unless this would hinder comparability).

Review of Basic Findings

For many years, national leaders believed that the average citizen cared little about foreign affairs and held ill-considered, contradictory opinions when crises loomed. Women, these leaders assumed, were particularly uninterested and illinformed because their primary concerns centered close to home (Almond, 1950). Thus, policy decisions were based primarily on elite male opinion. On rare occasions when women tried to influence U.S. foreign policy—such as when the Women's Peace Party proposed mediation for World War I or Women's Strike for Peace protested atmospheric nuclear testing—policymakers ignored them, ridiculed them, or tried to "educate" them through public relations campaigns.

Recent research has challenged each of these components of conventional wisdom. Although opinion surveys continue to show a lack of detailed knowledge about international events, they also reveal that U.S. citizens do care about the broad outlines of foreign policy. Aldrich, Sullivan, and Borgida (1989) found that "peace stands with prosperity as an outstanding example of enduring goals held by the public. . . . [W]ith the exception of the period between 1973 and 1980, foreign issues have been commonly cited as among the most important problems facing the nation" (p. 1114).

Lack of knowledge about international relations may motivate citizens to develop a set of abstract beliefs to guide their reactions to world events (Hurwitz and Peffley, 1987). In response to assertions that popular ideas about foreign policy resemble fickle moods more than rational opinions, some scholars have argued that general attitudes fit into one of several relatively stable and coherent "belief systems." Wittkopf and Maggiotto (1983) categorized elite and mass beliefs using a fourfold typology defined by level of support for militant and cooperative internationalism. A follow-up study (Wittkopf, 1987) showed that distribution of respondents among the four categories depended primarily on degree of involvement with foreign policy: elites and attentive public supported all forms of internationalism; mass audiences favored militant internationalism; and inattentive respondents subscribed to isolationist views. Comparison of data from the 1974, 1978, and 1982 Chicago Council on Foreign Relations (CCFR) polls led Wittkopf to conclude that the most important characteristic of post-Vietnam popular opinion was its "remarkable stability over diverse circumstances" (p. 153).

These studies reported no meaningful differences in women's and men's ideas about foreign policy goals and guiding axioms.

Wittkopf's 1987 follow-up does not explore gender differences because his data for 1978 and 1982 do not include the sociodemographic characteristics of the respondents. Wittkopf and Maggiotto (1983) found that mean scores for white males were slightly negative for cooperative internationalism and vaguely positive for militant internationalism, whereas mean scores for white females and all nonwhites tended to be slightly positive. But race and gender explained less of the variance than the leader/mass distinction. This was supported by a second study (Bardes and Oldenick, 1978) that explored five dimensions of foreign policy attitudes and found no gender differences worth note.

These conclusions are in sharp contrast to another body of research that finds large and stable gender differences about the use of force in specific situations. Tom Smith (1984) studied 285 questions on surveys given between 1937 and 1983 by six polling services. More men than women selected the forceful alternative in 87 percent of the cases. The largest gender gaps (up to 30 percent more men indicating approval) concerned questions about activities that are considered manly, such as gun ownership, hunting, and boxing. Direct use of force for law enforcement and military involvement showed a 10 percent average difference. Questions related to what Smith termed "indirect use of force," such as military spending, showed a relatively small gap, while the few reversals mostly dealt with situations where women supported forceful responses to interpersonal violence against other women.

Shapiro and Mahajan's (1986) study of poll questions from the last three decades also found that the gender gap on policies for the use of force has consistently been moderately large, usually twice as great as sex differences on other types of issues. The gap became progressively smaller when they divided the questions into ones that obviously dealt with force, ones that were ambiguous, and ones where force was clearly irrelevant. Because the size of the difference on ambiguous issues (abortion, criminal punishment, and so forth) was closer to that for nonforce questions, Shapiro and Mahajan hypothesized that there must be an obvious choice between forceful and nonforceful options for a large gender gap to emerge.

The force/nonforce choice is perhaps most obvious when military intervention is at issue. In 1981, the Roper Organization asked a series of questions about hypothetical situations where the president might use U.S. troops (Bensen, 1982). Scenarios in which intervention received more total support than opposition were (1) another group of U.S. embassy employees taken hostage, (2) Soviet invasion of Western Europe, and (3) Soviet invasion of West Berlin.

Respondents divided evenly in the case of Communist takeovers in Central America and definitely rejected military action in response to an Arab invasion of Israel, a Soviet invasion of Poland, and a North Korean invasion of South Korea. When the answers were separated by sex, however, women showed decisive support for intervention only in the case of another hostage-taking (57 percent for, 24 percent against). A mere 2 percent more women approved than opposed intervention to protect Western Europe (42 percent for, 40 percent against); in all other cases, the majority opposed use of force.

Asking about hypothetical or potential uses of force is different from inquiring about ongoing military action. The Roper study of attitudes toward intervention found that military action caused the presidential approval rating to rise more among men than among women because "men seem to consistently favor more militaristic solutions to problems than women." This has been called the "rally-round-the-flag" effect, in which presidential approval ratings jump dramatically after fighting starts or the United States is involved in some other type of sharp, dramatic, and focused international event. During the Korean and Vietnam wars, women were much more likely to think that military action had been a mistake and to support U.S. withdrawal (Baxter and Lansing, 1983). Gallup polls showed only modest increases in approval ratings by either sex after the invasions of Grenada and Panama (*Gallup Poll Monthly*, December 1983, p. 18, and January 1990, p. 17). Neither conflict lasted long enough for us to know if women would have become disenchanted more quickly than men.

Attitudes toward nuclear weapons policies are more complex because some people think a large nuclear arsenal increases the chance of war, while others believe it reduces that probability. Several studies have assessed sex differences in nuclear attitudes, but no consensus has been reached. Some evidence suggests a "macho pride" factor that increases support for nuclear weapons development and a "tenderness" factor that correlates with opposition to nuclear arms. Mark Jensen (1987) systematically tested hypotheses about support for nuclear weapons use, nuclear restraint in the face of provocation, and nuclear weapons development. He found that the only significant gender difference was a lower level of male support for nuclear restraint. An interesting sex-related difference did show up in another study that asked people why they had not selected "threat of nuclear war" as the most important problem facing the United States in 1983. Men responded that there would never be a nuclear war twice as frequently as women did.

Women, by contrast, were twice as likely to say that they did not choose it because they thought that nuclear war was out of their control.

Defense spending is another policy domain where one finds mixed results. In a study designed to assess sex differences in support for government spending between 1973 and 1984, Cynthia Dietch (1988) found that some years showed slightly greater female support for military spending and others somewhat higher rates of male support, but that in none of the years was the difference statistically significant. This result is consistent with Smith's argument that military spending does not trigger a large gender gap because it is a matter of "indirect force." However, it could also be seen as another instance where support for defense spending fluctuates depending on whether a person feels that arms provoke or deter conflicts.

Women in the United States are not unique. Welch and Thomas (1988) examined data from a 1983 British election study and found that although there was no major gender gap on overarching ideology and partisan affiliation, there were substantial differences in attitudes toward the use of force. For example, 17 percent more women than men believed that Britain should remove its troops from Northern Ireland, and 7 percent more women said that they felt less safe with U.S. nuclear weapons on their soil. Interestingly, women did not differ significantly from men in their attitudes toward maintaining a British nuclear deterrent and reducing military spending. This, along with the finding that women support stiffer punishment for criminals yet are less likely to advocate the death penalty, convinced Welch and Thomas that the gaps they found really did spring from different attitudes toward the use of force, rather than from a more "tolerant" or "appeasing" outlook on life (p. 35).

Current Trends

The gender gap in popular attitudes toward the use of force continues to grow in both intensity and importance. In a longitudinal study of hundreds of opinion poll questions asked between 1948 and 1981, the editors of *Public Opinion* (1982) found that differences on what they called the "force dimension" expanded over the years. Significant and sustained variations on what they called the "compassion" and "risk" dimensions developed after the mid-1970s, suggesting a new gender gap concerning the ends, as well as the means, of foreign policy.

Fite, Genest, and Wilcox (1990) analyzed CCFR data from 1975–1986, using instruments designed to measure both belief structures and attitudes toward force. They found some gender differences on both goals and means during the early years, but only those questions relating to use of troops showed substantial gaps. The gap on use-of-force questions increased slightly during the 1980s. More important, significant differences on policy goals emerged, with women being less concerned than men about containment and more interested in altruistic goals (keeping the peace, combating world hunger, and fostering international cooperation). But despite their more altruistic orientation, women were slightly less supportive of economic aid because they feared that it would hurt the domestic economy or lead to U.S. military involvement overseas.

The Gulf War displayed the gender gap at its widest. In a Harris poll taken in early December 1990, men were evenly divided on the wisdom of attacking Iraqi forces (48 percent for, 48 percent against), whereas women opposed military action by 73 percent to 22 percent. Similar chasms existed regarding "surgical" air strikes. Men approved this tactic by 57 percent to 40 percent, whereas women rejected it decisively, 63 percent to 29 percent. The sexes did not differ significantly in support for less obviously lethal strategies, like giving economic pressures more time to work. In particular, women were no more willing than men to avoid a confrontation by allowing Saddam Hussein to keep a piece of Kuwait. Because 61 percent of the respondent pool opposed force before the Gulf War began, Harris concluded that "for the first time, women alone have turned public opinion about a war. They have swayed the polls against President Bush's using military force in the Gulf" (p. A35).

Obviously, this negative public opinion failed to prevent the war. Once shooting started, women were not immune to the "rally-round-the-flag" effect. However, polls from the end of January 1991 showed that women were evenly divided on the wisdom of continuing to fight or seeking a settlement (47 percent to 46 percent), whereas men strongly favored by 66 percent to 28 percent a continuation of the war (Hart and Teeter, 1991). When the emphasis was shifted from whether the United States should use the tools of war or diplomacy to whether it should pursue the objective of removing Saddam Hussein from power, an increased number of women supported the continuation of the war (56 percent for continued fighting to 36 percent for stopping the war once Iraq had left Kuwait). Looking at ends rather than means did not significantly alter the male response; support for continued fighting increased only slightly to 69 percent for and 25 percent against (CBS News Poll, 1991).

Cautions

Modern opinion survey methodology presents a picture of the similarities and differences in the sexes' thought patterns that seems much more scientific than the impressionistic assertions characterizing the early suffrage debates. In many regards, being able to ask large numbers of people what they think about a particular issue is an improvement over a situation where politicians simply claim widespread silent support for whatever they are about to propose. However, there are several reasons to be cautious when generalizing from findings that women and men have usually held similar ideas about broad outlines of U.S. foreign policy, but do not always support the same specific means to reach those goals.

Survey research designers must decide whether to give a few fixed alternatives, provide scales to indicate strength of feeling, or allow open-ended answers. Most of the studies cited in this chapter that dealt with attitudes toward the use of force offered three choices: "yes/approve," "no/oppose," and "don't know." This type of closed-ended research design makes it possible to process the data quickly and provide simple, striking figures. However, the results are not always meaningful. For example, knowing that a certain percent more women than men object to a particular policy does not say anything about the intensity of respondents' support or opposition. Nor is one usually told whether attitudinal differences between the sexes are greater or smaller than those within each group. Most important, summary statistics rarely give any indication of why respondents chose as they did. Yet, it seems crucial to know if those who oppose the use of force do so because they believe that it is unnecessary, ineffective, or inappropriate to the issue at hand. For example, one of the questions used by the editors of *Public Opinion* to illustrate the gender gap on the force dimension asked respondents: "Do you think it will be best for the future of this country if we take an active part in world affairs, or if we stay out of world affairs?" Thirty-nine percent of female respondents thought that the United States should be less active, while only 28 percent of the males thought that this was true (Opinion Roundup, 1982, p.

29). This question is measuring support for activist or isolationist foreign policies, rather than support for forceful or diplomatic forms of international involvement.

Surveys often use leading questions and oversimplify complex issues. For example, a May 1990 Gallup poll included an item that read:

> Since WWII, the policy of the United States has been to maintain our military strength throughout the world in order to help governments that might be overthrown by communist-based forces. Do you think we should or should not continue to follow this policy? (p. 10).

In addition to exaggerating the continuity in postwar policies, this question is ambiguous in several ways. It is not clear whether it deals primarily with general values such as anticommunism and militant internationalism or with the merits of using military forces as a tool to strengthen friendly governments. It is also impossible to know whether maintaining military strength refers primarily to defense spending, U.S. conventional intervention, or nuclear weapons development. Asking people to reply "yes" or "no" to such an ambiguous question may well mask important divergences in general beliefs about international relations or overestimate differences in attitudes toward force as a tool of foreign policy.

The wording of survey questions frequently ignores views that are outside the mainstream of the current policy debate. A November 1990 Gallup poll queried the following:

> If the current situation in the Middle East involving Iraq and Kuwait does not change by January, would you favor or oppose the United States going to war in order to drive the Iraqis out of Kuwait? (p. 16).

Asking "should the United States fight now?" ignored the deeper issue of why the situation was structured as it was, with massive troop deployments and a much-publicized ultimatum. It also finessed important questions about what U.S. war aims actually were and whether a war was the best way to pursue them. Someone whose main concern was to prevent Iraqi nuclear weapons development might support an attack even if Hussein started to withdraw, whereas one whose primary objective was to promote lasting peace in the Middle East could easily believe that the way in which the war was conducted would be as important as when it began.

Part of the reason for the gender gap on questions relating to the use of force is that women select the "don't know" or "no opinion" options more frequently than men. In Smith (1984), for example, more women than men chose those options on 86 percent of the questions. This has often been taken as a sign that women know or care less about questions of war and peace. However, the high rate of "don't know" answers among women may indicate that women feel less compelled to hold an opinion regardless of how illinformed they actually are. It also may reflect a serious design problem where unique features of women's world view are not well reflected by questions that are framed in terms that make sense to male pollsters and policymakers (for an expanded treatment of this idea in the context of research on moral development, see Gilligan, 1982). Concerning women's higher "don't know" rate, Shapiro and Mahajan (1986) suggest that "Some of these responses may not occur because of the low salience of the issue but rather because of the difficulty that politically attuned respondents may have in making their opinion fit one of the categories offered in closed-ended survey questions" (p. 57).

This interpretation is borne out by the fact that while women's "don't know" rate declines significantly on most issues when they enter the labor force, working outside the home has much less impact on the frequency of "don't know" answers for questions relating to the use of force (Fite et al., 1990; Shapiro and Mahajan, 1986).

Explanations of the Gender Gap

Although methodological imperfections may mask or magnify the size and shape of gender-related differences regarding the use of force, some significant differences clearly exist. Why women and men have disparate views of violence and what this implies for the future of U.S. foreign policy are less clear. Subsequent chapters in this volume will provide a more detailed look at popular attitudes toward women who use force for private and public purposes and attitudes toward the use of force among women in the foreign policy elite. The remainder of this chapter will focus on opinion survey research about the causal relationships regarding gender, mass opinion, and foreign policy.

One possible explanation for the gap is that more women than men oppose the use of force not because of a direct female/male difference but because being female increases the probability of belonging to a group with its own reasons for disliking militant international policies. For example, if poor people tend to be negative toward interventionist policies because of the cost or the risk to enlisted relatives, and if disproportionate numbers of women are poor, then gender would only be indirectly responsible for attitudes toward the use of force.

There is little evidence that the opinion gap develops primarily from the effects of intervening variables such as income or education level. These factors are frequently treated as background variables. However, it makes little sense to think of a sequence in which one's income or education level causes one to become female. Instead, it is more plausible to think in terms of a developmental sequence where women's life conditions lead to greater economic vulnerability or lower education levels and then to particular attitudes toward the use of force. Fite et al. (1990) found that controlling for socioeconomic status did not alter the gap. Holding partisanship and ideological self-identification constant reduced the gap slightly, but not enough to suggest that more women oppose the use of force primarily because more women are politically liberal. Welch and Thomas (1988) found similar results when they checked for intervening variables in their British sample. Structural factors (income, education, and occupation) did not have a significant impact either. Situational constraints (marital status, involvement in the paid labor force) also had little effect, possibly because working women have more exposure to political issues but less time to educate themselves about foreign policy matters.

A study testing the hypothesis that men's much higher rate of military service accounts for their approval of forceful solutions (Schreiber, 1979) found a positive correlation between veteran status and positive attitudes toward the military and military spending. As a group, veterans were no more likely than other men to approve of public or private displays of force. However, World War II–era veterans were more likely than same-age nonveteran males to own guns, whereas Vietnam-era veterans were more likely than their nonveteran counterparts to approve of police violence against political demonstrators.

The main debate about the source of the gender gap is between those who ascribe it to traditional female values and those who attribute it to progressive feminist views. Both groups agree that the gender gap is the result of a particular type of woman's social experiences, not of biological characteristics that all women share. But they differ both in their normative assessments and in their predictions about how the women's movement will affect the size and nature of the gender gap.

The first group maintains that women oppose the use of force because they have been socialized to be passive, timid, and apolitical. As women become "liberated," these theorists expect them to become more like men. For example, John Mueller (1973) predicted:

> if the effect of women's liberation is to change the attitudes of women, making them more assertive so they can compete in a male-oriented society, a correlative result may make them more hawkish on war and foreign policy. . . . the quintessential dove among women is not the liberated activist, but the unassertive little old lady who can't bring herself to support wars because they aren't "nice" (p. 147).

The alternative explanation (Conover, 1988) takes a more positive stance. Fewer women advocate force not because they lack whatever accounts for male belligerence but because they have unique biological and/or sociological factors that make them more caring and compassionate, more concerned with preserving interpersonal relationships, and less willing to believe that "might makes right." In this model, women's special values are usually submerged under the dominant values of male-oriented society. Women express the same values and policy preferences as men unless they develop a strong enough feminist consciousness to allow their "woman-centered perspective" values and preferences to emerge. These theorists predict that, as women become more "liberated," they will think less like male members of the dominant culture, and the gender gap will grow.

Several of the studies did try to test the traditional female socialization and feminist orientation hypotheses. Smith (1984) credited traditional socialization with having the greatest effect on the opinion gap because the largest differences in approval rates were on activities such as hunting, which are socially approved for men. He concluded that feminist ideology had no impact because he found neither changes in the male/female gap after the late 1960s nor significant opinion differences between feminists and nonfeminists of either sex. However, he failed to specify what he used as an indicator for feminism or whether he expected that the women's liberation movement should have increased or decreased the gap.

Welch and Thomas (1988) found that socialization had a greater effect than immediate constraints or structural factors. This result does little to resolve the traditional socialization versus feminist-orientation debate, though, because their socialization measures include aspects of traditional female sex roles such as nurturance, which some feminists also embrace. Furthermore, because Welch and Thomas studied data from a single election survey, it is impossible to know how changing levels of support for these values have affected attitudes toward the use of force.

Data from the 1984 National Election Study (NES) were examined in a study designed specifically to test the importance of feminist orientation. Pamela Conover (1988) found that women who identified with the women's movement and supported its basic goals were responsible for the vast majority of the gender gap in public opinion. Apart from the question of Central America, nonfeminist women did not differ significantly from men on any of the foreign policy options, whereas feminist women stood apart on each foreign policy item. Conover concluded that "while it is not very surprising to find that feminist women are more liberal than men in general, it is startling to discover that there are enough feminists who are liberal enough to create almost on their own the appearance of a widespread gender gap" (p. 1005).

If there is a critical divergence between feminist and nonfeminist women's foreign policy preferences, it is possible that there are also crucial differences among men. Unfortunately, Conover's data did not include a direct measure of feminist identity for men, and her attempts to use indirect measures to study feminist and nonfeminist males' compassion levels produced contradictory results.

Cook and Wilcox (1991) reanalyzed the 1984 NES data to determine whether opinion differences are the product of a unique woman's perspective or the result of values such as equality and political liberalism that could be held by men and women alike. They found that both "feminist sympathy" for men and "feminist consciousness" for women are strong predictors of values and policy preferences. However, gender still seems to influence attitudes toward use of force. When the policy preferences of feminist women and men are compared, only the war and peace issues show a consistent pattern of gender effects.

Implications and Conclusions

If the gender gap in opinions concerning the use of force is to be more than a statistical curiosity, differences in popular attitudes must be able to elicit changes in policy. There are at least three possibilities worth considering. First, the sociodemographic changes that are bringing more women into foreign policymaking positions could result in decisions favoring more pacific behavior. Second, democratic political process could translate women's attitudes into a mandate for policies that resolve conflicts through nonviolent means. Third, women opposed to the use of force could explicitly adopt political strategies to publicize gender differences and insist that leaders do more to include feminist perspectives and values.

The first possibility, that increasing the proportion of women in the military and foreign policy bureaucracies will lead to less belligerent actions, is the subject of several selections later in this volume. The way to reconcile the gender gaps in mass attitudes with those authors' generally skeptical conclusions about women's impact in elite positions is to remember that there is no single and distinct "woman's point of view." As long as the number of women admitted to the inner circle is small, the few who self-select and are chosen will tend to share the dominant perspective of those already in place. Furthermore, when the opinion gap is wrongly taken as evidence that the average female is unassertive and eager to avoid conflict at all costs, women who want to succeed will have an incentive to distance themselves from these negative images by expressing opposite opinions. Only if the proportion of decisionmakers opposed to the use of force were large and the prevailing ideology attributed their support for nonviolent conflict resolution to positive factors would one expect to see major changes in behavior coming from the top levels of the foreign policy institutions.

The possibility that grassroots opposition to forceful action will automatically be translated into more peaceful policies takes one into a large literature on the relationship between public opinion and U.S. policy outcomes. (For useful overviews, see Kegley and Wittkopf, 1991, pp. 279–322, and Weissberg, 1976. For information specifically about women's ability to translate their opinions into political action by elected officials, see Poole and Ziegler, 1985.) It can be briefly summarized by saying that whereas traditional models of democratic decisionmaking rely on a number of unrealistic assumptions, models that completely discount popular opinion are also inaccurate. However, the role that mass opinions play in the policymaking process is complicated and poorly understood. A desire to avoid public opposition often constrains political leaders from pursuing certain options, such as continuing atmospheric nuclear tests or openly sending a large American intervention force to support the contras in Nicaragua. Leaders also use polls to decide when to propose a new policy and what arguments to use to support it. In-house polling agencies may even manipulate questions to increase apparent support for their candidate's positions.

In short, even though it is possible to find correlations between changes in opinion and changes in policy, it is difficult to determine causality (Page and Shapiro, 1983). One could argue that President Reagan began responding to Soviet arms control overtures in the end of his first term because he knew that many women opposed his arms buildups and objected to his talk of winning a nuclear war. However, this would require one to demonstrate not only that disproportionate numbers of women held these attitudes, but also that Reagan believed that he needed their votes, sought their support by showing more interest in arms control, and would not have taken the steps in the absence of these women's strong opinions. Frankovic (1982) found partial support for the first step in this causal chain when she showed that the gender gap in the 1980 election could be almost completely explained by controlling for women's greater unwillingness to be more forceful with the Soviet Union even if it increased the risk of nuclear war. However, much work remains to be done.

Problems with the first and second options lead to a dilemma about whether or not one should accentuate those gender differences that do exist. The choice is between (1) increasing women's access to decisionmaking positions by reassuring conservatives that there are no relevant differences in most men's and women's approaches, (2) increasing the size and strength of the antiforce pressure group by forming an alliance built on similarities between progressive women's and men's views, or (3) increasing women's moral claim to leadership by emphasizing that they have distinctive views and values that would humanize domestic and foreign policy. Stoper and Johnson (1977) provide an excellent analysis of the history, benefits, and potential cost of arguing that women are naturally different from and morally superior to men. Ultimately, the choice between these options is a political and strategic decision that cannot be answered by reference to opinion survey statistics alone.

Note

The author appreciates helpful suggestions on earlier drafts offered by Richard Boyd, Ellen Riggle, and Nancy Schwartz, as well as research assistance provided by Sarah Lewis and Karen Hultgren.

chapter 4

Women in Groups and Organizations: Implications for the Use of Force

Jill M. Bystydzienski

This chapter discusses sociological knowledge that has implications for the extent to which women may use force against others. It focuses on women's status and roles in groups and organizations, and specifically on whether there are gender differences in group and organizational behavior. Studies of women in politics are then examined in an attempt to predict how greater participation of women might change government and military policy.

Women in Groups

There is much evidence that all-female groups behave differently from all-male groups. Research findings from laboratory experiments and field observations indicate that women in female groups are more oriented toward immediate relationships and less toward achievement and are less aggressive and more cooperative and trusting than men in male groups (Cattell and Lawson, 1962; Constantini and Craik, 1972; Sikula, 1973; Kanter, 1981). Women's groups tend to be less hierarchical than men's groups (Kanter, 1977) and in work organizations tend to be less mobility-oriented (Kanter, 1977; Westwood, 1984). Conversations in women's groups typically focus on interpersonal relationships, whereas all-male groups tend to discuss action-oriented events (Spender, 1980). Women in female groups take turns talking or engaging in an activity, whereas men in male groups compete aggressively for the limelight (Brock-Utne, 1985, p. 100). Gender differences have been found to exist in groups of children and adolescents (Brock-Utne, 1985, pp. 99–101; Thorne and Luria, 1986; Eder, 1987) and to persist in adult groups (Schaffer, 1981, pp. 88–92).

Such differences may be interpreted as the result of socialization of women for family roles and men for the public sphere. However, as a number of feminist researchers have pointed out recently, women's orientations and behavior in female groups also can be seen as realistic responses to women's structural situations: the opportunities and limits of the status and role demands women are subjected to in the family and in the world of work (Kanter, 1981, p. 412; Chase, 1987, p. 10). For instance, women in all-female work groups often indicate that they find advancement undesirable, and this has been interpreted in the past as women's "fear of success" stemming from traditional sex-role socialization (Horner, 1972). A more plausible explanation, however, indicates that in most cases women's chances for advancement are very limited (Chase, 1987), and when a woman does get promoted to a supervisory position she is frequently placed in the awkward position of mediating between male management and her female friends (Costello, 1985; Westwood, 1984). Similarly, women's emphasis on interpersonal relationships in all-female groups may stem from an accurate perception of blocked opportunities, which may result in seeking gratification through peer involvement (Richardson, 1981, pp. 207–210).

When women and men are together in groups, the two sexes also tend to behave differently. In general, research shows that men tend to dominate interaction in mixed-sex groups both verbally and nonverbally. Women typically speak less than men (Fishman, 1978; Spender, 1980); men are responsible, on the average, for more than 90 percent of interruptions that occur, and women frequently abandon a subject that interests them in favor of what men wish to talk about (Zimmerman and West, 1975; Kramarae, 1980; Kollock, Blumstein, and Schwartz, 1985). Men typically take up more physical space and spread their arms or legs sideways and outward more than women do (Robertson, 1989, p. 325). Men also are more likely to touch women than to be touched by them (Henley, 1973).

In mixed-sex groups, men display more aggression than women, although some studies have indicated that women either are learning to be more aggressive or are becoming more willing to display aggressive behavior (Schafer, 1981, p. 90). Men appear to be more aggressive when initiative is required, but women also become aggressive in response to direct aggressive behavior from another person (Taylor and Epstein, 1967; Hokanson and Edelman, 1966; Schafer, 1981). However, women express their aggression differently than men do; they tend to display nonverbal aggression such as glaring, whereas men are more likely to display verbal or physical aggression (Harris, 1974).

Because men dominate interaction in mixed-sex groups, they influence the agendas for discussion and the outcome of decisions.

Research has shown, however, that numbers of women in a group may make a difference in the extent to which women's influence is felt. In groups with highly skewed sex ratios, when women are few, they become isolated and invisible (Kanter, 1981). In groups where women compose less than 15 percent of the total membership, they do not influence group processes in any significant way (South et al., 1982; Spangler et al., 1978; Yoder et al., 1989). However, in groups that are between 15 and 30 percent female, women "have potential allies among themselves, can form coalitions, and can affect the culture of the group" (Kanter, 1977, p. 209). Other researchers point out, however, that numbers alone are misleading because women need to be in the powerful (leadership) positions within groups in order to affect group decisions (Cook, 1987; Epstein, 1983; Ferree, 1987).

Gender differences in behavior in mixed-sex groups are subject to a structural interpretation. Even if the numbers of women are nearly equal to those of men, men and women may not, in fact, influence group processes equally, particularly if their status external to the group is inconsistent with their group position. The resulting behavior, including frequency of participation and leadership, may reflect status and power differences, in addition to, or even more than, socialized sex-linked personality traits.

The research on women in groups indicates in general that women are less likely than men to use force against others, as, for example, giving orders or using physical aggression. Women's groups are less hierarchical, more interpersonally oriented, and more cooperative than men's, and in mixed-sex groups, men dominate interaction and decisionmaking. Sex-role socialization and, more important, women's lower status and relative lack of power keep women from taking equal part with men in groups.

Women in Organizations

Studies of women in organizations have focused largely on places of work and, in particular, on women in female-dominated occupations and in male-dominated strata (Chase, 1987). There also have been some studies done on women's organizations (e.g., Bystydzienski, 1989a; Freeman, 1979).

In most contemporary organizations, women are found predominantly at the lower levels. In 1988, employed women in the United States were grouped largely in two occupational categories:

administrative support (which includes clerical workers) and service (Rix, 1990, p. 357). While more women have been entering traditionally male domains in recent decades, women generally do not hold positions of power and authority within occupational hierarchies, and the relatively few women in management tend to be concentrated in lower-paying positions and in less-prestigious organizations (U.S. Department of Labor, 1991). For the most part, world labor markets continue to be sex-segregated, with women performing less-valued work and concentrated in support functions (Waring, 1988).

Those who have studied women in modern organizations have pointed out that most are found at the bottom of hierarchies, in jobs that offer little room for advancement, typically being supervised by men, and working almost exclusively with other women (Benson, 1978; Costello, 1985; Melosh, 1982). In these female-dominated employment situations women tend to develop work cultures that help them cope with the structural constraints of the workplace (Chase, 1987).

Do these female work cultures differ from those developed by men in male-dominated, low-level occupations? There is some indication that they do. While in both cases people seek creative ways to overcome the constraints of their work environments, and they both adapt to and resist imposed circumstances, women differ from men in the specific ways they interpret their tasks and form social relations at work. For instance, women's work cultures tend to be outwardly more cooperative and conformist than those fashioned by men. In the classic experiments at the Hawthorne Western Electric plant in the late 1920s and early 1930s, the groups that cooperated with management were all-female, whereas the group that established a production quota and was aggressively controlling and suspicious of management was all-male (Kanter, 1981, p. 411). Although women's work groups tend to be more conciliatory toward management and tend to define their work grievances more narrowly than male groups (Westwood, 1984), closer examination of women's work experiences has revealed that they also resist poor and oppressive working conditions (Chase, 1987). Women's resistance, however, is often manifested differently than that of male workers, who tend to respond in overtly aggressive ways such as restricting output or striking. Women are more likely to import a "domestic" culture into the workplace by "celebrating major life events together and developing warm and familial friendships which both appropriate and extend beyond work time" (Westwood, 1984, p. 6). This is not to say that women never develop more militant postures or go on strike, but that they tend to respond to the constraints of their work situations by drawing on their experiences outside of work and thus humanizing the workplace. In their more aggressive stance toward unsatisfactory working conditions, men are also drawing on experience. However, it is important to remember that because men hold higher social status than women, they can use it to their advantage vis-à-vis management, which is usually also male. Hence, female and male work cultures can be understood as responses to work conditions, responses that are shaped by the different experiences and positions of men and women.

Women also bring their life experiences (from personal and family spheres) into organizations they create for themselves. Studies of women's organizations (e.g., women's movement organizations, Freeman, 1979; battered women's shelters, Rodriguez, 1988; the Girl Scouts, Helgesen, 1990) have found that they tend to be low in hierarchy, have little role specialization, and have few formal rules. Those organizations established by women for women that are explicitly feminist[1] are the least bureaucratic (Ferguson, 1984; Rodriguez, 1988), and there is evidence that even in the more formally run women's organizations female executives eschew traditional hierarchies in favor of a more participatory, "circular" type of management (Helgesen, 1990).

Studies of women in male-dominated sectors of organizations, in management and the professions, have shown that the structure and culture of these higher-level occupations create problems for women that men do not have to face (Chase, 1987; Cook, 1987; Epstein, 1983; Kanter, 1977). For one thing, while numbers of women in these male-dominated occupations are increasing, women are not reaching the top positions (Cook, 1987; U.S. Department of Labor, 1991). Because women, particularly at the top levels, are relatively scarce in these occupations, they are subjected to "performance pressures because of their visibility, the heightening of boundaries around male collegial groups, and 'role encapsulation'—the tendency of their male coworkers to treat them in stereotypical ways" (Chase, 1987, p. 6). Moreover, as some have pointed out, organizational structures of these occupations are established to suit a traditional male lifestyle, with a wife at home and thus with no extra responsibilities outside of work (Hochschild, 1975). This taken-for-granted aspect of management and the professions impedes the careers of women with families. Many researchers also have shown that the power of these occupations resides in male collegial groups, "old boy networks," and in associations that generally exclude women in subtle and overt ways (Clark and Corcoran, 1986; Kaufman, 1984; Lorber, 1984; Reskin, 1978). Gender discrimination, rooted as it is in the status of women in a male-dominated society, follows women into the world of work and creates visible barriers to their advancement.

The same barriers that make it difficult for women to demonstrate competence and to advance in male-dominated occupations influence women's exercise of leadership. Given the existing sex-stratification patterns in organizations, when the rare woman occupies a top position, she may not be able to exercise authority effectively (Kanter, 1981). Whether there are major sex differences in leadership style is still an open question. Some studies have found none (e.g., Crozier, 1965; Megaree, 1969; Powell, 1988), while others have emphasized women's reluctance to assume visible leadership, their minimization of authoritative exercise of power, and their maximization of subordinate autonomy (Helgesen, 1990; Kanter, 1981; West, 1976).

Given the conditions under which women work in male-dominated organizations, it is small wonder that studies dealing with the presence of women find that it makes little difference to the functioning of these organizations (Kanter, 1981; Frank, 1977). Since powerful positions are occupied largely by men, women have limited opportunity to influence decisions and policies. Most research on women in contemporary male-dominated organizations suggests that women develop two major patterns of adaptation: cooptation and segregation. The first applies to those structures and occupations where women work alongside men but which are male-dominated. Here, women accept male definitions of the situation and try to blend into the male organizational culture. The second pattern manifests itself in groups of female workers who become effectively isolated from the organizational mainstream and cultivate female friendship, support, and cooperation in order to cope with low status and poor working conditions. Both patterns preclude women as a group from having an independent effect on the structure and culture of mainstream organizations. The implications of these findings for women's use of force appear straightforward: women are excluded largely from positions where decisions to use force would be made, and in the rare cases where they are in places of power, they are likely to go along with such decisions.

Are we to conclude, then, that the increasing presence of women in male-dominated organizations has made no difference? Some recent feminist research appears to suggest otherwise. This research attempts to understand women as "subjects" and thus tries to view their organizational existence from their own point of view (Chase, 1987). From this perspective, it becomes clear that the two patterns of adaptation developed by women to cope with their conditions of work are complex and contradictory. For instance, women who appear to have been coopted into male-dominated organizational strata are often painfully cognizant of the contradictions in which they are involved. On the one hand, they are frequently aware of the structural impediments to their full integration and yet the only way they can function is to ignore that knowledge (Chase, 1987, p. 17). Women are thus often simultaneously "immersed in and estranged from" (Westkott, 1979, p. 422) their occupations. The resultant tension arising from a disjuncture between consciousness and behavior has the potential of transforming the workplace.

Some recent studies of women in traditionally male occupations have begun to suggest that the influx of women may be changing some fields. A survey of many occupations by Cihon and Wesman (1987) revealed that women and men performed the same occupations differently, with women placing more importance on cooperation with coworkers and expressive aspects of work relationships. A study of women in architecture found that female architects used a more holistic, socially responsible, and flexible approach to design and planning than their male counterparts (Kennedy, 1989). A study of women prison guards showed that women did not perform the role as men have performed it traditionally; rather, they tended to be more flexible and to develop friendly relations with, and to provide support for, inmates (Zimmer, 1987).

There is evidence that women may be changing some aspects of occupational and organizational structures, but the questions that remain are, what would constitute a meaningful transformation, and under what conditions can women bring about a significant change?

In an organizational context, transformation of existing structure and culture would require a full integration of women, but not on men's terms. The association of managerial and professional qualities with maleness and of low-prestige occupations with femaleness would need to cease as organizations would no longer advantage men over women (Chase, 1987, p. 20). Moreover, women would need to be able to bring into organizations a different perspective or point of view stemming from their own experience as women. Factors that would facilitate this integration might include significant numbers of women at all organizational levels and the extra-organizational existence of independent women's groups with a feminist consciousness and agenda. The next and last section of the chapter focuses on these questions by examining women's attempts to transform politics.

Women Changing Politics

Politics is an important institution on which to focus, particularly in reference to the use of force, as it is within this realm that decisions are made about the utilization of power that affect entire nations. Historically, throughout most of the world, women have been excluded from the political realm and only in recent decades have made some inroads into this male domain.

Researchers who have focused on the increasing numbers of women in political parties, caucuses, governments, and other political organizations have tried to assess the effects of the growing female representation on governmental and military policies (see, e.g., Bystydzienski, 1992a). It is widely assumed that women as a group have something different from men to contribute to politics. Because most human societies for at least the last two thousand years have had a division of labor by sex, women and men have developed different ways of acting and thinking. Thus, for example, women's life-sustaining and preserving activities performed in the realm of the family and immediate community might lead them to take a stronger stance than men against the use of military force (Ruddick, 1989). It is expected that by bringing more cooperative, caring, and less hierarchical values into mainstream politics, women will transform the existing system into a more responsive, democratic one.

In politics, as in economic work organizations, the full integration of women would require not just their numerical or "descriptive" representation, but a "substantive" representation as well (Pitkin, 1967). Women, thus, would need to be able to express their views and concerns and to incorporate them into the agendas, policies, and decisions made by the political organizations they entered.

In the United States, as well as in many other countries, feminists have placed considerable hope on the notion that getting more women into the formal political system would make a difference. For instance, in the United States, the coalition known as the Feminist Majority has actively encouraged women to run for office and women voters to vote for female candidates (Feminist

Majority Report, 1991). In Japan, the last decade has witnessed a growth in the women's movement and an unprecedented support among women for women political candidates (Ling and Matsuno, 1992). But does greater numerical female political representation result in substantive representation? The answer, as we have seen in the discussion of women in male-dominated organizations, is that numbers alone are not enough for women to have an effect on policies and decisions.

While some studies have suggested that female representation has to be at least 15 percent for women to influence group processes (South et al., 1982; Spangler et al., 1978; Yoder et al., 1989), there have been governments with substantially higher female representation where women had no voice. For instance, in the governments of Communist Poland and the Soviet Union women made up a quarter and a third of political representatives, respectively, at the national level, but had no influence as women on the monolithic political structures. This was partly because of the inflexibility of the system and its lack of acceptance of diverse views, as well as because women did not occupy important positions of power and were only selected to fulfill the ideological principle of more equal gender representation (Regulska, 1992). Traditional views and unequal treatment of women persisted in these countries despite a public rhetoric of gender equality (Bystydzienski, 1989b). Most important, the Polish and Soviet women lacked training in grassroots women's movements and did not have a feminist agenda to bring with them into the realm of formal politics. Once the monolithic governments fell in these two countries, women did not enter the newly formed, more democratic structures as women's representatives; in fact, in Poland women got only 14.8 percent of parliamentary seats in the 1990 election, and there were no women at all in the ruling cabinet formed in 1991.

The cases of Norway and Japan, on the other hand, illustrate that women can have an effect on politics whether their numbers are large or small, as long as there exist grassroots movements to train and encourage women to run for public offices and provide support and pressure for change from outside the existing political system. Norway has recently achieved a 47 percent female representation in the ruling cabinet, has a 35 percent female representation in parliament, and has over 30 percent at the local level (Royal Norwegian Embassy, 1990). Japan's female representation is minuscule by comparison: 5.9 percent at the national level and only 2.3 percent in municipal councils (Kubo, 1990). However, despite the enormous difference in women's numerical representation, in both countries a strong women's presence has been felt in the political realm.

Although Norway historically has had some female involvement in politics, particularly at the local level, women's political representation did not become significant until the 1970s. A well-organized women's movement dedicated to getting more women elected to Norway's local and national legislatures was the crucial factor in this achievement (Bystydzienski, 1987). Moreover, the movement recognized that women as a group had something unique to bring into politics by virtue of their different experiences as women living in a male-dominated society (Bystydzienski, 1992b). Beginning in the late 1960s, activist women, aided by most of the political parties and the government, organized election campaigns to get more women into politics. These campaigns were so effective that in the course of two decades female representation more than tripled at the national level, from less than 10 percent in the 1960s to 35 percent in the late 1980s. At the municipal level, women's representation rose from 5 percent in 1963 to 30 percent by 1986 (Forde and Hernes, 1988). The increasing number of women began in the 1970s to have an effect on government policies and legislation.

In 1978, Norway adopted an Equal Status Act, which is the only legal provision of its type in the world because, unlike its equivalents in other countries, it is not neutral according to gender. The opening paragraph of this document states: "This Act shall promote equal status between the sexes and aims particularly at improving the position of women" (Ministry of Consumer Affairs and Government Administration, 1985, p. 5). The Act also acknowledges that it is not possible to achieve equal status between men and women merely by prohibiting discrimination and indicates that affirmative measures must be taken to rectify discrepancies between the sexes in education, at work, and in politics. The lack of gender neutrality of the Act is directly attributable to the influence of the female politicians who were involved in drafting the document and to a strong women's movement that insisted that the Act reflect a view of equality in accordance with women's interests (Bystydzienski, 1992b). The further establishment of an "Ombud" (or commissioner's) office to enforce the provisions of the Equal Status Act and the addition in 1981 of a provision aimed at increasing the number of women on all publicly appointed committees, boards, and councils made the Norwegian Act a document with teeth, unlike those of most other countries.

Women's views and concerns have been reflected in many other political measures and policies in Norway. By the mid-1980s, several political parties officially accepted sex quotas (at least 40 percent representation of each sex among party candidates in elections), while the remaining parties did so unofficially. Despite a worsening economy in the 1980s because of the fall of North Sea oil prices, the Norwegian government increased its emphasis on families. Child-care subsidies have grown, and paid parental leave was raised from sixteen to eighteen weeks. Provisions were made also for parents to take up to ten days each (single parents, twenty) from work for family emergencies (Overholser, 1987, p. 16).

The growing responsiveness of the Norwegian political parties and government to women's issues coincided with the increasing number of women in public offices. As more women entered the Norwegian Parliament and county and municipal councils, they brought specific women's concerns to governmental discussions, debates, and legislation. Many of these women received their political training in the women's movement and were sympathetic to the views and demands of women; many considered themselves feminists. They thus took a feminist agenda developed by the women's movement into establishment politics, where it had a significant impact (Bystydzienski, 1992b).

There is some indication that in Norway women in politics have been able to promote a more peaceful stance on a number of issues than did previous governments and organizations that had fewer women as members. While the country has had a tradition of social justice and peace, the growing number of feminist women in politics have pioneered as well as supported sound environmental policies, antinuclear power provisions, and development aid targeting women in Third World countries.

Japan has not had the same steady influx of women into political offices as Norway. In fact, the highest number of women elected to the Japanese National Diet (about 8 percent) took place in 1947, the first election in which women were allowed to vote (Robins-Mowry, 1983, p. 95); Japanese women have yet to surpass this record. Nevertheless, women's political activism continued after World War II and intensified in the subsequent decades.

Japanese women have had a history of pacifist and antimilitaristic actions. There was a strong feminist opposition to Japan's involvement in both world wars and to the government's military expansionism in China in the 1930s (Bingham and Gross, 1987). Although a full-fledged peace movement did not develop in Japan until the 1960s, women carried on their antiwar stance from earlier in the century during the post–World War II period. Their activism was renewed by the nuclear devastation at Hiroshima and Nagasaki as well as by the postwar U.S. military occupation. During the late 1940s and the 1950s, women staged protests near U.S. military bases aiming to reclaim lost land and to stop prostitution (Caldecott, 1983). Later, as the Japanese peace movement took hold, women demonstrated in large numbers against nuclear weapons and the use of nuclear energy (Pharr, 1981).

By the 1960s, many Japanese women were involved in civic organizations such as the Parent-Teachers Association or housewives' associations. These groups provided women with organizational training and became important avenues for networking. Many women who had served in civic organizations subsequently joined political parties, became involved in political campaigns, and even ran for public office (Bingham and Gross, 1987, p. 296). Japanese women also became active in environmental and consumer movements. Women led the Anti-Minamata Disease campaign during the 1960s (Bingham and Gross, 1987, p. 296) and later spearheaded numerous demonstrations and protests against industrial pollution, deforestation, and disposal of hazardous wastes. Since the 1960s, Japanese women also have formed consumer cooperatives that at first focused on ways to increase the quality and reduce the cost of consumer goods and now increasingly serve as avenues for recruiting and promoting political candidates (Kubo, 1990). It is the co-ops, run and staffed mostly by women, that have become centers of the grassroots Japanese women's movement.

Japanese women thus have had three decades of social activism before they began to focus on political offices, to organize campaigns to bring more women into politics as candidates, and to convince women to vote for their own sex. Several corruption scandals in the ruling governments and the introduction of a proportional representation system for elections to the Upper House of the Diet in 1980 aided Japanese women in their resolve (Ling and Matsuno, 1992).

Research on women in politics in Japan indicates that female politicians have brought a different dimension into political offices. They focus more than their male counterparts on quality-of-life issues, including problems of everyday life faced by families and individuals. Their down-to-earth approach makes politics more understandable to the general public, and there is widespread belief, especially among female voters, that gender can make a difference in terms of how politics is conducted (Ling and Matsuno, 1992). The relatively few women politicians have given a great deal of attention to the problems of the environment, and in 1991, when the Japanese Diet was debating whether to give several million dollars to the United States to cover expenses incurred by the Gulf War, it was the female representatives who argued most vehemently for spending the money on refugees from the Gulf region.

The Japanese case clearly shows that in order for women to make a difference in politics, grassroots training and a recognition of and commitment to women's views and concerns must be fostered among those running for political office. Although numerous women with such backgrounds help immensely to bring about change, numbers alone will not suffice.

The importance of a link between women's, especially feminist, organizations and female politicians should not be underestimated. There is evidence from the United States (where female politicians are relatively few) that female legislators who are involved with women's organizations are most active in representing women's issues and concerns in their work; they are notably more likely than men and than other women politicians to work on legislation aimed at helping women (Carroll, 1992).

Summary and Conclusion

The sociological studies of women in groups and organizations have indicated that even though structures occupied by women only are substantially different from those filled by men only, in mixed-sex situations women generally do not exert much influence as women on group processes and organizational decisionmaking because they are typically excluded from positions of power. Moreover, even when women do attain more influential positions, their lower social status interferes with their ability to insert their views.

It has been assumed widely that more equal numbers of women in male-dominated groups and organizations should bring about a balance of male and female perspectives. However, as the case studies of women in politics reviewed here have shown, numbers alone are not a sufficient precondition for a "women's effect." It is clear that just getting more women into elected offices will not bring about significant change. Women entering the political realm need to have training in grassroots women's movements and to have a feminist agenda to bring with them. While in office, they need to work with other female politicians and women's groups and organizations outside the system.

As the cases of Norway and Japan indicate, women can make a difference in politics provided they are backed by women's organizations and see themselves as representatives of women's interests and concerns. Under such conditions women can insert more peaceful views into political agendas and perhaps even influence military policies in the direction of lesser use of force.

Note

In this chapter, "feminism" refers to a general perspective that recognizes the oppression of women by men and seeks to reduce sex inequality. Thus an explicitly feminist organization is one that officially endorses this view.

chapter 5

Handgun Ownership Among U.S. Women and Its Consequences for Social Judgment

Nyla R. Branscombe, Susan Owen

The United States has been designated the "gun culture" by one prominent historian (Hofstadter, 1970). Although the number of weapons in private hands in the United States cannot be determined precisely, evidence from a variety of sociological sources indicates that as of 1980 there were approximately 120 million guns, with every other household possessing one (Wright, Daly, and Rossi, 1983). Approximately one-third of the guns owned by U.S. citizens are easily concealed handguns, purchased for the stated purpose of self-defense.

In the past, weaponry of all sorts, and guns in particular, were primarily a male-only domain (Arkin and Dobrofsky, 1978), but increasing numbers of U.S. women have been purchasing guns (Quigley, 1989). On the assumption that women are an insufficiently tapped consumer group, Smith and Wesson, the largest U.S. handgun manufacturer, began in 1989 to market a new line of weapons—the Ladysmith, a .38 caliber revolver—designed specifically for women. This company expects sales of handguns to women to continue rising (with another 15 to 16 million making this purchase during the early 1990s), and their advertisements, found in many national women's magazines, emphasize how a gun allows a woman to protect herself and her family (Pero, personal communication, April 1989). Although estimates vary considerably across sources, somewhere between 12 million and 42 million American women currently own a gun (Quigley, 1989).

This ongoing social change in the gender composition of gun owners in the United States has received little research attention, although what is known about the psychological and sociological factors involved will be examined in this chapter. Specifically, research on attitudes toward guns, the motivation behind their purchase, the characteristics of women who do buy guns, observers' inferences about women who own guns, and the judgments made about women who use guns will be examined.

Attitudes Toward Guns

Guns, and the violence that can result from their use, have received considerable media attention. Debates between anti–gun-control supporters and advocates of gun-control laws abound. The National Rifle Association, a prominent anti–gun-control organization, argues that guns protect their owners against crime. Pro-control advocates, on the other hand, suggest that guns do not protect their owners against criminal victimization but that they actually stimulate crime and other forms of aggressive behavior (Berkowitz, 1974). If guns were not so easily accessible, according to the pro-control advocates, then fewer gun-related violent deaths, including suicides (for which firearms usage is increasing; see McIntosh and Santos, 1982), would occur. In an attempt to understand how individuals differ in their beliefs about guns, Branscombe, Weir, and Crosby (1991) developed a scale to measure these two perspectives on gun ownership—that guns provide their owners with protection and guns stimulate violence—as well as the more general issue of whether gun ownership is (or should be) a basic U.S. right.

Men and women differed in their responses to these three attitude dimensions, with males displaying more positive attitudes toward guns, relative to females. This is consistent with prior research suggesting that men are more tolerant of aggressive stands on both domestic and international topics than are women (Eagly and Steffen, 1986; Kelley and Schmidt, 1989; Oskamp, 1977). Women are more likely to perceive guns as a stimulant to crime, and they are less likely than men to believe that guns protect their owners from victimization. In addition, women are less likely to endorse gun ownership as a general right that the U.S. public should possess.

To understand why people differ in their attitudes toward guns, a variety of other factors were also assessed. People who believe that gun ownership is a basic right and who believe that guns are protection from criminal victimization tend to be politically conservative; display pride in their U.S. identity; perceive themselves as sports fans; and possess more negative attitudes regarding women's roles, behaviors, and characteristics (e.g., believe an unmarried mother is morally a greater failure than an unmarried father, and a woman who refuses to bear children has failed in her duty to her husband). People who agree with the idea that guns stimulate crime tend to be politically liberal, have less pride in the United States, do not consider themselves sports fans, and strongly endorse feminist attitudes (e.g., believe that women have the right to compete with men in every sphere of activity).

Political conservatism, high self-esteem, and pride in one's national identity uniquely predict beliefs about gun ownership as a citizen's right. Believing that others are not trustworthy, having little self-perceived personal independence, and disagreeing with feminist ideas are the strongest predictors of agreement with the notion that guns provide protection from victimization. Political liberalism and a low frequency of experiencing anger are the best predictors of acceptance of the possibility that gun availability stimulates crime.

Thus, we see a constellation of psychological characteristics that are related to attitudes toward guns among both men and women. However, men in general report more positive attitudes toward guns than women do. What are the major factors that differentiate between male and female gun owners? Why is the rate of U.S. women purchasing guns increasing, yet the rate among men remaining relatively constant?

Fear of Victimization and Actual Risk

Fear of victimization may be one factor underlying the increase in gun ownership among women. Fear of criminal victimization is, however, not strongly related to actual vulnerability or risk (Maxfield, 1984). In the United States, young, single, minority males who live in urban areas have the highest likelihood of being victims of interpersonal violence and of sustaining injury as a consequence of that victimization. Their assailants are likely to have similar demographic characteristics (Gottfredson, 1984; Hough and Mayhew, 1983; Skogan and Maxfield, 1981). In contrast to their high level of actual risk of criminal victimization, these men report feeling reasonably safe or very safe on the streets alone after dark. Although fear increases with age and varies by area of residence, overall, men's reported fear is approximately one-third that of women's (Chambers and Tombs, 1984; Hindelang, Gottfredson, and Garofalo, 1978; Hough and Mayhew, 1983; Maxfield, 1984; Skogan and Maxfield, 1981). Thus, even though men of all ages appear to be at greater risk of criminal victimization by strangers than are women, men report feeling safer than women do.

Women actually constitute a "low-risk" population with respect to interpersonal criminal violence by strangers, according to the results of government-sponsored victimization surveys (Stanko,

1987). The demographic characteristics of women and men who have been victims are generally the same, although there is one major difference between the two. Men report same-gender assailants. Women, on the other hand, are not victimized by other women; they are victimized by men, who frequently sexually assault them in addition to the battering that male victims experience. Criminal violence for women takes on elements of sexual violence and is often an action by a man known to a woman. Women are more likely to be physically assaulted, beaten, and killed in their own homes "at the hands of a loved one than anyplace else or by anyone else in our society" (Gelles and Strauss, 1988, p. 5). Yet, stereotypical images about criminal violence remain focused on violence occurring outside, on the street, or by home intruders, all of whom typically involve strangers. Despite their reported low risk of such forms of victimization, women constitute the group most fearful of such crime (Balkin, 1979; Dubrow, 1979; Rigor and Gordon, 1981; Smith and Uchida, 1988). Thus, for the most part, women have more fear of criminal victimization by strangers than do men, although the type of crime they fear from unknown street assailants and burglars is actually where they are least at risk.

Women's fear of crime is indeed proportionate to their subjective estimates of their risk of rape (Rigor and Gordon, 1981), a crime they are at considerable risk of experiencing by someone known to them. Recent surveys estimate that between one-third and one-half of all U.S. women will be victims of rape or attempted rape during their lifetimes (Russell, 1982; Koss, Gidycz, and Wisniewski, 1987). Again, however, just as with other forms of criminal victimization, the fear is primarily of sexual assaults from strangers, which are actually more likely to be committed by someone known to the victim. We will now examine how women cope with their elevated fear of victimization.

**Women's Strategies for
Protecting Themselves from Crime**

Precautionary strategies are mechanisms for coping with feelings of vulnerability and insecurity. Tyler (1980) found that perceived personal vulnerability of criminal victimization is strongly related to crime-prevention behavior. Individuals who have been victimized tend to perceive themselves as more vulnerable after the event than they did before, and they are likely to change their behavior as a means of avoiding future victimization (Perloff, 1983). Women's precautionary strategies for avoiding victimization have traditionally involved social isolation (i.e., not going out at night), the use of "safe" men (i.e., men known and trusted by that woman, who serve as escorts) as protection from other men, and the use of other precautionary strategies when they are out alone at night (Rigor and Gordon, 1981).

Conflicting recommendations concerning how a woman should respond if and when she is attacked are rampant (Morgan, 1986). Despite the mixed messages concerning the value of resistance versus passivity, enrollment in self-defense classes is rising, as is the number of women purchasing guns to use as weapons (Bales, 1988; Gibbs, 1988; Quigley, 1989). The purchase of a gun for protection against criminal victimization is a precautionary strategy that many women report they have already undertaken or they are actively considering for the future (Branscombe and Owen, 1991). With more women becoming socially and economically independent of men (U.S. Bureau of the Census, 1979) and assuming the traditional male roles of protector and provider by becoming heads of households and/or homeowners, they are also taking responsibility for their own safety. Either these women are not willing to use traditional precautionary strategies, those strategies are not available to them, or they perceive the traditional precautionary strategies as unlikely to be successful. For example, it is difficult to differentiate "safe" men from "unsafe" men, as evidenced by the fact that most rapes are committed by men known to women (Koss et al., 1987). In addition, recent survey research indicates that up to 67 percent of dating relationships involve some kind of violence (Gelles and Strauss, 1988), domestic violence is the major cause of injury to women under forty in the United States (Basow, 1986), and approximately 14 percent of women experience marital rape (Finkelhor and Yllo, 1985; Russell, 1982).

Characteristics of Gun Owners

Smith and Uchida (1988) report that people who purchase guns for self-protection have had a household member victimized in the last year, believe crime is increasing in their neighborhood, believe that police service is poor in their area, and tend to live in urban centers. Male gun owners have been found to have a high need for power, to be more willing to approve of the use of force, to have had more experience with violence, and to be more fearful than male non–gun-owners are (Lizotte and Bordua, 1980). Men who do not own guns are more sociable and have a higher need for affiliation, relative to male gun owners (Diener and Kerber, 1979).

The little research that has examined the characteristics of women who own guns suggests that single urban women who own guns have a pessimistic perception of others, favor the use of force to resolve societal and social problems, are Protestant, and have been victims of criminal violence. This implies that fear of victimization is an important motivator for gun purchases among women, as neither occupation nor education distinguished female gun owners from females who do not own guns (Williams, Marolla, and McGrath, 1981).

What determines a woman's choice of gun ownership as a self-protective strategy, among the many possibilities that could be selected (i.e., home burglary alarm systems, owning a large dog, and so on)? Lizotte and Bordua (1980) suggest that family socialization determines gun ownership, particularly among males. People who have been raised in households where guns are present and who therefore have experience with firearms are most likely to choose a gun for self-protection. This difference in familiarity and experience with weapons among men and women might explain why women are more likely to believe that guns stimulate crime as opposed to the notion that guns protect them against crime (Branscombe, Weir, and Crosby, 1991). Women in general have simply had less exposure to guns during their early years than men have. Even though the evidence that handgun ownership does actually provide real protection from criminal victimization is inconsistent (Wright et al., 1983), gun ownership might provide a sense of psychological security for some people (Yeager, 1976), especially those who have been previously victimized.

To summarize, it appears that, among women, choosing a gun for protection against crime is a growing phenomenon. This change in gun ownership appears to mirror other social changes that have been simultaneously occurring (e.g., in women's increased participation in the work force and the growing number of women who are heads of households). Much remains unknown about the motivations underlying gun purchases among both women and men, however. Fear of victimization (regardless of actual risk potential) appears to be a critical factor for women who choose to adopt this nontraditional self-protective strategy, based on the limited literature that is available. Familiarity with guns may also be an important determinant in specifically choosing a gun for self-defense purposes. It appears that although a gun may not provide any real protection against the most common types of victimization events that women are likely to experience, it may act as a method of calming fears related to vulnerability and victimization.

Are there any important social consequences for those women who choose a gun as a self-protective strategy? The notion that a woman should not own a gun for self-protection because it can be easily taken away from her and, as a consequence, be used against her ignores the fact that women who do own guns are more likely than men to acquire professional training to learn to use them safely and competently. Nevertheless, the issue of how women gun owners are viewed by others is an important one. The following sections review a series of studies that investigated the perceptions of male and female gun owners, as well as the judgments made about those who injure another person with a gun.

Consequences of Gun Ownership for Social Inferences

Traditionally, gun ownership has been primarily male, a role ranging from playing with toy guns to enactment of actual military roles (Arkin and Dobrofsky, 1978). Men have almost exclusively occupied hunting and offensive roles, as well as that of protector. Furthermore, as a result of Freud's influence on everyday culture (see Brenner, 1974), guns come to be identified symbolically as the essence of masculinity (e.g., served as a penis symbol). Thus, gun ownership is inconsistent with stereotypes of American women. The consequences of this deviation from expectancies were examined in two studies: one involving a college student sample and the other involving a larger community-based sample (Branscombe and Owen, 1991). The influence of gun ownership on social inferences concerning three important components of expectations about men and women—the roles they occupy, their physical attributes, and the traits they possess—were investigated.

It was expected that because weapons ownership is consistent with social expectations for men, ownership or nonownership would have less impact on how men are perceived than on how women are perceived. Guns are symbols of aggression, and it is more socially acceptable for men to behave aggressively than it is for women to do so (Eagly and Steffen, 1986). Hence, gun ownership is consistent with expectations for men and should have relatively little impact on the inferences made about them. There is one caveat to this reasoning, however. If respondents infer that a gun-owning male cannot defend himself without a weapon (he is an inadequate male), then gun ownership might reduce his perceived "masculinity" relative to a non–gun-owning male.

In contrast to men, it was expected that relatively large differences would occur in the inferences drawn about women who own a gun and those who do not. Because gun ownership is consistent with male behavior, this type of stereotype inconsistency in women should lead people to assume such women also possess other masculine attributes. Thus, it was anticipated that female gun owners would be "masculinized" by gun ownership, taking on the psychological and physical attributes of males as a result of this violation of expectancies for females. Other research not directly involving the use of weapons has made the point that both men and women are closely scrutinized, are perceived differently, and are often penalized for behaving in a way that is stereotype inconsistent (Branscombe and Weir, 1992; Clary and Tesser, 1983; Costrich, Feinstein, Kidder, Marecek, and Pascale, 1975; Kelly, Kern, Kirkley, Patterson, and Keane, 1980; Fiske, 1982; Pyszczynski and Greenberg, 1981).

Although the demographic characteristics of the two samples studied varied widely, the results were virtually identical, with the community sample showing slightly stronger effects of gun ownership on social inferences than the college student sample. In both studies, participants were randomly assigned to indicate on scales of 0 to 100 percent the likelihood that either a male or a female who either owned a gun or for whom no mention of a gun was made possessed various traits, roles, and physical characteristics.

Women who were said to own a gun were perceived as equally likely to possess male physical traits (e.g., they were broad-shouldered, muscular, and tall), positive male traits (e.g., they were independent, bold, and decisive), and negative male traits (e.g., they were reckless, forceful, and aggressive), as were males who were described as gun owners. However, women who do not own guns were assumed to possess significantly fewer of these characteristics than were men who do not own guns. Thus, females who own guns gain in terms of the male stereotypic traits that they are believed to possess, while there is a tendency for males who own guns to lose some of these male stereotypic qualities. Females who are said to own a gun were also assumed to be just as unlikely as males to occupy female-dominated roles (e.g., secretary, homemaker). Women who do not own a gun are, however, assumed to be more likely to occupy such roles, relative to men. Finally, gun ownership reduces the likability of the owner, and this was particularly true for women. When gun ownership was not mentioned, women were perceived as more likable than men. Gun ownership eliminated this difference.

Both men and women with negative attitudes toward guns made more negative inferences about gun owners than about non–gun-owners, regardless of the gun owner's sex. However, the differential effects of gun ownership on social inferences drawn about women and men did not depend on the participant's attitude toward guns. It appears that gun ownership is indeed inconsistent with the stereotype of women, and, of course, gender stereotypic expectancies are very widespread throughout the population.

Thus, women who own guns are "masculinized," whereas gun ownership has relatively little effect on inferences about men, although there was a tendency for male gun owners to lose some of their masculine qualities. It is possible that the image of a man with a gun depends on the motive that is inferred for its ownership. If participants in the two studies assumed that the male gun owners possessed the gun because they were unable to defend themselves by simply relying on their own physical abilities, then this perceived loss of masculinity relative to males who do not require such external assistance would be easily explained. For the average woman, perhaps the very idea of self-protection is inconsistent with social expectancies, leading females with guns to be perceived as different from women who do not own guns. Traditionally, women have relied on men to protect them rather than assuming this role themselves. At any rate, the perceptions of women who own guns resemble those of men and on the whole are less positive than those made about women who do not own guns.

It is likely that many women who already own a handgun, or who intend to purchase one in the future, implicitly realize that such ownership is inconsistent with stereotypes and that they might be socially penalized for it. The gun manufacturer Smith and Wesson is providing a toll-free anonymous telephone service for women wanting to learn more about how to use and where to buy their product. According to Smith and Wesson representatives, some of these new female buyers do not want anyone to know that they are buying a weapon because it would bring shame and embarrassment (Pero, personal communication, April 1989). We turn now to the issue of how men and women who actually use the gun they own to injure a home intruder are perceived.

Social Judgment Consequences
When a Gun Is Used to Injure Another Person

People who use a gun against a burglar who invades their home are very likely to receive considerable scrutiny from the police, the media, and even the court system. With more women purchasing handguns to protect themselves and their families against home intruders, making judgments of such events is an important social issue, particularly given that women who simply own a gun are less liked and are assumed to be more like men than women who do not own guns. Given the increase in gun ownership among women, such judgments will probably be required increasingly in the future.

Does gun ownership provide any real protection against crime? Are homeowners who possess a gun during a burglary of their residence more or less likely to be injured by the intruder? Kleck and Bordua's (1983) review of interview studies with convicted burglars indicates that these prisoners do report being keenly aware of the possibility that a homeowner might possess a gun and use it to injure them. Although the percentage of burglars who are foiled by an armed homeowner is exceedingly small (2 percent), this risk is, if anything, slightly greater than the probability that a burglar will ever be convicted and imprisoned (Wright et al., 1983). Nevertheless, the likelihood of injury to the homeowner does appear to be somewhat elevated when the homeowner is armed (Williams et al., 1981). Regardless of whether widespread gun ownership serves as an effective deterrent to burglars, many citizens believe that it does serve this function (Branscombe et al., 1991).

The circumstances in which the use of deadly force by one human being against another is legally justified varies by state in the United States, although for the most part three conditions need to be met. Specifically, the shooting of another person (e.g., a home intruder) can be deemed justifiable and legal if it can be demonstrated that the intruder had the ability, opportunity, and intention of causing grave bodily harm or death to the occupant of that residence (see Kates and Engberg, 1983, and Lafave and Scott, 1972, for further legal discussions on the use of deadly force).

This section will present two studies that investigated the judgmental consequences of the use of a gun by a male or a female homeowner (Branscombe, Crosby, and Weir, in press). It was assumed that because the stereotype of men is that they are more competent than women, especially in a traditionally male domain such as use of weaponry, a male homeowner who used a gun incompetently would be more likely to be perceived as guilty of a crime than would a male homeowner who was competent in the use of a gun. In the first study the incompetent male gun user did not actually injure the intruder, but the competent male shooter did. That is, the bullet was said to have hit the intruder or to have missed him. We expected that the incompetent male shooter would be perceived as more guilty than the male shooter who was stereotype consistent and successfully used the weapon to injure an intruder. The opposite was, however, expected for female shooters. Stereotypically, females do not own guns, and if they do, they are expected to be incompetent in their use. Therefore, female homeowners who shot an intruder competently were expected to be perceived as more guilty of a crime than were incompetent female shooters. In both cases—that of the incompetent male shooter and the competent female shooter—violation of people's stereotypes were expected to increase perceived guilt and blame for the outcome.

In the first experiment this idea was tested by having either a male or a female homeowner hit or miss a burglar who was in the home attempting to steal a stereo. In the second experiment the scenario was altered slightly. In the later study, in all cases the homeowner's bullet always hit the thief who was breaking into a car in the homeowner's driveway. The competence manipulation involved hitting the thief either as a result of skill in the use of a gun or because the bullet ricocheted off the ground and hit the thief (i.e., skill versus luck). Degree of confidence that the homeowner was guilty of a crime and degree of perceived harm to the intruder were measured in the first study. In the second study, blame assigned to the homeowner for the incident, homeowner likability, and severity of the punishment advocated for the homeowner were measured. In addition, in the second study, the extent to which participants believed that guns provide their owner with protection was assessed several weeks before the experiment was conducted.

As expected, results from the first experiment showed that incompetent female shooters were less likely to be perceived as guilty of a crime, relative to competent female shooters. On the other hand, competent male shooters were less likely to be perceived as guilty of a crime compared to incompetent male shooters. The competent female shooter was perceived as producing more injury to the intruder than was the competent male shooter. The incompetent male was perceived as producing more injury than was the incompetent female. In other words, people who deviated from sex roles were perceived as producing more serious outcomes and as being more guilty of a crime.

Results from the second experiment also supported our hypotheses and were consistent with what was found in the first study. For persons who strongly believe that gun ownership provides them with protection from crime, homeowners who violated those stereotypes, especially skilled female shooters, were evaluated less positively, were considered more to blame for the outcome, and were perceived as deserving greater punishment than were either of the stereotype-consistent targets—the skilled male shooter or the unskilled female shooter.

Previous research (Branscombe, Weir, and Crosby, 1991), reviewed earlier in the chapter, revealed that the belief that guns provide protection against crime is uniquely predicted by disagreement with feminist beliefs. Thus, it is likely that persons of both genders who agree with traditional gender stereotypes are the most likely to blame a competent woman shooter, relative to a competent man who shoots an intruder. His behavior is consistent with gender and attitudinal expectancies, whereas hers is not.

Conclusions

Stereotype-based expectancies guide judgment and decisionmaking processes concerning what women who own guns are like, how they should be treated if they do use deadly force with a gun, and evaluations of their actions. In this research, events involving guns were not simply judged based upon their consequences. If that were the case, in the first study both male and female homeowners who hit the intruder should have been judged similarly. They were not. In fact, perceived severity of the consequences depended on how consistent the person's actions were with gender and attitudinal expectations. People were also not just using perceived threat of bodily harm when evaluating the actions undertaken by the homeowner. If so, then female homeowners, by virtue of their smaller size, should have been perceived as less likely to be guilty of a crime and as less blameworthy or punishable for their actions. Particularly in the second homeowner shooting experiment, we found that skilled female shooters were considered the most blameworthy and deserving the highest punishment when the event was inconsistent with the perceiver's attitudinal expectancies. People are often unaware that their stereotypes are guiding their inference and decisionmaking processes (see Branscombe and Smith, 1990), but nonetheless stereotype effects were clearly observed in the present research.

Whether the conclusions drawn here would hold for women whose roles require the use of force such as military or police officers is an open question. Role-based expectancies may be stronger than gender-based expectancies in some cases. Further experimental work involving the perception of military or police women and men who use guns to defend themselves in the course of their jobs could easily address this issue. In addition, we cannot be certain whether the differential desire to punish a homeowner for using a weapon to injure an intruder would be observed among trial judges either in deciding guilt or innocence or in making sentencing decisions themselves. However, as Parisi's (1982) review of the research on sentencing decisions in the criminal justice system indicates, sentencing is generally equal for males and females when the seriousness of the offense is controlled for, although occasionally it appears that "negative (punitive) treatment is accorded females for 'manly' crimes" (p. 215). It appears that although women may be treated more leniently when the crime is stereotype consistent, such as shoplifting or check fraud, there is evidence that when women commit crimes that are not expected of women such as violent crimes (e.g., murder and assault), their punishment is more severe (Chesney-Lind, 1987). Not only are women punished more severely than men for these crimes, but when determining their sentences, judges more harshly punish women who do not fit the societal norms for women. In other words, women who are not married, who do not have children, or who are not economically dependent on someone such as a father or husband receive more severe sentences than do married women with children (Edwards, 1984). Ironically, the demographic characteristics of women who receive more severe sentences are precisely those of women who are choosing guns as a self-protective strategy.

Summary

Increasing numbers of women are choosing handguns as a protective strategy against potential criminal victimization. Little is known about the sociological and psychological characteristics of these women. What is known is that many women who choose to arm themselves fear victimization and may have experienced an assault during the past year. While research suggests that possession of a gun provides little real protection against the kinds of crime that women are most at risk of experiencing, possession of a gun may provide psychological security for the owner. However, our research indicates that there are consequences for women who either own a gun or use one during a burglary of their home. Women who own guns are perceived as being psychologically and physically similar to men, compared with women who do not own a gun. Women who own guns are also disliked more than women who do not own guns. Women who skillfully use a gun to thwart a burglary are more likely to be viewed as guilty of a crime relative to women who are incompetent, particularly by perceivers who believe that guns should provide their owners with protection from such forms of criminal victimization. So, even though a gun may provide a sense of security against rape and other violent crimes, it can have potentially severe consequences for the perception of women, especially if they actually use it to protect themselves or their possessions. Women who violate traditional gender role stereotypes by using a gun may expect to be penalized by the legal system for doing so.

chapter 6

Women in Law Enforcement

Barbara Carson

The legitimate use of force has been described as acts causing pain or injury that are socially approved (Collins, 1974; Goode, 1971; 1972). Such acts are endorsed by our society when force is used by individuals appointed to maintain social control, such as military personnel, or, as is the focus of this chapter, police officers. Historically, employment in these occupations has been denied to females, and in the case of police officers, it is issues surrounding the use of force that have been used to justify this exclusion.

This chapter will trace the historical evolution of the role of police and the reasons that an emphasis on the use of force led to the conclusion that women were not suited for the job. It will be seen how women in the early 1900s redefined the nature of police work by reducing the importance of the use of force, thus allowing for their own entrance into the profession. A review of current practices will show that contemporary female police officers use force differently than male officers do. Finally, a brief review of current thought on policing will show that women's approaches to social control and the use of force are now becoming the recommended standards for all police officers, regardless of their sex.

The Legitimation of Force in Policing

Scholars analyzing the legitimate use of force, or as it is sometimes called, legitimate violence, argue that it is typically a rational human response. Such acts are usually goal-oriented and entail behavior incorporated into everyday systems of actions (Ball-Rokeach, 1980). These acts may be sanctioned by laws, court systems, economic systems, and community norms (Goode, 1971, 1972). Definitions of legitimate and illegitimate use of force tend to vary depending upon historical period, context, and circumstances (Williams, 1981).

Police officers in the United States are allowed to use more force than other citizens on the assumption that police are thereby enabled to maintain order and control. So, for example, police are authorized to carry guns and are allowed to use them in situations where most citizens are not. This access to legitimate force has been permitted ever since the establishment of modern policing in the United States.

Police departments in this country were first formed after an experiment in London (Walker, 1992), where Sir Robert Peel established the first modern police department in 1829. The British had rejected the idea of police for more than five hundred years, fearing that a quasimilitary organization would deny citizens personal liberties, but by the early nineteenth century the desire for safety in the street and a civil society prevailed, and the London government agreed to try the idea of fulltime police officers (Reith, 1943).

In this British model, job requirements to become a police officer were stringent. One had to be healthy, strong, literate, law-abiding, an outstanding citizen in the community—and male. Considerable screening ensured that these officers were men who refrained from any "ungentlemanlike" behavior, such as swearing or drinking alcohol (Lundman, 1980).

When the first police departments were created in the United States (Boston in 1838, New York City in 1845, and Chicago in 1851), much of the organizational structure and job responsibilities were modeled on the London police force, but the criteria for hiring the first U.S. police officers were very different (Walker, 1977). In the United States, police work was a political patronage job (Miller, 1973). Men who supported the winning political party were eligible to be hired as police officers. Whenever there was a change in political rule (such as a new mayor from a different political party), a whole new police department was hired (Walker, 1992). "Ungentlemanlike" behavior was common among police in the United States. Lack of intelligence, poor health, and a criminal record did not prevent a man from becoming a police officer (Reith, 1980; Walker, 1977).

The duties of the first police departments were much different from those of police departments today. They were neither responsible for nor concerned about the investigation of crime. Their purpose was to maintain order—to make the streets safe and to control groups of people defined by others as undesirable (Cox, 1974; Lundman, 1980)—and it was hoped that patrolling would prevent crime.

The first police departments in the southern states were

community organizations established to maintain the institution of slavery (Wintersmith, 1974). Their job was to arrest any slave who was not on the master's property and to inspect community houses, looking for runaway slaves. There was great concern that because black slaves outnumbered free whites, the slaves might organize and start a rebellion. Southern police departments were created to make sure this did not happen: i.e., to serve as slave patrols (Williams and Murphy, 1990).

Local police departments in northern communities were also created to control undesirable segments of the population. There was a strong fear among property owners that the undesirables of their community might be dangerous and that they should be monitored and punished if necessary. Many northern police departments were created to stop race riots and to force labor back to work (Lundman, 1980; Walker, 1992). The first state police organization was created in Pittsburgh, Pennsylvania, with the specific purpose of getting rioting, striking members of labor back to work.

From the beginning, police were not only allowed the legitimate use of force for social control. Adhering to the sexual division of labor at that time, when men were considered the protectors and women physically and morally weak, women were not allowed to be police officers (Martin, 1980).

Introduction of Women into Policing

Women began to be hired as police officers in the late nineteenth century; they quickly appeared in departments throughout the United States. However, the type of work done by women officers was much different from that done by men, and this division of labor remained until the 1970s. Also, while most police departments today have female officers, the percentage of females is still extremely low.

In 1893, the mayor of Chicago appointed the first woman to work in a police department. She was Maria Owens, the widow of a former patrol officer. Her duties were to assist male detectives when they were working on cases involving girls or adult women (Lunneborg, 1989). She had no arrest powers.

The first woman to be a sworn officer with arrest powers was Alice Stebbins Wells, who was a graduate of a theology seminary and had been a social worker in several church-related social work positions. She felt strongly that social workers should engage in preventative and protective activities, particularly for the benefit of women and children. She argued with the chief of the Los Angeles police department that she could better achieve these goals if she had police powers of arrest. In 1910, she was hired with the duties of supervising and enforcing laws concerning juveniles and women at dance halls, skating rinks, movie theaters, and other public recreational facilities. Although she could arrest people, she could not wear a uniform or carry a gun (Horne, 1980).

Wells lectured to women's organizations throughout the United States, arguing that all departments should hire female officers. She spoke to groups such as the American Female Reform Society, the Women's Christian Temperance Union, and the League of Women Voters. She argued that women were needed as police officers to save wayward youth and helpless women from the evils of industrialism, alcohol, and other abuses. (Like other early advocates, she believed that women in policing were simply extending their roles as mothers by serving as guardians of children and protectors of public morals.) Wells also pointed out that for some police tasks, such as settling family disputes, doing clerical work, and performing certain kinds of undercover vice work, women were actually better suited for the job than men (Lunneborg, 1989).

Communities across the country soon responded to Wells's call. In 1912, the New York Police Department hired Isabella Goodwin as its first female detective, and by 1915, 25 cities in 20 different states had female police officers. By 1929, the International Association of Police Women, created by Wells and some colleagues in 1915, had 593 women police officer members from 154 different cities in the United States and representatives from 29 different countries (Cox, 1974). The goal of this organization was to advocate that police departments hire women for duties concerning women and children as victims and offenders (Horne, 1980).

The trend of hiring at least one female police officer in all major U.S. city departments continued, but for many departments one female was considered enough. In 1960, there were only 2,400 female police officers nationwide, and in 1971 women still constituted less than 1 percent of all sworn officers in 16 of the 32 largest cities. In fact, some police departments at the time were under quota orders to hire no more than 1 percent female officers (Horne, 1980).

For many decades, female police officers did different work than men did. Women officers remained focused on issues related to women and children, and these officers continued to emphasize providing services for the prevention of crime rather than merely responding to crime after it occurred—such an orientation to social welfare was a novel approach to law enforcement.

Frequently, within police departments there were separate women's bureaus or juvenile bureaus that were staffed primarily by female officers (Hutzel, 1933). Female officers were typically well-educated, white, upper-middle-class, reform-minded social workers. In some cities the officers were not actually called police even though they had the sworn powers of arrest. They were called safety workers (Lunneborg, 1989). Female officers did not compete with males for jobs. Women and men had separate promotion lists and different pay scales. Women received lower pay than men, even though they were typically required to have more education to qualify for a given job (Horne, 1980). Female police officers were rarely exposed to any aspect of police work involving the use of force. A general perception of women's inability to use force was the major reason for the rarity of female police officers. Some pretraining physical ability tests for becoming an officer were beyond the ability of women. Minimum height and weight requirements made it virtually impossible for most women to qualify for applying to be police officers.

Most significantly, male police officers were strongly against allowing female police officers. Studies have found that male officers did not believe women were physically capable of doing police work or of providing adequate backup for male police officers. Male officers argued that because women are smaller and weaker than men, they were less able to perform the job, and that women did not have the emotional fortitude for the work. However, federal legislation in the early 1970s allowed these perceptions of women's abilities to become empirical questions. Numerous court cases resulted, opening the way for more women to become police officers and for women to become integrated into mainstream police work, including the right to use force.

In 1972, Congress amended Title VII of the Civil Rights Act of 1964. Title VII prohibits discrimination on the basis of race, creed, color, sex, and national origin, and the 1972 Amendment extended this coverage to include public employees. This act also created the Equal Employment Opportunity Commission to enforce the new rules, to investigate complaints, and to sue on behalf of complainants. Another legislative act, the Crime Control Act of 1973, prohibited discrimination against women in the employment practices of any agency that received funding from the Law Enforcement Administration Agency (LEAA), at that time a major funder for most U.S. police departments.

Under these new federal rulings, police departments could still refuse to hire a woman if they were able to show that she could not do the job. For example, tests of physical strength might still be lawful even though they have disproportionate impact on women as long as the tests measure skills essential to the job. These tests had to be good predictors of an employee's performance on the job.

More court suits were filed when females tried to gain entrance into police work under these new rulings, and the results of the suits were fairly consistent. First, it could not be demonstrated that physical ability is essential to police work (*White* v. *Nassau County Police Department*, 1975; *Officers for Justice* v. *Civil Service Commission*, 1975; *Blake* v. *City of Los Angeles*, 1977). Much of police work is providing services to the public, and when force is necessary, guns can be used effectively by both males and females. Second, it could not be shown that physical strength is predictive of good police work (*Harless* v. *Duck*, 1980). Third, height and weight standards for employment in police departments were found to be unreasonably discriminating against females and their use to be in violation of Title VII (*Smith* v. *Troyan*, 1975; *Smith* v. *East Cleveland*, 1972; *Hardy* v. *Stumpf*, 1974). (Research sponsored by the Police Foundation and the International Association of Chiefs of Police found no conclusive relationship between height and effective police performance [White and Bloch, 1975].)

These cases had profound effects on police departments throughout the United States. Because the legislative statute allowed courts to mandate increased employment based on judicial findings of denial of Title VII protections, many police departments were given court-ordered quotas of specified percentages of new hires that must be female. These same court-mandated federal guidelines also helped integrate people of color into police work. Many quotas are still in effect today.

After the federal rulings, the FBI reported that between 1972 and 1979 employment of women as police officers doubled, from 1.5 percent of all police officers to 3.4 percent (FBI, 1981). By 1987, women composed 7.6 percent of all metropolitan officers, representing more than thirty-six thousand women (FBI, 1988).

The introduction of women into mainstream police work was followed by a flood of studies analyzing how female police officers' work compared with male officers', and even though the courts ruled that the use of force was a very limited part of police work, many of the studies focused on women's ability to use physical force.

When Women Entered Police Work

Considerable research has documented that on most issues the first women to enter policing were effective as police officers (Bloch and Anderson, 1974; Milton, 1972; 1974; Sichel, Friedman, Quint, and Smith, 1977). In addition, there has been substantial confirmation that the public responds favorably to female police officers on patrol (Bloch and Anderson, 1974; Milton, 1972, 1974; Sichel et al., 1977). For example, Bloch and Anderson's (1974) comparison of female and male officers found that women officers give fewer traffic tickets and make fewer arrests than male officers. However, female arrests are more likely to result in convictions, indicating a higher quality of arrests. In addition, women receive fewer citizen complaints regarding unbecoming conduct. These researchers conclude that women officers in the 1970s were beginning to develop a style of policing different from that of male officers but that both successfully accomplished the requirements of the job.

Some research found that in specific aspects of policing, women were not as successful as men. Some of the first female officers tried to emulate the styles of male officers in interaction with citizens. For example, they attempted to be gruff, even to the point of lowering their voices. Frequently, these strategies were not effective for the female officers (Nieva and Gutek, 1981). This emulation of men is a common reaction among the first women who enter various male-dominated work environments, and frequently it fails (Kanter, 1977).

To understand the difficulties the first female police officers faced in creating a style for handling potentially violent situations, the context in which they were working must be analyzed. The major problem confronting these females was their coworkers—male police officers. Typically male police officers, even in the 1970s and 1980s, did not agree with the federal court decisions that women were capable of doing police work.

Male officers had several views on the integration of women into mainstream policing. First, they felt that women did not belong in all areas of policing. They argued that the public wants an authority figure during times of crisis and that females are too emotional and unstable to provide one (Bloch, Anderson, and Gervais, 1973; Remmington, 1983). As discussed earlier, research on the community's reaction to female officers did not support this contention. Second, male officers felt that female partners were not skilled in the use of force and, therefore, it was risky to have females as partners (Cox, 1974; Remmington, 1983). Addressing this last point, Grennan (1987) empirically tested the premise that having female partners increased police vulnerability to victimization. He analyzed more than three thousand violent confrontations experienced by patrol teams in New York City. He found that mixed patrols (one female and one male) were no more likely to experience injuries than all-male patrols. Also, in mixed patrols neither the female nor the male suffered any more injuries than the other.

Nevertheless, the existence of these stereotypes made work for policewomen extremely difficult. For example, Wexler and Logan (1983), investigating stress among female officers in a large California police department, found the most commonly cited problem by female officers was the negative attitudes of their male coworkers.

The stereotypes probably also contributed to Garrison, Grant, and McCormick's (1988) findings about women's assignment to patrol duty. Patrol is considered the backbone of policing and is usually required before advancing to higher levels of authority in police work. Garrison et al. found that the percentage of women in patrol work was 1.5 percent in 1971 and only 4.5 percent in 1985. More often than not, women were assigned to nonpatrol duties or, as also found by Steel and Lovrich (1987), nonhazardous assignments.

Even for those few female officers who were given some exposure to potentially violent situations, opportunities to gain experience and develop appropriate responses were frequently restricted by the reaction of male coworkers. Substantial research documents that male officers were extremely protective of female officers who were in potentially violent situations (Bloch and Anderson, 1974; Cox, 1974; Martin, 1980; Miller, 1973; Sichel et al., 1977). This protectiveness went so far as to actually block the female officers from ever gaining experience. For example, several studies found that when female officers indicated over the radio that they were approaching a potentially dangerous situation, they never had to call for backup. Upon hearing that females were possibly going to be involved in the use of force, several male officers would automatically show up without being dispatched. Furthermore, when males came to the scene, they typically took over and sent the female officers to do the paperwork (Heffner, 1979; Martin, 1980; Remmington, 1983).

Women in Policing Today

More recent research on female police officers' performance has documented that women are now starting to find their own effective approaches to social control. Even though the style for many may be different from that of male officers, there is now little discussion regarding whether females are appropriate for police work. As noted by Lunneborg, "No one argues seriously today that there is no role for women in the police" (1989, p. 13).

Regarding physical strength, Diskin's (1985) analysis of women at the Federal Law Enforcement Training Center at Glyncoe, Georgia found that women enter with lower levels of fitness, especially upper-body strength and cardiovascular endurance. However, women's improvement exceeds that of men. Once women become habitual exercisers, there is a 38 percent improvement in upper-body strength, and women usually can benchpress more than 80 percent of their body weight by the end of the training. Ironically, there is considerable evidence that female police officers' approach to their job does not require physical strength as much as male officers'. In developing their own style of police work, female police officers are much less aggressive than male officers (Bloch and Anderson, 1974; Sherman, 1975; Jones, 1987). Female officers are skilled at diffusing potentially violent situations through verbal means rather than by the use or threat of physical force.

Recently, Hunt (1992) documented the fact that ideas regarding female officers' inabilities to use force still exist in police departments, and she provided new information on the persistence of these stereotypes in spite of contradictory information. In her participant-observer study of a large police department, she found that some male officers still believe that women are neither physically strong enough nor brave enough to handle police work. There are still claims that women cannot handle violent offenders or provide adequate backup and coverage for a partner. However, when Hunt pushed for further information and asked for descriptions of actual events, she discovered that the accusations were disguises for other concerns male officers had about female officers.

Hunt found that male officers feared that because female officers relied on verbal persuasion more than on physical force for conflict resolution, they would not condone the use of extralegal force occasionally used by male officers. Male officers expressed fears that female officers might cooperate with federal investigators and expose excessive brutality on the part of male officers. A related concern was that female officers might reveal other forms of police corruption, implying that women have higher moralities than men.

Finally, Hunt documented that there was actually little concern about female officers being able to do the job or being capable of using force. Instead, male officers did not want females to be police because they were afraid it would destroy the public belief that policing is an exciting and dangerous job. Female officers might reveal the true nature of contemporary police work: that it is primarily a service-providing occupation, that little time and effort are actually spent on investigating crime and apprehending criminals, and that, for the most part, the police are not very effective at solving or even stopping crime.

Conclusions

Police departments were first created in the United States to maintain order and control undesirables. Much of the job focused on the use of physical force, and, consistent with the gender-based division of labor at that time, women were seen as unable to engage in the use of force necessary for the job. Women eventually gained entrance to the profession by creating a specialized role for themselves, one which, again, was consistent with characteristics of gender roles at that time—to protect and help women and children.

When women first entered policing, they were segregated from mainstream police work. While this allowed for their entrance into the profession, it also allowed them to develop new ideas on the nature of policing. Horne (1980) states that in this isolated environment, women were able to experiment and become innovators of new policies and programs.

The first women who entered policing were highly educated and dedicated to social reform. They focused on improving the welfare of community members and preventing crime, as opposed to strictly maintaining public safety and controlling criminals.

These innovations have become the foundation for current thought on contemporary approaches to policing. For example, there is much support today for what is called "community policing," which focuses on developing strong cooperative ties between police and citizens (Green and Mastrofski, 1988; Kelling, 1988). Also, "problem-oriented policing" is frequently advocated (Eck and Spelman, 1987; Goldstein, 1990), an approach that recommends addressing conditions that cause people to become criminals rather than simply coping with them after they have broken the law. Both approaches are similar to what Alice Wells and other female police officers were doing decades ago.

A further trend in contemporary policing is to restrict the use of physical or deadly force as much as possible (Blumberg, 1989; Walker, 1992). Police today are still granted more authority to use legitimate violence than the ordinary citizen, but there is considerable effort in all areas of policing in the United States to use force only as a last resort. The emphasis on verbal skills and a less aggressive approach to policing, as is demonstrated by many female officers, is now becoming the standard for the way all police should act.

part 2
The Role of Women: The Evidence

chapter 7

Women in the Armed Forces
Mady Wechsler Segal

There is a cultural ideal in most societies that men are the warriors. This ideal persists despite the fact that women in many nations have participated in military operations and even in warfare as combatants (Goldman, 1982; Segal, Li, and Segal, 1992; Stanley and Segal, 1992). Public discourse and other forms of social life are socially constructed to support a perception that women are not combatants. The steadfastness of this belief demonstrates the social construction of reality.

It is not the purpose of this chapter to present an exhaustive review of the historical evidence on women in military operations. Rather, a brief summary is provided of some of the conclusions of cross-national and historical research. Some of the highlights from the history of women's involvement in the armed forces of the United States are described. Special attention is given to the changes associated with the all-volunteer force of the past twenty years. These changes are dramatized by the varied roles played by uniformed women in recent military engagements in Panama, Grenada, and the Gulf region. The latter, in particular, has led to increased public visibility and policy debate with regard to women's military positions.

Despite the increased numbers and roles for women in the U.S. armed forces over the past twenty years, gender-based exclusions persist and military organizations are still resistant to full incorporation of women. As has happened in the past in many nations, the diminution of military threat has led to a downsizing of the military, which in turn reawakens pressures to limit women's participation in the armed forces. The resolution of current issues will affect women's future military roles.

Historical Overview of Women in
the U.S. Military and Other Nations

Although the military historically has been a masculine institution, when there are shortages of qualified men and especially during times of national emergency, most nations have increased women's military roles. Women's involvement in military activities can be traced back to ancient times (see Stanley and Segal, 1992, for examples). Historical accounts document the participation of individual female soldiers in civil wars, revolutions, and partisan and resistance movements from the fifteenth through the nineteenth centuries in many nations, including the United States.

In the twentieth century, responding to the demands of World War I, women were employed by military forces in both nursing and non-nursing capacities in unprecedented numbers. This was true, for example, in Germany, Russia, the United Kingdom, and the United States. The U.S. navy and marine corps established women's units in 1917 and 1918, respectively. The uniformed women were granted military status and were assigned to jobs women normally held in civilian society, such as telephone operator and clerk; some were stationed overseas. Because these units were established to meet specific personnel needs in order to free men for combat, the units were temporary and the women were demobilized after the war.

In World War II a major shift occurred in the nature of women's military participation. Not only did they serve in large numbers, but their roles expanded. Women worked in war industries and performed a wider variety of functions for the armed forces, such as medical personnel, drivers, and social workers. Nursing services were organized within the military of several nations. Women's corps were established to perform non-nursing functions, and some countries even enlisted women along with men in the regular branches of the armed forces. As the war progressed, women's activities expanded beyond the usual roles women play (health care, administration, and communications) to include technical and combat support jobs.

In the United States, numerous women were employed in civilian industry essential to the war effort, as well as in uniformed military service (Campbell, 1984; Gluck, 1987; Holm, 1982; Treadwell, 1954). Women's organizations were formed for all services, with their original designations implying their intended temporary nature (e.g., Women's Army Auxiliary Corps). Although women were mainly assigned to traditional fields, small numbers served in almost every specialty, excluding direct combat. For example, some were airplane mechanics, parachute riggers, and weapons instructors.

U.S. women were prohibited from serving as offensive combat personnel, but they were deployed to foreign theaters and were thus exposed to danger. Nurses stationed in the Philippines and Guam were taken prisoner by the Japanese, and others were captured by the Germans.

One group worthy of special attention was the Women's Airforce Service Pilots. These women performed the demanding and often dangerous mission of transporting military aircraft overseas. Although the pilots were uniformed and subject to military discipline, they were regarded as civilians. In 1977 they were granted military veteran status. This is an interesting example of the social construction of what constitutes a military role—and how such definitions can be changed after the fact.

During World War II, U.S., British, and Soviet women were involved in espionage and sabotage activities, and women were active in resistance organizations in France, Italy, Russia, and Yugoslavia. Women were conscripted in Germany, the Soviet Union, and the United Kingdom.

Had the war not ended in 1945, civilian nurses in the United States would have been drafted. The bill to conscript nurses had been passed by the House and had cleared the Senate committee (in March 1945). The termination of the war in Europe in May 1945 reversed the shortage of military nurses that had led to the need for conscription.

Germany during World War II provides another interesting example of the maintenance of social definitions of women as not in the military despite the roles they play in armed services. Some of the women conscripted wore uniforms, were under military authority, and performed functions within the armed forces that in other nations were considered military. However, these women were labeled civilians.

In all these nations where World War II had increased women's military participation, the end of the war, like the end of other military crises in other times and places, saw a return to limitations on women's military roles. Generally, women serve as a reserve labor force, both civilian and military. What has happened in the past in many nations is that when the armed forces need women, their prior military history is recalled to demonstrate that they can perform effectively in various positions. There is a process of cultural amnesia regarding the contributions women made during emergency situations, until a new emergency arises and then history is rediscovered.

One common pattern is for women to be involved in military and paramilitary activities in revolutionary movements but to be relegated to more traditional female status after the revolution is successful. For example, some Israeli women served in guerrilla activities and combat operations during the War of Independence (1947–1948), and this is probably the source of the commonly held misconception that Israel permits women to serve in combat. The reality is that since the formation of the state and the Israeli Defense Force, women have been excluded from direct combat. Further, this policy was the result of cultural and political factors and not because of any military failure resulting from men's or women's actual behavior in combat (Gal, 1986). (Israel does conscript women, though fewer women than men actually serve and their conditions of service differ from men's.)

In the United States, legislation after World War II provided for continuing the women's armed services but severely limited military women's numbers and activities. As in other areas of social life in the United States following World War II, women were expected to return to more traditional roles (Campbell, 1984). Despite some modification of these laws in the 1960s and 1970s, U.S. women's contemporary military roles are still constrained by exclusions prescribed by this legislation.

Since the combat exclusion laws were passed in 1948, women in the navy and marine corps have been prohibited from being assigned to duty on aircraft engaged in combat missions and from serving other than temporary duty on combat ships. Women in the air force have been prohibited from serving on aircraft engaged in a combat mission. There are exceptions to these exclusions for physicians, nurses, chaplains, and attorneys.

The army has no statutory prohibition against women in combat, but policy has been developed to be consistent with what is viewed as congressional intent. This policy has been changing in recent years. Rather than explicitly prohibiting women from engaging in combat, army policy prevents women from being assigned to units or jobs in which they would routinely be engaged in close combat.

These exclusions, however, do not protect women from the risk of exposure to combat. Women in the air force are prohibited from flying fighter planes but are permitted to fly tankers, which would be targets in the event of war. Navy women serve on support vessels, such as supply ships, which are also likely targets. Women in the army serve in military police, mechanical repair, transportation, intelligence, signal, and other support specialties that would bring them into battle.

Women in the U.S. Armed Forces in the Past Two Decades

Despite the combat restrictions and the lack of wartime necessity, the representation of women in the military has increased dramatically since 1970. In 1971 there were approximately 43,000 women in uniform (30,000 enlisted and 13,000 officers), constituting only 1.6 percent of total active-duty military personnel. By the end of 1980, nine years later, there were about 173,000 women, or about 8.5 percent of total active-duty forces.

Table 7.1 shows the percentage of women in each of the services in 1989. Of the active-duty force of more than 2 million, 225,859, or approximately 11 percent, were women. Their representation was highest in the air force (13 percent) and lowest in the marine corps (5 percent). These figures now provide a baseline of women's representation in the military before the current drawdown of forces. In December 1990, women numbered 223,297 and constituted about the same overall 11 percent of active-duty forces (Rogers, 1991).

Table 7.1 Women as a Percentage of Active-Duty Military Personnel by Service

	Army	Navy	Marines	Air Force	Total
Officers	12.6	10.5	3.3	12.5	11.5
Warrant officers	2.9	1.4	4.4	—	2.8
Enlisted personnel	11.1	9.6	5.1	13.5	10.7
Total	11.1	9.7	5.0	13.3	10.7

Source: Defense Manpower Data Center

Differences among the services in the proportion of women are primarily because of the differential occupational distributions in the services. Since women are excluded from some combat positions, the larger the number of such positions there are in a service, the fewer the number of women the service can admit. Further, women are not equally distributed throughout the job categories that are open to them. Table 7.2 shows that a number of enlisted women are employed in every occupational area but that they are concentrated in administrative and medical specialties, which is to be expected, given the preponderance of women in comparable civilian jobs. The absence of medical personnel in the marines (which gets its medical support from the navy) contributes to the smaller percentage of women in the corps than in the other services.

The Contemporary Situation in Other Nations

Policies and patterns of women's roles in the armed forces of other nations show much recent change. The United States was on the forefront fifteen years ago in integrating women into the armed forces. The U.S. military still has the largest percentage of women (about 11 percent). However, there are now six NATO nations that have gone beyond the United States, in some ways, in integrating women into their armed forces. Some or all combat roles, including direct-offensive combat positions, have been opened to women (at least in principle) in Belgium, Canada, Denmark, the Netherlands, Norway, and the United Kingdom (Segal and Segal, 1989; Stanley and Segal, 1988).

Some of the changes taking place in other countries and the rationales for the policy changes are interesting and relevant to the United States. For example, the United Kingdom is now allowing women to train as fighter pilots and to serve on all types of ships. In the course of developing this policy, an alternative considered was maintaining a gender exclusion for "combat" ships, while opening "support" ships to women, in order to minimize the danger to women. However, the British experience in the Falklands War was that casualty rates aboard "support" ships were greater than on combat ships, resulting in the Royal Navy considering all of its ships to be combat ships.

Table 7.2 Occupational Areas of Enlisted Personnel, June 1989

Occupational Area	Number of Women	Total Personnel	Women as a Percentage of Total	Percentage of Women
Infantry, gun crews, and seamanship specialists	7,544	304,871	2.5	3.9
Electronic equipment repairers	11,450	178,547	6.4	6.0
Communications and intelligence specialists	20,977	172,180	12.2	10.9
Health care specialists	25,872	100,308	25.8	13.4
Other technical and allied specialists	4,338	42,469	10.2	2.2
Functional support and administration	68,301	277,473	24.6	35.5
Electrical/ mechanical equipment repairers	16,376	368,849	4.4	8.5
Craftspersons	3,716	72,401	5.1	1.9
Service and supply handlers	18,771	163,975	11.4	9.8
Nonoccupational	14,921	113,375	13.2	7.8
Unknown	107	431	24.8	0.1
Total	192,373	1,794,879	10.7	100.0

Source: Defense Manpower Data Center

U.S. Women's Involvement
in Recent Military Engagements

The expansions in women's military roles in the previous two decades have led to greater likelihood that women would be involved in military engagements and in roles that are not "traditional" for women. In December 1989, women participated in the U.S. invasion of Panama during Operation Just Cause. Approximately 800 of the 18,400 soldiers involved in the operation were women (Moskos, 1990). Their roles were varied and included piloting helicopters to ferry troops—some while under enemy fire from the ground.

The missions and experiences of some of the female soldiers involved in the Panamanian operation fueled a renewed debate about women in combat. For example, there was controversy over whether a military police captain was in combat when she led her unit in attempting to capture a military dog kennel believed to be occupied by armed and firing members of the Panamanian defense forces.

But attention to the participation of women in Operation Just Cause pales by comparison with media coverage and potential policy impact of the roles played by women in Operations Desert Shield and Desert Storm. Further, the generally acknowledged high quality of women's performance in their jobs demonstrates the lack of validity of many recent arguments expressing reservations about women's abilities to perform their assigned missions. (See Mitchell, 1989, for a diatribe against the expansion of women's military roles in the 1970s and 1980s.) Some military women and civilian advocates are optimistic that these demonstrations will result in greater opportunities for military women, whereas others are more pessimistic based on the historical record (WIIS, 1991).

As shown in Table 7.3, approximately 41,000 women were deployed to the Gulf region between August 1990 and February 1991 (Eitelberg, 1991). Women made up about 7 percent of all military personnel deployed (including all ranks and active-duty and reserve personnel combined). The army employed the vast majority of these women.

One interesting aspect of women's representation in Gulf War operations was the difference between active-duty and reserve forces, especially among officers. Although women were 5.6 percent of

**Table 7.3 Women in the Active and Reserve Forces by Service:
Percentage of Officers and Enlisted Personnel in Operations Desert Shield/Storm**

Service	Percentage Who Are Women[a]		
	Active	Reserve	Total
	ENLISTED		
Army	7.9	14.7	9.4
Navy	3.1	12.3	3.6
Marine Corps	1.6	0.1	1.5
Air Force	5.6	10.1	6.4
TOTAL			
Percent	5.6	12.2	6.8
Number	23,481	10,858	34,339
	OFFICER[b]		
Army	8.8	22.4	12.4
Navy	7.1	26.7	9.4
Marine Corps	1.4	1.5	1.4
Air Force	7.3	21.0	10.2
TOTAL			
Percent	7.3	21.3	10.3
Number	3,585	2,858	6,443
	TOTAL		
Army	7.9	15.7	9.7
Navy	3.5	14.9	4.2
Marine Corps	1.5	1.0	1.5
Air Force	5.9	12.4	7.0
TOTAL			
Percent	5.8	13.4	7.2
Number	27,066	13,716	40,782

Source: Eitelberg, 1991 who used data provided by Defense Manpower Data Center.
[a] Includes military personnel in theater any time between August 1990 and February 1991.
[b] Includes both commissioned and warrant officers.

active enlisted personnel in the theater of operations, they were 12.2 percent of reserve enlisted forces. The contrast is even more marked among officers: 7.3 percent of active-duty officers were women, compared to 21.3 percent of reserve officers.

The experiences of Operations Desert Shield and Desert Storm demonstrate that the policy excluding women from offensive combat roles does not provide complete protection from death or capture: thirteen American women were among the 375 U.S. service members who died, and two women were prisoners of war (Eitelberg, 1991).

Current Issues and the Future

The increased participation of women in the armed forces in the past two decades clearly has been a response to personnel demands associated with the all-volunteer force in the United States. Shortfalls in the enlistment of men beginning in 1973 led to several policy changes, including lowering accession goals, lowering standards for enlistment of men, greater emphasis on personnel retention, and increases both in the numbers of women and in the occupational specialties open to them. Similar shortages of men in other nations recently have had similar effects.

Changes in the military itself, such as greater emphasis on technology and higher support to combat ratios, have contributed to women's greater representation (Segal and Segal, 1983; Segal, 1992). Further, women participate in the armed forces to an extent compatible with cultural values and structural patterns of gender roles. Greater acceptability of military women is indicated by various social changes. Perhaps most important is that equality of citizenship rights and obligations is being extended to previously disadvantaged groups, including women. This can be seen in laws prohibiting gender discrimination.

As both a cause and a consequence of greater citizen equality between the sexes, there has been movement away from traditional gender stereotypes and structural sex segregation in civilian society. There has been decreasing emphasis on women's family roles and increasing labor force participation, including participation in traditionally male arenas. Research shows that a majority of the electorate favors expanded military integration of women to include some combat roles from which they are excluded (Davis, Lauby, and Sheatsley, 1983).

Nevertheless, civilian occupational sex segregation is still strong, and resistance to expanding women's military participation remains. Given the historical tendency to view women exclusively as a reserve military labor source to be tapped when men are in short supply, the current military personnel reductions are likely to be accompanied by renewed debates on the benefits and shortcomings of female personnel.

While Congress passed legislation as part of the 1992 defense authorization bill repealing the laws banning women from serving as pilots in combat, the services have not yet acted to train any women as fighter pilots. Further, the Senate version of the bill (to which the House agreed in compromise) included a plan to appoint a presidential commission to consider the issue of women in combat, including ground combat in the army and marine corps. The commission was due to report back in November 1992. Some of the people appointed to the commission have been outspoken opponents of expanded military roles for women, especially combat, and none has been an advocate of opening combat positions to women.

The issue of whether women should be allowed to volunteer for combat roles has been in public discourse in the United States since the 1970s (Segal and Hansen, 1992). The arguments for and against allowing women in combat have not changed much since then. They include consideration of differences between men and women (on the average) in physical and psychological traits (especially aggression), the potential impact of women on the cohesion of military units, and cultural values regarding gender roles (e.g., Feld, 1978; Hooker, 1988; Quester, 1982; Segal, 1982; Tuten, 1982; Webb, 1979). Proponents of expanded roles for military women stress citizenship equality and its relationship to military service. Those who oppose expansion stress negative impacts of women on military effectiveness or possibly on the women themselves (Segal and Hansen, 1992).

The issue of women in combat also raises questions regarding women's family roles. The Gulf War deployment brought military family issues into the public eye, with particular attention to the fact that mothers can be sent to war, including those who are single parents and those married to service members who also deploy. Although legislation was introduced during this period to prohibit the deployment to a combat theater of sole parents and both members of a dual military couple, this legislation was opposed by the armed services and by military women's advocates, and it died. Even though there is a potential for public opinion to develop opposing the deployment of such parents, public attention to the issue was short-lived.

There is also the potential for attention to the effect of pregnancy on military assignments. One policy that could be reinstated is the practice that existed until the 1970s of discharging women from service when they become pregnant. An alternative policy is to allow pregnant women and women with children to remain in service only after completing their first term of enlistment. In other words, under this policy first-tour military women who became pregnant would be discharged. At this time, there is no active consideration of such policies, but it would not be surprising for discussion to surface. The current downsizing of military forces has created pressure to find ways to choose who should be separated from the services and to retain those who are likely to cause the fewest problems; pregnancy may be seen as detrimental to optimum performance.

Other aspects of downsizing and force structure decisions will have implications for the future role of women in the military. For example, because women are concentrated in some military specialties, especially in support units, the degree to which these positions are reduced will affect women. Decisions to transfer support functions more to the reserves than to active-duty forces will decrease the representation of women in the active forces and further increase their representation in the reserves—where they already account for larger percentages of personnel.

It would be consistent with women's military history for the representation of women in the U.S. armed forces to be reduced during the downsizing, especially in active units. Although the Department of Defense and the services themselves have made public statements indicating that it is official policy to retain the current representation of women in the armed forces (Rogers, 1991), resistance to change has been evident throughout the past twenty years and may resurface during the drawdown.

There are already indications that women's representation may decrease. Rogers (1991) reports a decrease during the first three quarters of fiscal year 1991 in the proportion of women among new enlisted accessions of 2 percent (compared to the same period the previous year) from 15 percent to 13 percent. She notes that women's representation is affected by policies excluding them from some specialties; further, the jobs that women tend to fill are more likely to be abolished in the downsizing.

As in the past, women's new roles in the armed services have not been fully institutionalized and women have not caused any fundamental change in the masculine culture of the organizations. Pressures to develop policies that would reduce women's participation in the military may be negated by vigilance and political pressure by advocates for military women. It remains to be seen whether such activism will be evident and how effective it will be.

chapter 8

Women in Weapons Development: The Manhattan Project

Ruth H. Howes, Caroline L. Herzenberg

In modern warfare, high-technology weapons symbolize national power. Women have traditionally been invisible in the defense technology establishment and are thought to have played little role in designing and producing modern weapons, notably nuclear warheads and the systems that deliver them. To determine whether women have indeed played no role or were simply overlooked in historical accounts, we have examined the research project that developed the first nuclear explosive.

The Manhattan Project

Histories of the Manhattan Engineer District, the code name assigned to the massive secret research effort that led to the development of the U.S. atomic bomb during World War II, rarely mention technical work performed by women on the project. Less formal accounts stress the lives of the wives who struggled to maintain a semblance of normal family life in secret cities that resembled military camps (Fermi, 1954; Wilson and Serber, 1988). The reader retains the impression that all of the technical work on development of nuclear energy and nuclear weapons was performed by male staff members, while women filled support roles as wives and mothers. Members of the Women's Army Corps served as stenographers and supply clerks, and occasionally wives held part-time jobs in the lab.

In actuality, women were involved in essentially all technical aspects of the development of the atomic bomb. No woman sat on the committees that directed the project, although in the summer of 1946, Gertrud Nordheim was appointed to a group of consultants to the theoretical division at Los Alamos, which included many of the major theoretical leaders of the project, such as physicists Fermi, Weisskopf, Feynman, and Teller (Truslow and Smith, 1961). On the other hand, many women were directly involved with the scientific developments that led to the atomic bomb, in roles ranging from leading scientific projects to serving as highly skilled technicians.

We have identified and studied about seventy of the women who worked in various scientific capacities in the Manhattan Project and related activities. About thirty of them worked at Los Alamos, about twenty-four at Oak Ridge, and still fewer at the University of Chicago, Columbia University, Hanford Reservation, and other sites. Several women worked at more than one of these locations. Significant contributions to the progress of the technical programs at these labs originated from the work of these women.

The data presented here on the roles filled by women during the Manhattan Project have been collected from accounts in the published literature; from interviews with individuals who worked on the Project and their family members, colleagues, and friends; and from questionnaires sent to lists of women who worked at the Clinton Engineering Works (today Oak Ridge National Laboratory) and at Los Alamos. In the nearly fifty years that have elapsed since the Manhattan Project, many participants have died, married, or moved so often that the addresses on file for them are no longer correct. Thus, this account cannot offer a complete view of the participation of women in the construction of the first atomic bomb; however, the sample of female participants contacted is large enough to give a reasonable picture of the kinds of technical work carried out by women.

The Manhattan Engineer District

Following the discovery of nuclear fission in Europe, a number of physicists rapidly realized that nuclear fission might provide a source of tremendous energy. Scientists such as Leo Szilard and Enrico Fermi recognized that it also might be possible to exploit this physical process to construct an entirely new type of super weapon, much more destructive than any conventional one. They managed to persuade the U.S. government to establish a project to look into that possibility. Fermi performed initial experiments at Columbia University in New York, but moved to Chicago, where in December of 1942 his group produced the first self-sustaining chain reaction.

With the realization that only one isotope of uranium, the rare uranium-235, underwent fission, a second aspect of the project began to investigate means to separate uranium isotopes in sufficient quantities to build a weapon. The project grew, until by the end of the war it consisted of three major laboratory sites as well as individual experiments in several universities, notably Columbia University, the University of Chicago (from which the research was moved to a site in the Chicago forest preserves and then to what is today Argonne National Laboratory), and the University of California at Berkeley. Los Alamos Laboratory in New Mexico was charged with the engineering design of the atomic weapon. The Clinton Engineering Works (today Oak Ridge National Laboratory) produced enriched uranium-235 by the gaseous diffusion method, while the Hanford Site in Richland, Washington held the giant nuclear reactors and fuel purification plants used to produce the radioactive fissile element plutonium.

Women performed scientific work at all of these sites. Most of them were quite young, recent Ph.D.s or graduate students, so, although they were aware of the technical goal of the project, they did not work as senior scientists.

The Physicists

The most distinguished female physicist involved with the Manhattan Project was future Nobel-laureate Maria Goeppert Mayer. A theoretical physicist who taught half-time at Sarah Lawrence College, Mayer joined the isotope separation project at Columbia University in 1942. Her work consisted of theoretical studies of the thermodynamic properties of uranium hexafluoride gas, which was used in the diffusion process for the separation of uranium isotopes. She also conducted theoretical investigations of the possibility of using photochemical reactions for isotope separation. Although a senior member of a research group, she was not given a full-time appointment (Dash, 1973; Sachs, undated).

At least one of Mayer's students, Susan Chandler Herrick, obtained a job with the project through Mayer's influence. Herrick worked in Mayer's group on problems in uranium chemistry, including the synthesis and crystallization of compounds of uranium and the development of techniques to produce single crystals from a few hundreds of milligrams obtained from a mass spectrometer without losing any appreciable amount of the precious uranium-235. She found that it was possible to grow crystals of cesium zinc uranylnitrate from saturated solutions. She also did some work on the problem of the pinholes in the nickel barriers used in diffusion plants. Both Mayer and Herrick were aware that they were studying the separation of uranium isotopes for the purpose of constructing a bomb.

Mayer's theoretical work also focused on the energy emitted by a nuclear explosion as electromagnetic radiation. She calculated the opacity of uranium and called attention to the enormous energy released as electromagnetic radiation. At the time, her results were considered unimportant; however, they provided the basis for the eventual successful design of the hydrogen bomb. At the University of Chicago after the war, she began the work on the origin of the elements that led to her recognition of nuclear magic numbers and the development of the shell model of the nucleus. In 1963, her accomplishments in clarifying the structure of atomic nuclei by the development of the theory of nuclear shell structure were recognized by the award of the Nobel Prize in physics (Brush, 1985; Hellmans and Bunch, 1988).

Another physicist, Leona Woods Marshall, was completing her Ph.D. in molecular spectroscopy at the University of Chicago in 1942. Enrico Fermi's group moved to Chicago to begin construction of the first atomic pile (nuclear reactor), designed to prove that there were conditions under which a nuclear chain reaction would occur, with the ultimate objective of producing plutonium by a chain reaction (Brown and MacDonald, 1977). Leona Woods participated in the design and building of this first nuclear reactor as a member of the famous team of Enrico Fermi, working under the stands of Stagg Field at the University of Chicago (Libby, 1979; U.S. Department of Energy, 1982; Rhodes, 1988; Howes, in press). Woods was drafted to assist with construction of the boron trifluoride detectors used to monitor the flux of neutrons from the pile. She completed her Ph.D. after going to work with Fermi's group and was present on the memorable day (December 2, 1942) when the atomic pile operated to produce the first self-sustaining nuclear fission chain reaction. (Her name appears on the label of the Chianti bottle that records the celebration of this success.)

Following its initial operation, the atomic pile was dismantled, moved, and rebuilt in a remote area of the forest preserves outside Chicago. Woods, who in July 1943 had married John Marshall, also a physicist, followed the pile. She continued to conduct experiments on the operation of the pile and the neutrons it produced until the birth of her first son in 1944. She hid her pregnancy under overalls and a denim jacket and worked until two days before the baby's birth. Then Leona Woods Marshall moved to Hanford to join her husband in overseeing the operation and construction of the plutonium production reactors there. Fortunately her mother was willing and able to accompany her to Hanford to help with child care. For the remainder of the war, Marshall devoted herself to assisting with the production of plutonium for the new weapon (Libby, 1979).

Another young Chicago Ph.D. in nuclear physics, Elizabeth Riddle Graves, who was nicknamed "Diz," moved in 1943 with her husband, Al Graves, to Los Alamos, where she was assigned to work on the Cockcroft-Walton accelerator. Her husband had been recruited from the University of Texas at Austin, where she had not been able to find work because of nepotism rules, and he insisted that she be allowed to work at Los Alamos. Because she had worked on neutron-scattering experiments with Samuel Allison at Chicago during her dissertation, Diz Graves worked with colleagues on experiments designed to choose a neutron reflector to surround the core of the atomic bomb so as to scatter fast neutrons back into the fissioning core of the bomb and keep the neutron flux high. No one had measured the effectiveness of a variety of materials in scattering high-energy neutrons. As one of the few physicists in the country with actual experience in fast neutron scattering, Graves was a welcome addition to the group making those critical measurements.

She is described by her colleagues as hard working and competent, capable of asserting herself when necessary, and an independent thinker with a basically conventional outlook. She had a sense of humor, and a tale circulated of her winning a bet that she could persuade a very proper European physicist to precede her through a door in spite of his unfailing insistence on proper manners—a trick accomplished by telling him that she had ripped her dress. A more telling story of her determination records her standing on the experimental floor, timing the labor contractions for her first baby with a stopwatch while trying to complete a set of experiments.

Pregnant at the time of the test of the first atomic bomb, Graves was assigned to monitor radiation away from the test site. She and her husband checked into a cabin in Harry Miller's Tourist Court in Carrizozo, New Mexico, with baggage that included a seismograph, a Geiger counter, a short-wave radio, and a portable electric generator. The tourist court was forty miles east of the Trinity test site, and the needle of their Geiger counter shot off scale as the radioactive cloud passed over the small town at about four o'clock in the afternoon (Lamont, 1965, pp. 193, 227, 230, 252). Fortunately the cloud passed over and the town did not have to be evacuated.

Following the war, Graves continued to do experimental nuclear physics at Los Alamos while raising a family. In 1946, eight men were involved in a severe radiation accident at a critical assembly test at Los Alamos, and Elizabeth Graves was asked to perform calculations to determine whether the radiation exposure was lethal. She was not informed until afterward that her husband had been among those involved in the accident and that it was his radiation exposure she had calculated (Rapoport, 1971).

A third physicist, Joan Hinton, had graduated from Bennington College. Her brother was at Cornell, so Hinton went there during two of Bennington's winter study periods. The cloud chamber on which she worked was in a basement lab next to the Cornell cyclotron. Hinton happily joined the cyclotron crew in their repair work. Cornell refused to admit a woman to its graduate program in physics, so Hinton began study at the University of Wisconsin. She had started construction of a cloud chamber when she was recruited by the physicists from the cyclotron crew at Cornell, who were by then at Los Alamos. Wisconsin cooperated by giving her a master's degree following a very informal examination in which she claims she sat on the floor of the lab, answered a few questions, and showed the committee a picture of her cloud chamber.

At Los Alamos she was assigned to work on building an enriched uranium reactor known as the "water boiler" for its cooling mechanism. Her group also tested assemblies of enriched uranium and later plutonium. The first version of the enriched uranium reactor was designed partly to provide a strong neutron source for experiments and partly to serve as a trial run in the art of building reactors. It was the first in a series of steps from the slow reaction first produced in the Chicago pile to the fast reaction in a sphere of active metal that makes a nuclear weapon (Brown and MacDonald, 1977).

The reactor group was mostly young and worked hard at physics while playing hard along with its irrepressible leader, Enrico Fermi. Among other exploits, Hinton sneaked in to observe the first explosion of a nuclear device, the Trinity test in New Mexico, by riding through the army guards at sunset on the back of the motor scooter owned by one of her fellow workers on the reactor.

Following the Hiroshima detonation, Hinton was stunned by the destructive force of nuclear weapons and joined the movement to internationalize atomic energy. She actively lobbied in Washington as part of the peace movement. To complete her graduate studies she selected Illinois because friends from the reactor group were going there. Illinois refused to admit a woman; however, Fermi and Allison invited her to Chicago, where she became part of an informal group that met to discuss new ideas in physics that interested Fermi.

Disgusted by what she perceived as the militarization of physics, Hinton decided to leave the field and travel to China, where her brother was working as a dairy farmer for the Chinese Communists under Mao. Hinton has continued to live in China and is today a leading designer of dairy farms.

Mayer, Herrick, Marshall, Graves, and Hinton are typical of female physicists in the Manhattan Project; of course, numerous other women physicists played interesting and important roles. Among them were the distinguished experimentalist Chien-Shiung Wu, later known for her work on parity, whose expertise in the nuclear properties of noble gases enabled her to help solve the problem of the "poisoning" of the chain reaction in reactors, by the buildup of noble gas fission products with extremely high neutron absorption cross sections (Lubkin, 1971; Yost, 1959; Brush, 1985; Howes, in press). Katherine "Kay" Way worked with Alvin Weinberg on the analysis of Fermi's data from the early atomic piles to see if the neutron multiplication factor could be made large enough to permit a self-sustained chain reaction, calculations that led to the construction of the historic pile under the University of Chicago football stands. Way later worked on poisoning of reactors and determination of reactor constants, collaborated in the development of the Way-Wigner formula for fission product decay, and did some theoretical work on reactor design that was used in the production reactors at Hanford (O'Neill, 1979; Artna-Cohen, Gove, and Martin, in press).

Jane Hamilton Hall worked at the Metallurgical Laboratory at Chicago and then as a senior supervisor for the nuclear reactors under construction at Hanford. Following the war she worked at Los Alamos on problems in neutron cross sections, and she eventually became an associate director of Los Alamos. She also was a longtime member of the General Advisory Committee of the Atomic Energy Commission (Sylves, 1987). Ella "Andy" Anderson participated in the Los Alamos cyclotron group and studied the actual fission process, including questions such as the number of neutrons produced per fission and the time delay before the emission of neutrons. She prepared the first sample of nearly pure uranium-235 received by the Los Alamos group for use in the experiments. After the war she did distinguished work in health physics at Oak Ridge.

Mary Argo, with her husband, followed Edward Teller into the Manhattan Project and worked in the group at Los Alamos that Teller established to investigate the possibility of building a weapon based not on nuclear fission but on nuclear fusion. Argo did calculations on deuterium-deuterium and deuterium-tritium burning. Mary Argo was the only female staff member officially invited to see the Trinity test. Another theoretical physicist at Los Alamos, Jane Roberg, also worked on the calculations for the fusion weapon.

Other female physicists on the Manhattan Project included Margaret Ramsey Keck, who was assigned to the implosion project and was involved in photomicrography and grain size determinations for improving the explosives used in the detonators of the weapons. Gertrud Nordheim, a German-educated theoretical physicist, worked at Oak Ridge on calculations of neutron diffusion in the atomic piles, and later, in the summer of 1946, she was appointed as a consultant in physics to Los Alamos along with her husband.

Women physicists also worked in parts of the Manhattan Project located around the country in universities. They included Helen Jupnik, who in 1943 obtained a leave of absence from her job at American Optical Company to go to Princeton to do experiments on resonance absorption of neutrons in uranium in order to ascertain the probable dependence of fission probability on neutron energy.

The Chemists and Metallurgists

Nathalie Michel Goldowski received a Dr.Sc. degree in physical chemistry from the University of Paris. Born in Moscow in 1908 to parents who were among the Russian aristocracy, she escaped with her mother from the Russian revolution in 1917. Her doctoral work centered on the corrosion of metals, and she went to work for the French air force, where she became chief of metallurgical development at age 32. Among her contributions was the idea of bolting strips of magnesium to the fuselages of French seaplanes. The air frames of the French planes were made of aluminum, which corroded badly. Because the magnesium was electropositive, it corroded before the aluminum, maintaining the integrity of the plane.

As Hitler occupied France, Goldowski again escaped with her mother, this time to the United States, where she worked as a research associate for Sciaky Brothers in Chicago until she joined the Manhattan Project there in 1943. Her work in the Metallurgical Laboratory was important in the development of an aluminum-bonded coating for the uranium slugs used in the Hanford reactors.

Uranium corroded too badly to be exposed to cooling water, so the uranium was canned in aluminum. Unfortunately aluminum covers for the slugs also corroded badly. The canning of the aluminum slugs had turned out to be one of the most significant problems faced at Hanford (Brown and MacDonald, 1977, p. 328). The new, noncorroding aluminum coating for the slugs developed by Goldowski was critical to the success of the plutonium production project.

Goldowski has been described as an interesting, intellectually uninhibited, flamboyant person. A large but very graceful woman, she wore her heavy straight black hair down her back and wore clothes bought in Paris. The purchaser of the car she used during the war remarked that it must have been one of her experiments in corrosion. Following the war, she left the project. Her Russian background could not be traced, and she did not become a naturalized U.S. citizen until 1947.

Chemists in the Manhattan Project included Hoylande Young, who was recruited as a research associate to Chicago in 1942, worked as a senior chemist in the Metallurgical Laboratory in 1945–1946, and edited papers that were later published in the National Nuclear Energy Series. She became director of technical information at Argonne National Laboratory (Nicholls, 1978; O'Neill, 1979). Isabella Lugoski Karle, now a distinguished crystallographer, worked in Chicago on the Manhattan Project (Julian, 1990). With her Ph.D. from the University of Michigan, she followed her husband to Chicago and was hired into the group run by Glen Seaborg that was studying the chemistry of transuranic elements. Using the best microtechnology of the day, she grew crystals of plutonium chloride for the first time, and with repeated experiments she demonstrated the stability of this plutonium compound.

Mary Holiat Newman was directed to the Columbia University branch of the Manhattan Project, where she worked on the development of components for the gaseous diffusion plant for the separation of uranium isotopes. Ellen Cleminshaw Weaver, also a chemist, followed her physicist husband into the Manhattan Project at Oak Ridge in June 1945, where she worked on fission fragment radioisotopes and on fission fragments from the atomic pile. She developed microanalytical techniques for separating rare earths.

With a B.A. in chemistry, Rosellen Bergman Fortenberg joined the laboratory at Oak Ridge in March 1944 and worked in analytical chemistry. Similarly, Ada Kirkley Perry became a technician at the Y-12 plant doing analysis of samples. At Hanford, Yvette Berry was recruited for work in the analysis of radioactive samples (Van Arsdol, 1958).

Lilli Hornig was working toward a Ph.D. in chemistry and followed her husband to Los Alamos. There she was assigned to a group researching plutonium chemistry, where she worked with another female chemist, Mary Nachtrieb. Following the dissolution of the group when plutonium-240 was discovered, Hornig transferred to the explosives division, where she worked on explosive lenses (Henriksen, 1986).

The Biologists and Biomedical Scientists

Several women in the Manhattan Project made important contributions to the early studies of the biological effects of radiation. Grace Morgan Happer, a physician, was recruited by her brother, Karl Zeigler Morgan, who headed health physics at the Clinton Engineering Works. After the laboratory opened to produce enriched uranium for the bomb program, Grace Morgan Happer became the first physician at the site (Goodwin, 1991). She participated actively in the development of early clinical studies of the effects of radiation and treated serious cases of radioactive contamination. Because she held an M.S. in organic chemistry from the University of North Carolina in addition to her M.D. from Women's Medical College in Philadelphia, she was able to work closely with the research community as well as to handle clinical and public health issues. Her husband remained in India, and her three- or four-year-old son lived with her while she worked at Oak Ridge during the war. At Oak Ridge she was constantly frustrated by the military mindset. In one instance, her efforts to reduce respiratory illnesses from dust by having a road blacktopped were met with refusal by the military commanders because it would draw attention to the operations—even though the dust clouds themselves could be seen all the way to Knoxville, a major city about twenty-five miles away.

Miriam Posner Finkel, who had received her Ph.D. in zoology from the University of Chicago in 1944, was recruited by the Metallurgical Laboratory and, with her colleagues, took over all short- and long-term studies of the toxic effects of radiation on animals that had been injected or otherwise treated with samples of the nuclides, including in particular plutonium.

Anne Perley, a biochemist, was recruited to the Health Physics group at Los Alamos in July 1944. There she joined the team charged with monitoring workers for exposure to radioactive nuclides such as plutonium and polonium. At the time of the radioactive accident that took the life of Louis Slotin, she was the only person equipped to determine sodium and inorganic phosphorus in small amounts of blood and urine so that the radioactivity induced in these elements by the high neutron dose could be measured.

Edith Hinckley Quimby, already a distinguished scientist at the time of World War II, worked part-time on the Manhattan Project at Columbia University in New York, where she studied the medical effects of radiation exposure.

The Mathematicians and Computing Personnel

The theoretical division at Los Alamos was formed to develop nuclear and hydrodynamic criteria relating to the design of the atomic bomb and to predict the detailed performance of the weapon designed (Brown and MacDonald, 1977). The division was hungry for people who could do these tedious calculations with accuracy. Just as many of the early female astronomers began their careers by doing calculations for observatories, many of the women in the Manhattan Project and at Los Alamos in particular were involved in such calculations. One leader of the division said, "We hire girls because they work better and they're cheaper."

The design of the implosion type of atomic bomb involved complex calculations tracing the path of the shock wave from the detonation of the explosives through the fissile core of the weapon, as well as many other kinds of calculations. Modern computers make such calculations easy, but during World War II, they were done using electric calculators, which did one step at a time. Later, the project used IBM electronic calculating machines, which could be programmed by a plug board to do one or two arithmetic steps and which were fed stacks of punched cards, thus greatly speeding up the calculations.

Among the early computing personnel at Los Alamos were Mary Frankel, Josephine Elliott, Beatrice Langer, Kay Manley, Mici Teller, Jean Bacher, and Betty Inglis (Metropolis and Nelson, 1982). Some of the women involved in computations had backgrounds similar to that of Frances Wilson Kurath, who held a bachelor's degree in mathematics and had married a physicist on the project, Dieter Kurath. Most of these women (including E. De Le Vin, Josephine Elliott, Betty Inglis, Margaret L. Johnson, Beatrice Langer, Mici

Teller, Frances Wilson, and E. Wright) were in the theoretical division's Group T-5 (computations), while others (including Naomi Livesay and F. E. Noah) were in Group T-6, IBM computations (Brown and MacDonald, 1977).

A typical woman recruited to the computing division, Naomi Livesay held a B.A. in mathematics from Cornell College in Mount Vernon, Iowa, and a Ph.M. in mathematics from the University of Wisconsin, which she obtained in 1939. Following her graduation, she took a job with Princeton Surveys in Princeton's School of Public and International Affairs to work on the mathematical analysis of survey data. The data were processed on IBM electrical calculating machines, which she learned to program and operate. After six months, she found the job boring and obtained a Rockefeller Foundation Fellowship at the University of Chicago. On learning of her fellowship, her superiors at Princeton finally offered her the chance to enroll in graduate courses, but by then Chicago was more appealing.

Following a year at Chicago, in the fall of 1940, Livesay was offered a post as a teaching assistant at the University of Illinois. (Women were hired for these jobs because many male faculty were being pulled into war-related research.) In mid-1944, she was recruited to the Los Alamos computing group (Metropolis and Nelson, 1982). A new group was being formed to do calculations related to the implosion weapon, and because the group would be using IBM machines, Livesay was ideal for its requirements. She supervised a crew of GIs and civilians who kept the machines running twenty-four hours a day. When the shock wave hit an interface between two materials, the calculations were carried forward by hand because it was not worth reprogramming the machines. Livesay and Tony Skyrme of the British mission would do the calculations across the interface by hand and compare their results to correct errors. They would then take their results back to the machine.

Locating errors made by the machines was constantly necessary. They were located in a room facing an unpaved New Mexico road that carried heavy truck traffic, and dust was a constant problem. As psychological pressure to complete the implosion calculation built, Livesay was authorized to obtain extra help, and she recruited Eleanor Ewing (Ehrlich), whom she had met at the University of Illinois. Ewing held a B.A. and M.A. in mathematics from that university. As part of her mathematics program, she was encouraged to enroll in physics. As she walked into the classroom with a male acquaintance, the professor called out, "Miss Ewing, we do not mix sexes in physics. We have the girls' row down in front, please." Not surprisingly, she was the only woman in the class. Despite her ability in math, her slower lab partner was made team leader. After a year of physics, she switched to an insurance course, where she was still the only woman but the academic climate was warmer. After she obtained her M.A. in 1943, Ewing was hired by Pratt and Whitney Aircraft in Hartford, Connecticut, to teach elementary mathematics to women who were interested in becoming engineering aides to help the war effort. On being recruited by Livesay, in late August 1944, her introduction to the Manhattan Project came from her immediate superior, who sat cross-legged on top of a table and announced that she had come to the mesa to make an atomic bomb. Ewing's first impression was that she might have to undertake the project alone, and she couldn't even remember what an atom was.

Nurses, Technicians, and WACs

In addition to the women who worked in chemical analysis at Oak Ridge and Hanford and those doing the calculations of the theoretical division at Los Alamos, there were female nurses involved in the care of early cases of radiation exposure. Women worked as technicians in a variety of jobs at Los Alamos and Oak Ridge, frequently as the only woman in a group. Since wartime security insisted that project participants not discuss their work with anyone, other women on the project often did not know what work their friends were doing.

Civilian women technicians included Eleanor Eastin (Hawk) Pomerance and Grace McCammon Estabrook, who worked at the Y-12 plant in Oak Ridge; Jean Klein (Hurwitz) Dayton; Rebecca Bradford Divan; and Jeanne Brooks Carritt and Frances Dunne at Los Alamos.

Typical of the female technicians, Frances Dunne started the war working as a senior aircraft mechanic with an A license at Kirtland Field in Albuquerque, New Mexico. She attended various colleges but obtained no degree. Her outstanding mechanical ability and her small hands prompted George Kistiakowsky to hire her for work with the explosives group. With the title of explosives supervisor, she was the first and only woman to actually work at the explosive sites at Los Alamos, along with a group of thirteen tech sergeants from the Special Engineer Detachment. She did not realize until 1945 that their project was an atomic bomb, but she understood the explosives end of the operation; her group did the explosives testing for both Fat Man and Little Boy. She would reach inside the cavity of an explosive to assemble the trigger and then serve as the technician in charge of the explosive test. She did the countdown and actually pressed the button that detonated the charges. The mockups of the bombs were tested for air, land, and sea delivery by running them through a large tank of water and shooting them off a wooden frame. The mockups used in the test were much smaller than the eventual bomb, and thus Dunne's dexterity was essential. The group was the final assembly team for Fat Man and Little Boy, although Dunne did not go to the South Pacific.

No account of the women who worked on the Manhattan Project would be complete without mention of the members of the Women's Army Corps, the WACs. In the period from 1943 through 1945, there were WAC members assigned to units at Clinton, Hanford, Los Alamos, and other project installations, and some of them were involved in highly technical and scientific work (Jones, 1985). According to the official history of Los Alamos (Hawkins, 1961), nearly half the WACs there in May 1945 were working as scientists or technicians, and the percentage employed as scientists was higher than the percentage of civilian employees or members of the men's army in the Special Engineer Detachment.

Probably the most accomplished scientist among the WACs was Mary L. Miller, who held a Ph.D. in physical chemistry from Columbia University (1934). She was a research associate at the school of medicine of Washington University in St. Louis when the war broke out. She decided to enlist as a private in 1943 and was stationed at Los Alamos. Her talent and qualifications placed her in charge of a laboratory group, but she insisted on maintaining her low military rank.

Other WACs in the Manhattan Project included Lyda Speck, who worked at the Van de Graaff accelerator at Los Alamos and succeeded in publishing some of her technical work in the *Physical Review* after the war; Myrtle "Batch" Bachelder, who worked in analytical chemistry and spectroscopy to determine the purity of materials used in the preparation of uranium and plutonium at Los Alamos; Evelyn S. Walker, who worked with metal oxides and plastics; and Miriam White Campbell, who drew up the detailed plans for the assembly of the bomb, Little Boy.

Conclusions

The roles played by women in the scientific and technical work of the Manhattan Project were as varied as those of their male colleagues. This sampling of the women who were there clearly indicates not only that they were notably present, but also that they made significant contributions to the successful construction of the first nuclear weapons. Most of the women interviewed recalled their days in the Manhattan Project as a time of life when they felt terribly alive and vitally involved in their work. Nearly all of them expressed a desire to support the U.S. war effort. Few of them seem to have considered the consequences of their work until after the war. Manley (1990) quotes several women from Los Alamos who describe having concerns over the consequences of the work much later. They felt that the construction of a nuclear weapon was warranted by the wartime situation and that they would do the same thing again. Their attitudes are not unlike those of their male counterparts. Only Joan Hinton seems to have become active in the effort to obtain civilian control of nuclear technology.

The absence of women from the leadership of the defense technology establishment is probably a result of social factors rather than an unwillingness of women to work on weapons development or a lack of ability to perform this type of physical research. Several of the women, such as Diz Graves, who rejected an appointment to the Atomic Energy Commission to care for her husband, and many who stopped working to raise children, abandoned promising careers for family concerns. Others pursued their careers in universities or switched fields. The "glass ceiling" found in the defense technology establishment thus appears to be primarily an outgrowth of the social roles expected of women rather than an indication of female inability or unwillingness to participate in the construction of weapons of mass destruction.

Note

Ruth H. Howes gratefully acknowledges the support of a Faculty Academic Year Research Grant from Ball State University.

chapter 9

Women and National Security Policy
Frances G. Burwell, Meredith Reid Sarkees

> National security policy refers to those objectives and programs
> whereby the government seeks to ensure the nation's security and
> survival in a potentially hostile international environment. It is a
> somewhat narrower concept than foreign policy, which refers to the
> totality of objectives and programs whereby the government seeks to
> cope with the external environment (Kegley and Wittkopf, 1987, p. 81).

This duty of a state to protect its citizens and territory from physical
harm has long been seen as the basic tenet of international relations
(Morgenthau, 1990). Consequently, the use of military force against
another country is one of the most momentous decisions a national
government can make. The consequences, in terms of lives lost,
money and resources spent, and influence enhanced or depleted,
can be enormous. As a result, the decision to use military force,
whether it involves a fullscale conflict or a single punitive bombing
raid, is usually taken at the highest level of government. In the U.S.
system, such a decision is generally made by the president, with the
advice of the National Security Council.

When the involvement of women in this decision is considered,
one fact that becomes immediately obvious is the almost total
absence of women as significant players. Usually, those closely
involved in the decision to launch a military operation are men. On
the other hand, it is also clear that a growing number of women are
entering the national security policy community. During the last
thirty years, women throughout U.S. society have moved into
"nontraditional" occupations (i.e., those previously restricted to, or
dominated by, males). The U.S. government, including the national
security agencies, has seen significant changes in the gender
composition of its work force, as have most other sectors of society.
The number of women in the Foreign Service, on legislative staffs,
and in the agencies generally has increased throughout the past two
decades. Lest this be overstated, it must be noted that fewer women
are still entering the field than men, but the change is not
insignificant.

The focus of this chapter is to examine what effect this increase in the number of women involved in the national security policy community might have on a decision to authorize the use of military force. The examination of the issue will focus on three subsidiary questions: How is national security policy currently being made? Where are women located within this process? And what types of impact do women have? In particular we will examine the participation of women in the making of national security policy: to describe the extent of women's involvement; to detail the number of women in different agencies and at different levels; and to examine some factors that may increase their participation rate or that may contribute to their career advancement or lack of it. Also, the views of female national security professionals will be discussed. Earlier chapters have described the widespread belief in a "gender gap" over the use of force. There is a significant body of research indicating that women, as part of the overall population, are less likely than men to favor the use of force. The corresponding assumption is that including more women in the process will necessarily result in more peaceful foreign and national security policies. This expectation will be addressed in the context of the perspectives of high-ranking women within the foreign policy establishment.

The National Security Process

The decision to use force at the national level in the United States is a result of a process that includes a variety of agencies with disparate constituencies and functions. The term "national security community" is very broad, with rather ill-defined boundaries. It could conceivably include not only those executive branch agencies concerned with determining and implementing policy, but also the military forces charged with actually providing security in the physical sense. It could include the Congress, with its extensive staff, which can greatly affect national security policy through its power to declare war and its budgetary power. It might even include nongovernmental groups, especially public interest groups, the defense industry, and research institutions, all of which certainly affect the debate over the use of force and at times have great influence on government decisions. However, since the military and the public have been addressed in other chapters, the focus on the national security community in this chapter will be rather circumscribed. It will include the National Security Council and its staff, the Department of State, the civilian sectors of the Department of Defense, and Congress, particularly the members of committees concerned with national security policy, their staffs, and the staffs of those committees.

In gauging the extent of women's participation in major national security decisions, a critical question to ask is whether the process is centralized or decentralized. Are major decisions made primarily among a small circle of presidential advisers, perhaps acting on limited advice? Or is the involvement of large sectors of the bureaucracy encouraged, with advice and options flowing upward? In the first case, only the very top layer of the national security community will be involved, along with a few close personal advisers to the president. In the second case, analysts and experts who are relatively new in the bureaucracy can have a major impact by framing the terms of the debate and identifying potential courses of action. The extent to which women are active players in a government decision to use force will depend on an appropriate match between the type of policy process and the presence of women in the relevant positions. If the first case is applicable, women must be among the relatively small circle of presidential advisers; if the second case is applicable, they could be effective even at relatively junior levels in the bureaucracy.

During the postwar period, many observers of the policy process have written about the increasing power of the presidency and the declining influence of other government forces in major foreign policy decisions. Particularly in national security policy matters, the president has relied increasingly upon his own personal staff and the Executive Office of the President (including the National Security Council) at the expense of both Congress and the bureaucracy (Kegley and Wittkopf, 1987). However, as Leslie Gelb cautions, in examining the policy apparatus, we find one stark truth:

> that personalities and abilities are far more important than structure and process, and that these factors will determine who will make policy and decisions under the president. . . . The only safe prediction on organization is that however the formal system is constructed, actual power will gravitate to the person whose policy views and styles prevail with the president. . . . If a president wants to create a decisionmaking system that encourages competing views over which he presides and decides, he can do that. Similarly, if he wants to stress the image and the fact of harmony or professionalism or division of labor, he can do that as well (1988, pp. 236–237).

As a result, we shall restrict our examination to the Bush administration, examining how these agencies have interrelated in making national security policy. President Bush, as the consummate insider, seemed more likely than his predecessor to use the bureaucracy, allowing the careerists an avenue for security policy input. On the other hand, Bush has also demonstrated a very "hands-on" style of leadership, which has reflected a willingness to override normal bureaucratic channels (Deibel, 1991). Along these lines, Bush has adopted a more restricted, hierarchical, policymaking model, which concentrates national security policymaking within the hands of a few close personal advisers and which tends to exclude both the bureaucracy and Congress. "The Bush White House seeks to exploit divisions in government to the advantage of the White House" (Rose, 1991, p. 313).

In terms of the president's relations with Congress, during the first two years of the Bush administration there were no major national security nor foreign policy confrontations between the president and Capitol Hill. However, the seeds of potential conflict had been sown by both the president's campaign to reassert presidential prerogatives and Congress' intention to play an assertive foreign and defense policy role (Sinclair, 1991). Bush had already proven willing to resist congressional initiatives, successfully vetoing more legislation than any predecessor (Rose, 1991). The president's desire to exclude Congress from national security policy decisions was particularly evident during the initial stages of the Gulf War. As commander-in-chief, Bush originally ordered 200,000 troops into the region, and later increased the force levels to more than 400,000 without first seeking the support of Congress (Rose, 1991). The president's failure to include Congress, and especially to take key Democrats into his confidence, led to a full-scale congressional debate on the looming conflict, and especially on the value of continuing economic sanctions. Although there was significant opposition in the Senate, where the administration's measure passed by only fifty-two to forty-six, the debate and vote came late enough in the process that it did not provide an effective challenge to the president's primacy on this issue.

In terms of the national security bureaucracy, the Bush administration, unlike that of Ronald Reagan, has been for the most part devoid of officials with their own strong political agendas; instead, it has been characterized by insider politics (Rockman, 1991). Bush has treated the role and mission of career civil servants with respect, appointing cabinet officials who are not hostile to the statutory goals of their agencies. On the other hand, the president has also revealed a propensity for relying on a small group of personal friends (Aberbach, 1991). In general, Bush has followed the counsel of a limited group of advisers, including James Baker, Brent Scowcroft, and Dick Cheney, without bringing career officials or other legitimate players into the deliberations (Campbell, 1991).

Bush's political style has been characterized by George Will as stemming from his comfort with "a small set of entitled decisionmakers and his disdain for the politics of public persuasion" (Rockman, 1991, p. 26). As a result:

> Bush's inner sanctum has a fraternity air, what one top Republican calls "a male prep school, locker-room atmosphere." The president is very much a product of his upbringing and his generation, and in his closest councils he makes many important decisions with a group of likeminded men (Dowd, 1991, p. 1A).

This collegial atmosphere shuts out the bureaucracy and places a premium on personal loyalty, further reducing the likelihood that any new actors will be involved. Moreover, as one observer noted:

> Such shortcomings may not be limited to the White House; for while the president relies on Baker, Cheney, Scowcroft, and Sununu, Baker has been criticized for ignoring the Foreign Service in favor of a few top aides, all of them veterans of Baker's previous cabinet or campaign posts: Robert Kimmitt, Dennis Ross, Margaret Tutwiler, and Robert Zoellick (Deibel, 1991, pp. 19–20).

Another commented:

> The strained relations between Baker and the State Department's career diplomats are no secret; Baker relies on a small group of insiders and rarely seeks advice on foreign policy from career officers. In addition, Bush and Baker often bypass Foreign Service Officers in favor of direct contacts and personal relationships with other heads of state (Roberts, 1991, p. C6).

This emphasis on personal relationships with foreign leaders has been characterized as "Rolodex diplomacy" (Deibel, 1991, p. 6), and was particularly evident in Bush's successful efforts to galvanize world leaders and build the coalition against Iraq (Campbell, 1991).

Clearly, in the Bush administration, like others before it, national decisionmaking is centralized at the very top levels of the government. This is particularly true for a decision regarding the use of force, as was amply demonstrated during the Gulf War. Thus, whether individual women have any influence on this process will depend on their proximity to the president, either as members of his close circle of advisers or in some prominent role. For example, Margaret Tutwiler, the assistant secretary of state for public affairs, has a long association with Secretary of State Baker. Thus, it is likely that she does have an impact on policy beyond her public role of explaining U.S. decisions after the fact. Whether that role extends to questions concerning the use of force is unclear.

Where Do Women Work?

For women to be involved in the national security decisionmaking process, they must first be working in the relevant agencies and offices. Also, they must be present at the appropriate rank. Staff aides may be present as expert advisers or staff officers, but that is entirely different from being one of the actual decisionmakers at the highest level. This section will analyze some of the available data concerning where women work in the various institutions responsible for national security policy.

In discussing the data for the numbers and ranks of women in the national security community, it is first necessary to distinguish between the legislative and executive branches, which play different roles in policymaking and utilize radically different personnel systems. The congressional system is not really a system at all, but is instead composed of publicly elected officials who retain considerable autonomy in the hiring of their own staffs and those of the relevant committees. The executive branch, in contrast, is divided into several interlocking personnel systems, complete with complex hiring and promotion procedures, numerous grade levels, and fairly regular accumulation and reporting of data on the representation of women and minorities.

The primary personnel structure of the executive branch is the Civil Service. The portions of the Civil Service that are most relevant to our purposes are the GS system, the GM system, and the Senior Executive Service, or SES. In addition, the State Department includes the Foreign Service, which will be discussed later. The GS grades (with 1 being the lowest and 18 the highest) include mostly individuals with administrative, clerical, and technical responsibilities. The GM grades (which are parallel to GS 13–15) include those individuals with supervisory, managerial, or policy responsibilities. Generally, there are far fewer GM employees than GS employees in any agency. High-ranking GS employees (grades 16–18) number relatively few, and usually are lawyers, scientists, or technical experts with an advisory role in policy. Most of the individuals formerly in the GS 16–18 ranks were transferred in 1978 into the newly created Senior Executive Service, which comprises the high-level managerial and policy personnel throughout government. Above the SES and the Civil Service as a whole are the Executive Schedule, or political appointees whose positions require Senate confirmation. These individuals include the departmental secretaries, under secretaries, assistant secretaries, and other persons of similar rank.

Across the entire civilian federal work force women are 44 percent of employees. The GS and GM grades combined are 51 percent women, but within grades 13–15, where GM employees are found, the percentage of women drops to only 20 percent. In the SES, only 12 percent of employees are women (U.S. Office of Personnel Management figures, as of September 30, 1991. No separate breakdown is available for GS and GM employees across the entire federal work force). This pattern, in which women constitute a significant percentage of the overall work force but only a small percentage of the high-level managerial grades, is repeated throughout the national security community.

What follows is an analysis of the primary executive branch agencies involved in national security policy and the number and rank of the women working in those agencies. Of course, having numerous women working in a particular agency, even high-ranking women, does not necessarily mean that those individuals are involved in a governmental decision to use force against another country. However, the absence of women, especially at the high levels, is a clear indication that women are not involved in such decisions.

The Department of State

> The Department of State advises the President in the formulation and execution of foreign policy. . . . The Department of State's primary objective in the conduct of foreign relations is to promote the long-range security and well-being of the United States. The Department determines and analyzes the facts relating to American overseas interests, makes recommendations on policy and future action, and takes the necessary steps to carry out established policy (*U.S. Government Manual*, 1988).

The State Department has long had a reputation for being slow to hire and promote women in its work force, especially in the diplomatic corps. In fact, State has been sued successfully for sex discrimination on several occasions, most recently in *Alison Palmer et al.* v. *Baker* (1988), leading to an exhaustive examination of hiring and promotion procedures. Some changes have been instituted, but too recently for the impact to be adequately judged. Today the State Department compares somewhat unfavorably with the federal work force as a whole, having, for example, a smaller percentage of women in the senior grades but a slightly higher percentage of women in the middle-level managerial grades. However, State compares favorably with the other major national security agency, the Department of Defense, with slightly higher percentages of women at both the senior and middle ranks.

As of March 1991, the Department had 25,464 employees, divided into two separate spheres, the Foreign Service and the Civil Service (*Federal Civilian Workforce Statistics,* March 1991). The Foreign Service, comprising about 66 percent of all personnel in the State Department, sends individuals to represent the United States around the world: in embassies, at international organizations, and at various conferences and negotiations. Most of the professionals in substantive policymaking jobs in the department's Washington offices are from the Foreign Service. Finally, the Foreign Service includes those communicators, security personnel, and other administrative specialists who serve overseas. The Civil Service, about one-third of State Department personnel, manages the communications, logistics, and domestic end of foreign relations, largely from Washington, D.C. The personnel systems of the Foreign Service and the Civil Service are quite different. The Foreign Service has a rather unique system that involves entrance exams, periodic reviews, and a series of short-term assignments. The Civil Service is on a GS grade system, like many government jobs, and retains a formalized step system for promotions.

Table 9.1 details the distribution of women throughout the State Department's Civil Service. The percentage of women across the entire Civil Service is quite high—63 percent. But the vast majority of them are in grades GS 12 and below, with women representing 35 percent of GS 13–15. These numbers are higher, however, than comparable figures from the Department of Defense overall or from the Office of the Secretary of Defense. For grades 13-15, the State Department has a higher percentage of women than does the federal government as a whole. However, in terms of policymaking, the most influential positions are those in the SES. In 1970, there were three women in the Senior Executive Service of the State Department; in 1981 there were eight; in 1987 there were nine. However, taking into account the growth of the SES, there has been little or no progress in the percentage of women in it, fluctuating from 15 percent to 8 percent in 1987 and back to 12 percent of the SES in 1991. These statistics would seem to indicate that women encounter a "glass ceiling" that limits their entry into these levels.

Table 9.1 Department of State Civil Service Personnel

Grade	Total Employees	Women	(percentage of total)
Undefined	105	16	(15)
GS 1–4	442	340	(77)
GS 5–8	1,683	1,372	(82)
GS 9–12	1,737	1,160	(67)
GS 13–15	1,274	447	(35)
GS 16–18	0	0	
GS Total	5,136	3,319	(65)
SES Total	104	12	(12)
Total	5,345	3,347	(63)

Source: U.S. Department of State, *Multi-Year Affirmative Action Plan, FY 1990/92* (Washington: Department of State, April 1991).
Figures are as of September 1990.

The Civil Service, however, represents only a portion of the State Department's work force. The Foreign Service is the more visible personnel group, largely because of its role in representing the United States abroad. Also, members of the Foreign Service generally tend to be more involved in the making of foreign policy than do members of the Civil Service. The Foreign Service itself is divided into "generalists" and "specialists." Generalists are persons usually referred to as diplomats or Foreign Service officers (FSOs). Specialists are those with specific skills, such as security personnel, budgetary officers, and secretaries; they are not usually involved in foreign policy decisions. Thus, the statistics for Foreign Service specialists are presented in Table 9.2 mostly to illustrate the continued pattern of women in the lower and middle ranks and men in the senior grades.

Table 9.2 Department of State Foreign Service Personnel

Generalists

Grade	Total Employees	Women	(percentage of total)
SFS-CM	41	1	(2%)
SFS-MC	314	17	(5%)
SFS-OC	315	33	(10%)
Total SFS	670	51	(8%)
FS 1	807	140	(17%)
FS 2	978	220	(22%)
FS 3	917	263	(29%)
FS 4	1,153	367	(32%)
FS 5	371	134	(36%)
FS 6	65	26	(46%)
FS 7	2	1	(50%)
FS 8	0	0	
FS 9	0	0	
Total FS	4,284	1,151	(27%)
Total Generalists	4,954	1,202	(24%)

Specialists

Grade	Total Employees	Women	(percentage of total)
SFS-CM	0	0	
SFS-MC	16	2	(13%)
SFS-OC	45	0	(0%)
Total SFS	61	2	(3%)
FS 1	192	11	(6%)
FS 2	352	38	(11%)
FS 3	438	88	(20%)
FS 4	783	151	(19%)
FS 5	761	254	(33%)
FS 6	504	320	(63%)
FS 7	405	310	(77%)
FS 8	290	224	(77%)
FS 9	45	18	(40%)
Total FS	3,770	1,414	(38%)
Total Specialists	3,831	1,416	(37%)
Total	8,785	2,618	(30%)

Source: U.S. Department of State, *Multi-Year Affirmative Action Plan, FY 1990/92* (Washington: Department of State, April 1991).
Note: Figures are as of September 1990.

It is the Foreign Service generalists who are much more relevant to a decision regarding the potential use of force. They provide advice from U.S. embassies around the world, handle day-to-day operations with other governments, and generally implement U.S. foreign policy. The distribution of women throughout the Foreign Service generalist corps is provided in Table 9.2. The percentage of generalists who are women is small (24 percent) compared with the GS personnel in the Department of State overall or with the Office of the Secretary of Defense. In part, this is because some traditional female occupations (i.e., secretary) are not included in the generalist group but rather with the Civil Service or the specialists. Among the senior ranks of the generalists—the individuals most likely to be office directors, deputy assistant secretaries, or ambassadors—only 8 percent are women. This percentage is lower than that for the SES grades in the State Department overall, the federal government overall, and the Office of the Secretary of Defense. It is higher, however, than the percentage of women in the SES grades at the Department of Defense as a whole.

Thus, the Foreign Service generalist corps continues the pattern of very few women in the senior levels. It differs from the other agencies in not having a large group of secretarial/administrative personnel who are women. It also differs in having slightly higher percentages of women in the middle levels of FS 1 to FS 3 than are found among the GM 13–15 grades. This may have a significant impact on future representation of women in the senior ranks, because it represents an increasing percentage of women in the pool of individuals likely to be promoted to the senior grades. Of course, such advancement is not assured, and the issue of promotions was included in the sex-discrimination case brought against the State Department. In a recent appeal of a portion of *Alison Palmer et al.* v. *Baker,* the U.S. Court of Appeals found that women in State were hampered in promotions because of discrimination in assignments, merit awards, and performance evaluations (Havemann, 1990).

Among the Foreign Service generalists, the two groups likely to have more opportunities to address issues regarding the use of force are ambassadors and political officers. As the primary representatives of the U.S. government to another government, ambassadors provide advice to Washington and carry Washington's desires and concerns to the other country. Should hostilities become a possibility, the ambassador could be a major player, although that might take the form of giving advice rather than making decisions. In the case of Iraq, the U.S. ambassador, April Glaspie, was ordered not to return to Baghdad (she was in Europe when Kuwait was invaded), and she spent the war working at the State Department. Glaspie was unusual, however, in being a woman assigned as ambassador to a country of major importance to the United States. Currently most female ambassadors serve in smaller countries that have been somewhat peripheral to U.S. interests. The difficulty that women have in rising through the career ranks to the ambassadorial level is compounded by the increasing tendency of presidents to utilize ambassadorships for political patronage. For example, President Bush has cut the number of ambassadorial posts to career Foreign Service officers to 43 percent, down from 63 percent under Reagan (Sciolino, 1989). Of the eighty-eight positions filled by career members of the Foreign Service officer corps, only six were filled by women, an abysmal 7 percent of the total. In sharp contrast, 13 percent of politically appointed ambassadors were women. In August 1989, Charles Untermayer, the White House personnel director, claimed that the administration's appointment policies for ambassadors were in fact adopted to supplement the State Department's affirmative action program. However, in her congressional testimony, Mary Lee Garrison, co-president of the State Department chapter of the Women's Action Organization, noted the tangential impact of this policy on women.

> Certainly from the standpoint of female Foreign Service Officers, it is galling that historically approximately two-thirds of the female ambassadors have been political appointees. . . . We have no qualms about the inclusion of qualified women from outside the State Department ranks as ambassadors, but if you look at those women who have been appointed from outside the Foreign Service ranks to ambassadorial appointments, in most cases, their lack of qualifications is stunning. . . . It very much affects morale and cheapens the accomplishments of those women and minorities who have worked darn hard to get to those levels. It tars everyone who has appearance of being a woman or minority candidate with a brush of incompetence, and even more tragically, it presents to young people looking at the possibility of careers in the Foreign Service a very warped picture (*Hearings*, 1989, p. 49).

As a result, she claims that the brightest women have realized that their likelihood of obtaining an ambassadorship is increased if they leave the State Department and concentrate on political activity.

Political officers are those Foreign Service generalists who spend most of their careers analyzing political or military issues. The generalist corps is divided into four such groups ("cones" in State Department parlance): political, economic, consular, and administrative. Economic officers deal primarily with trade and monetary issues, consular officers work on visa and immigration issues as well as assisting U.S. citizens overseas, and administrative officers manage facilities, budgets, and personnel. After taking the Foreign Service written exam, which now covers four functional areas, a successful generalist candidate is put on a list for one area, for which s/he may be hired. It is quite rare, but not impossible, to switch cones mid-career. Therefore, the assignment is of great importance. The State Department has been criticized for assigning these cones on the basis of the exam alone, especially since the exam itself has come under continued criticism. The political and economic cones are those most involved in substantive policy formulation and are considered the most prestigious and the most likely to lead to promotion to the Senior Foreign Service. At the end of FY 1990, women were disproportionately represented in the administrative and especially the consular cones. Although they are 22 percent of all generalists, women make up 35 percent of the consular cone and 29 percent of the administrative cone. Table 9.3 shows the distribution of officers across the cones, by sex.

Table 9.3 Cone Assignments for Foreign Service Officers

	Percentage Male	Percentage Female
Total Foreign Service Officers	78	22
Political Cone	82	18
Economic Cone	80	20
Consular Cone	65	35
Administrative Cone	71	29

Source: U.S. Department of State, *Multi-Year Affirmative Action Plan, FY 1990/92* (Washington: Department of State, April 1991).
Figures are as of September 1990.

Of all female Foreign Service officers in 1990, 28 percent were assigned to the political cone and 28 percent to the consular cone; whereas of all male Foreign Service officers, 40 percent were assigned to the political cone and only 17 percent were assigned to the consular cone. That women FSOs have been disproportionately assigned to the consular cone has been recognized publicly in at least two places. In *Alison Palmer et al.* v. *Baker,* lawyers for the plaintiff found that between 1975 and 1980, 16.9 percent more females were assigned to the consular cone than expected, based on the proportion of new hires. A more recent acknowledgment came in the recently released Government Accounting Office (GAO) report on the Foreign Service that was requested by Congress. It stated that there are a "disproportionate number of minorities and white women in functional areas that employee groups consider to be less desirable" (*State Department,* 1989, p. 30). This overrepresentation of women in the consular cone could be a further obstacle to women's career advancement, since, as the GAO concluded, political and economic officers had the greatest chance of promotion. If political officers are those most likely to deal with issues regarding the use of force, then this distribution makes it even less likely that women will be involved.

The Defense Department

> The Department of Defense is responsible for providing the military forces needed to deter war and protect the security of our country. . . . Under the President, who is also Commander in Chief, the Secretary of Defense exercises direction, authority, and control over the Department, which includes the separately organized military departments of Army, Navy, and Air Force, the Joint Chiefs of Staff providing military advice, the unified and specified combatant commands, and various defense agencies established for specific purposes (*U.S. Government Manual,* 1988–1989).

The Department of Defense is one of the largest federal bureaucracies. Overall, the civilian work force of the Defense Department in the categories relevant here—GS, GM, and SES— totals 659,400. In addition, there are forty-one political appointees whose positions require Senate confirmation. This would include the secretary and deputy secretary, as well as the under secretaries, the assistant secretaries, and some other high-level positions. Also, a significant number of military personnel work in Defense Department offices (the status of military women is examined in another chapter of this volume). The Defense Department also includes numerous agencies that deal primarily with the technical aspects of national security policy, ranging from the Defense

Advanced Research Projects Agency (DARPA) to the Civilian Health and Medical Programs of the Unified Services (CHAMPUS). Most of their employees are technical experts rather than political decisionmakers. Table 9.4 details the number of civilian women in the Department of Defense overall.

Table 9.4 Department of Defense Civilian Work Force

Grade	Total Employees	Women	(percentage of total)
GS 1–4	78,360	60,286	(77)
GS 5–8	200,577	141,478	(71)
GS 9–12	291,816	97,296	(33)
GS 13–15	25,800	4,289	(17)
GS 16–18	7	0	(0)
GS Total	596,560	303,349	(50)
GM 13	33,036	6,228	(19)
GM 14	18,966	2,398	(13)
GM 15	9,359	790	(18)
GM Total	61,361	9,416	(15)
SES 1–2	130	19	(15)
SES 3–4	1,079	54	(5)
SES 5–6	273	15	(5)
SES Total	1,482	88	(6)
Total	659,403	312,853	(47)

Source: Department of Defense, September 1991.
This table does not include all DOD employees. In particular, hourly wage and blue-collar workers are not included, nor are consultants and other nonpermanent personnel.

Again the pattern appears in which women dominate the GS ranks, while men are the majority in the GM ranks and dominate the SES grades. In some cases, the presence of numerous women in the lower ranks might indicate improved chances that women will be well represented in the higher ranks in the future. This assumes, however, that the women currently in the lower GS ranks will be promoted. Unfortunately, most of the

GS women are at GS 10 or below, a level from which few people are promoted into the managerial/policy grades. The percentage of women among the high-ranking political appointees is 17 percent; higher than the percentage in either the SES or GM grades, which represent the top of the career Civil Service.

The two central bureaucracies for formulating Defense Department positions regarding foreign policy, including the use of force, are the Office of the Joint Staff (formerly the Office of the Joint Chiefs of Staff) and the Office of the Secretary of Defense (OSD). The Office of the Joint Staff actually has relatively few civilian personnel. Because it is intended to coordinate military options and planning across the three services, it is, not surprisingly, dominated by military personnel. The top level—that of the service chiefs themselves—is and always has been exclusively male. In addition, the personnel listings in the *Federal Yellow Book* (Winter 1992) show very few military women at all in the Office of the Joint Staff. Whether this will change in the future, as the growing number of women entering the military rise to the appropriate rank, is still uncertain.

Our focus, however, is on the civilians working on the Joint Staff. Of that population, fully 85 percent of the GS staff are women. In the grades below GS 12, which are dominated by administrative and secretarial staff, the percentage is even higher. However, in the GM grades (13–15) only 20 percent of the civilians are women, and both individuals in the SES are men. The Joint Staff—at least on the civilian side—clearly demonstrates a pattern of female administrative and clerical staff, with men in management and analytical positions.

The Office of the Secretary of Defense includes not only the immediate staff of the secretary and deputy secretary, but also the offices of the under secretaries for acquisition and policy and numerous other offices concerned with civilian and military personnel, legislative and public affairs, and intelligence. Table 9.5 details the number and percentage of women at various grades in OSD. It is consistent with the overall Defense Department patterns: the GS system is largely made up of women (95 percent), while the GM and SES grades are occupied mostly by men. However, OSD does have a higher percentage of women in those grades than does the Defense Department overall: 26 percent of the GM grades and 11 percent of the SES, rather than 15 and 6 percent, respectively. Of the eighteen high-level political appointees in OSD, however, none are women.

Table 9.5 Office of the Secretary of Defense Civilian Work Force

Grade	Total Employees	Women	(percentage of total)
GS 1–4	2	1	(50)
GS 5–8	331	319	(96)
GS 9–12	149	126	(85)
GS 13–15	9	7	(78)
GS 16–18	0	0	
GS Total	491	453	(92)
GM 13	137	25	(18)
GM 14	104	50	(48)
GM 15	528	101	(19)
GM Total	669	176	(26)
SES 1–2	21	5	(24)
SES 3–4	171	15	(9)
SES 5–6	83	9	(11)
SES Total	275	29	(11)
Total	1,435	658	(46)

Source: Department of Defense, September 1991.
This table does not include all DOD employees. In particular, hourly wage and blue-collar workers are not included, nor are consultants and other nonpermanent personnel.

National Security Council

> The function of the Council shall be to advise the President with respect to the integration of domestic, foreign, and military policies relating to the national security so as to enable the military services and the other departments and agencies of the government to cooperate more effectively in matters involving the national security (National Security Act of 1947, cited in Campus and Johnson, 1988, p. viii).

The National Security Council (NSC) brings together the most powerful and influential set of advisers for any president struggling with the decision of whether or not to use force outside the United States. The members of the NSC, or the "Principals Committee," consist of the president, vice president, secretary of defense, and secretary of state. Those specified as "statutory advisers" to the NSC are the director of the Central Intelligence Agency, the chair of the Joint Chiefs of Staff, and the director of the Arms Control and Disarmament Agency. The official title of the head of the NSC staff is assistant to the president for national security affairs. None of these positions has ever been held by a woman. Below the assistant to the president, the NSC staff is divided into "special assistants to the president" (i.e., those who head particular offices such as Soviet affairs or defense policy/arms control) and "directors," who are the analytical staff members working for the special assistants.

The only woman to have served as a member of the NSC was Jeane Kirkpatrick, who was U.S. ambassador to the United Nations during the Reagan administration. The person holding that position has not normally been a member of the NSC. Although Kirkpatrick was certainly a very visible member of the NSC, there is dispute about her effectiveness and the seriousness with which she was regarded by her male colleagues (Ewell, 1987). For the staff of the NSC, the picture is slightly better. Though a woman has never served as NSC adviser, several women have served as prominent staff members, including Condoleezza Rice and Madeleine Albright. Currently, of the twelve special assistants, the only woman is Virginia Lampley, who is special assistant for legislative affairs. Of the thirty directors, three are women. In addition, women run the information management office and the administrative office of the NSC (*Federal Yellow Book,* Winter 1992, pp. 121–122).

Although the NSC itself has played a major role in government decisions regarding the use of force, it has not been an avenue through which many women have been involved in such decisions. In the future, some increase in the number of women holding director positions can be expected, because these individuals are often seconded from other government agencies or brought in from research institutes or think tanks. As more women move into that recruitment pool, more of them will emerge as directors and special assistants. As for the head of the NSC staff, or the actual members or statutory advisers, there may be a much longer wait. Often those individuals have either risen to the top of a career ladder (such as Robert Gates at the CIA) or been long-time advisers of a president (such as James Baker at State). Few women have yet been included in either circle. One exception is Madeleine Albright, who was Michael Dukakis' foreign policy adviser during the 1988 presidential campaign. Had that campaign succeeded, she would have been a logical candidate for a high-level foreign policy post.

The Congress

Historically there has been a debate between Congress and the president concerning the extent of congressional involvement in national security policy. As was mentioned earlier, Congress has a legitimate role in national security policy, particularly because of its constitutional mandate to declare war. Additionally Congress has been able to utilize its tools of budget approval and, in the Senate, confirmation of appointees to develop a very active role in influencing national security policy. On occasion, ambassadorial appointments have been held up until the executive branch has answered congressional concerns about specific policies. Congressional restrictions on the disbursal of federal money have limited U.S. aid to the Nicaraguan contras and to multilateral institutions, affected the development and purchase of weapons systems, and determined the levels of aid received by countries around the world.

As such, women who work in Congress may very well be involved in national security issues. Unfortunately, one of the most striking things about women working in Congress is how few there are. (All figures in this section are based on the 102nd Congress.) Prior to the 1992 elections, the House of Representatives was 94 percent male, and the Senate was 98 percent male.

The most influential senators and representatives are those who belong to relevant committees. For national security policy, the committees would be the House and Senate Armed Services Committees, the House Foreign Affairs and Senate Foreign Relations Committees, the House and Senate Select Committees on Intelligence, the Defense and Foreign Operations Subcommittees, and the House and Senate Appropriations Committees. But representatives and senators are not the only individuals to affect national security policy from the Hill. Many of the policies are suggested, framed, and evaluated by staff members, who work both for committees covering particular issues and for individual members of Congress. See Table 9.6 for a breakdown of Senate and House Committee memberships and staff.

Not surprisingly, given that there are only two female senators, the representation of women on Senate committees is slight, although it does include both Senators Nancy Kassebaum and Barbara Mikulski. Representation on the House committees is somewhat better, although there are no women on the relevant subcommittees of the Appropriations Committee. As for the committee staffs, the available data indicate a

Table 9.6 Committees of the U.S. Congress Representation of Women Members and Staff

Senate Committees				
Committee	Total Members	Women Members	Total Staff [a]	Women Staff
Appropriations Committee				
Defense Subcommittee	18	0	10	2
Foreign Operations Subcommittee	13	1	4	1
Armed Services	20	0	37	6
Foreign Relations	20	1	8	1
Select Committee on Intelligence	17	0	5	1

House Committees				
Committee	Total Members	Women Members	Total Staff [a]	Women Staff
Appropriations Committee				
Defense Subcommittee	13	0	13	2
Foreign Operations Subcommittee	12	0	3	2
Armed Services	55	4	59	23
Foreign Relations	45	2	31	9
Select Committee on Intelligence	21	1	16	4

Source: Congressional Yellow Book, Winter 1992.
Note: a. Does not include those clearly identifiable as secretarial or administrative staff.

much higher percentage than among the members. This probably reflects the general increase in the numbers of women entering the field of foreign and defense policy (and the fact that it is much easier to be hired by a congressional committee than it is to run and win an election). However, the figures should be taken with caution. Gathering comparable data for the legislative branch is difficult, for no system comparable to the Civil Service or Foreign Service exists for the members of Congress and their staffs. Individuals with similar or identical titles might have very different responsibilities, depending on the needs of the committee or the member. Although those individuals clearly identified as secretaries were not included, many staff titles were vague enough to make it difficult, if not impossible, to distinguish those with purely administrative duties from those with analytical and substantive responsibilities. And, unlike the Departments of State and Defense, members of Congress are not required to file EEO reports on the racial and gender composition of their staffs. The gender of individuals has been decided based on names, and the wide variety of titles has made distinguishing analytical staff from secretarial/administrative staff far from foolproof (the major source for this section is *Congressional Yellow Book,* Winter 1992). Nevertheless, taken as a whole, these figures do offer a good, albeit not perfect, indication of the participation of women in congressional deliberations on national security policy.

The Gender Gap

The final issue to be addressed is whether changing the number of women in these national security policy establishments would in any way alter U.S. policy. As earlier chapters have noted, a significant argument has been made in much of the feminist literature that women are more peaceful than men; that their maternal instincts make women want to preserve life, not destroy it. Thus, in terms of national security policy, it is argued that women will be more supportive of peace initiatives and more opposed to the use of force. These theoretical expectations regarding dissimilar policy preferences between women and men have been augmented by studies of electoral behavior, which have indicated a gender gap in terms of women's support of candidates, women's support of political parties, and women's positions on major policy issues (see Chapter 3). Research on the gender gap was given impetus by the outcomes of the presidential elections in 1980, 1984, and 1988, and most recently by public opinion polls on the Gulf War. Concerning the war, it was argued that the gender gap had in fact become a "Gender Gulf" in that the difference between women and men favoring U.S. intervention was a full twenty-five points. The magnitude of this difference was cited as proof of women's strong commitment to peace (Roach, 1991).

However, these studies have focused on dissimilarities between women and men in the general public. It is a very different question to discover if the same types of policy disparities occur within the national security process itself. In contrast to the proliferation of studies examining the gender gap in mass politics, there has been relatively little written specifically addressing the question of foreign policy differences among elites. Probably the most well known are the studies conducted by Ole R. Holsti and James Rosenau (1981, 1984, 1988) concerning the foreign policy preferences of leaders in the fields of education, law, business, media, foreign service, public policy, and the military. Overall, their studies found little support for the existence of a gender gap. "On many of the issues that have dominated foreign policy discourse during the post–World War II era, differences among men and women are substantially less impressive than are the similarities" (Holsti and Rosenau, 1981, pp. 337–338). Subsequent research by Wittkopf and Maggiotto on an even narrower elite sample reinforced Holsti and Rosenau's conclusions, with type of position, political philosophy, and party identification being more significant than gender in predicting policy differences (Wittkopf, 1983). Even more applicable for our discussion is a recent study by McGlen and Sarkees (1993), who explicitly examined the policy preferences of women and men in senior policymaking positions in the Departments of State and Defense. In contrast to the predictions of the gender gap, they found that female policymakers tended to be more conservative than their male counterparts, with 44.8 percent of the women and only 27.8 percent of the men identifying themselves as somewhat or very conservative. In terms of specific foreign policy views on eighty-seven policy variables, there were significant differences between women and men on only nine policies, and, again in contrast to the predictions of the gender gap, women tended to take the more conservative and less-peaceful positions.

> Moreover, no clear picture of a unique women's view was apparent. If there was a pattern, it finds women taking the more conservative position. . . . for instance women were . . . more likely to downgrade the policy goal of strengthening the United Nations and less likely to support relying on the United Nations to settle international disputes. Similarly, women were more in agreement than men that revolutionary forces were controlled by China or the USSR; that detente allowed the USSR to pursue policies that promote conflict; that the government, not the press, tells the truth about foreign policy; that Third World conflicts jeopardize American interests; and that the U.S. has a moral obligation to prevent the destruction of Israel (McGlen and Sarkees, 1993, p. 23).

Similarly, in terms of foreign policy goals, their study found women more likely to downgrade peace as a foreign policy goal. It was only when the researchers controlled for department that they found any evidence of a gender gap, with the career women in the State Department diverging from the men on fifteen separate issues, including a reluctance to use force to solve international disputes (McGlen and Sarkees, 1993). Conversely, the female political appointees at State and Defense, as well as the careerists at Defense, took positions that were in fact more conservative than those of their male counterparts.

These findings reflect the conclusion that there are policy differences *among* women, rather than a specific women's view of national security. McGlen and Sarkees put forward several possible explanations. During the time of their study, at the end of the Reagan administration, a conservative ideological litmus test had been used to screen all political appointees, including the women. Additionally, it could be argued that the difficult struggle women face to survive in a hostile environment, in Defense particularly, encourages women to "fit in" to an overwhelmingly male organization. In the process, they may overcompensate, becoming even more conservative. In contrast, it may be possible that a process of self-selection is functioning, by which more conservative women, who favor the use of force, migrate into the Defense Department, while their more liberal counterparts feel more comfortable in the State Department (McGlen and Sarkees, 1993). Whatever the causative factors, it would seem that the findings from all of these elite studies indicate that women in such positions do not hold policy views that are significantly different from those of their male counterparts. Thus, there is little reason to believe that increasing the number of women in national security policy positions would fundamentally alter U.S. policy.

chapter 10
Women and the Peace Movement
Patricia Washburn

In the United States, leadership positions in the uniformed military services and the government departments that formulate policy governing the use of military force have traditionally been reserved for men. On the other hand, women have historically not only been associated with the peace movement but have served as leaders in the movement and the nongovernmental organizations (NGOs) associated with it. Any examination of women and the use of military force must document the leadership role of women in actively opposing its use.

The leadership role of women in the peace movement is reflected not only in the numbers of women who participate in the movement and the organizations that represent it but also in the structure of those organizations—indeed, because many peace organizations are predominantly female, we expect to find evidence of the less confrontational and hierarchical female management style that is documented in the sociological literature (see Chapter 4) built into the formal structure of these groups. Their leaders tend to be public figures much less frequently than the leaders of more pyramidal organizations. Formal credit for such accomplishments as the Nuclear Nonproliferation Treaty is often given to the political leaders, usually male, who respond to widespread pressure from the peace organizations rather than to the leaders of the movement itself. This further masks the leadership of women in these organizations and their importance as strategists.

To support these contentions, this chapter has three functions. The first is to give an overview of women working for peace in the nineteenth and twentieth centuries; the second, to examine some specific public policy implications of this work; and the third, to reflect on women's motivations for doing this work as determined from my research and the work of Ginger Hanks-Harwood.

A History of Women's Concern
for Peace in the United States

Although the focus of this chapter is on the nineteenth and twentieth centuries, women's concerns for peace and justice have their roots in several critical movements of our foremothers. In the colonial United States, Quaker women had been spreading the gospel as one of peace. They had supported both John Woolman and William Penn in their efforts to live in harmony with Native Americans. Many Quaker women were banished for their efforts, and some, including Mary Dyer, were martyred for their witness. As early as 1739, Anna Barbauld said, "When we pay our army and navy estimates, let us set down—so much for killing, so much for maiming, so much for making widows and orphans. We shall by this means know what we have paid our money for" (Harwood, 1991, p. 41).

Quaker women continued to advocate peace in the new United States. Harwood tells the story of Ellen McCarty, a Quaker minister in the 1830s, who held discussions with young military recruits on the moral issues of war and persuaded several to join the Society of Friends. Harwood notes, "Ordinary women within the Society of Friends were occasionally much more militant, missionary and active in the nonsectarian peace reform groups than were their more distinguished male colleagues" (1991, p. 56).

In September 1870, Julia Ward Howe suggested creating an annual "Mother's Day" that would be set aside for women's advocacy of peace:

> Arise then, women of this day. Arise, all women who have hearts, whether your baptism be that of water or of tears. Say firmly "We will not have great questions decided by irrelevant agencies. Our husbands shall not come to us, reeking of carnage, for caresses and applause. Our sons shall not be taken from us to unlearn all that we have been able to teach them of charity, mercy and patience. We, women of one country, will be too tender of those of another country to allow our sons to be trained to injure theirs." From the bosom of the devastated earth a voice goes up with our own. It says, Disarm! Disarm! The sword of murder is not the balance of justice (McAllister, 1991, p. 76).

Howe had her appeal translated into French, Spanish, Italian, German, and Swedish and began to lobby for a worldwide gathering of women. Convened in New York City in December of 1870, the gathering was attended by such luminaries as Lucretia Mott, John Stuart Mill, and Harriet Beecher Stowe. Howe then traveled to Europe to organize Mother's Day but met with mixed support. For several years there were celebrations on June 2 in such cities as London, Geneva, and Constantinople, but Howe's vision of Mother's Day did not capture the popular imagination. We "celebrate" a more commercial version, initiated by President Woodrow Wilson almost fifty years later.

The commercialized Mother's Day, however, has served as an occasion for protest and peace demonstrations, including one in Washington, D.C., in 1981, during which members of the National Mother's Day Coalition for Nuclear Disarmament distributed a brochure in response to the Reagan military budget, asking, "Is this the last Mother's Day?" Mother's Day has also been the occasion for a national day of mourning in 1987 and protests at the Nevada test site.

Historically, women have recognized that concerns for peace are not "passive." In her opening statement at the World Congress of Women in Behalf of International Peace, Julia Ward Howe said that "patience and passivity are sometimes the place for women—not always—If women did not waste life in frivolity, men would not waste it in murder" (McAllister, 1991, p. 77). Maria Weston Chapman said during the abolitionist struggle that "passive nonresistance is one thing, active nonresistance another. We mean to apply our principles" (Harwood, 1991, p. 57). The New England Non-Resistance Society, founded in 1838 by William Lloyd Garrison, stressed that one should refuse to cooperate with any government that did not reflect pacifist principles, and it advocated the abolishment of conscription as well as military titles, holidays, and memorials. The initial statement of principles was signed by an equal number of men and women.

Sarah and Angelina Grimké, two Quaker sisters, worked for justice and the abolition of slavery even though their family were slaveholders. Their brother Henry had fathered three sons by his slave mistress. One of them escaped to the North, where he was sheltered and supported by the sisters, eventually graduating from Harvard Law School. His daughter, Angelina Weld Grimké, was a playwright whose play *Rachel* was produced by the National Association for the Advancement of Colored People (NAACP) in the 1920s "to enlighten the American people relative to the lamentable condition of 10 millions of colored citizens in this free republic" (McAllister, 1991, p. 66).

The Grimké sisters were "eldered" for sharing the back-row bench with black members of their Quaker meeting, and they toured as paid staff for the American Anti-Slavery Society. In their public advocacy for justice, they often encountered abuse and sexism.

Sarah Grimké lamented, "I ask no favors for my sex. I surrender not our claim to equality. All I ask of our brethren is that they will take their feet from off our necks and permit us to stand upright on the ground which God has designed for us to occupy" (Harwood, 1991, p. 68).

In the 1830s, Quaker women initiated Olive Leaf Circles to create international bonds of friendship. Lucretia Mott collected more than 3,500 signatures showing U.S. support for the anti-slavery movement in England to be sent to the women of Exeter, England, and a series of tracts with peace articles reached approximately one million readers per month internationally. Later Mott formed the Philadelphia Female Anti-Slavery Society, which was both racially and religiously integrated. There seemed to be a lack of congruence between advocating the freedom of black slaves but not allowing female delegates to be seated at the World Anti-Slavery Convention. Out of women's frustration with their exclusion emerged the Seneca Falls Convention of 1848, which produced a Women's Declaration of Independence that stated:

> In entering upon this great work before us, we anticipate no small amount of misconception, misrepresentation and ridicule; but we shall use every instrumentality within our power to effect our object. We shall employ agents, circulate tracts, petition the State and National Legislatures, and endeavor to enlist the pulpit and press on our behalf.

The Seneca Falls Convention was an early example of the linking of peace and justice issues with feminism. Another issue that emerged with the Civil War was the tension between pacifism and the necessity for a "just war" to end slavery. Harwood (1991) notes that "the great American humanitarian peace movement had floundered on the rocks of practical application. . . . Social reformers were unprepared to resolve the issue of morality of the use of force to end structural violence."

Women began to organize in new ways. The Women's Christian Temperance Union (WCTU) became the training ground for many women during the latter part of the nineteenth century. Frances Willard became president of WCTU in 1879, when it was the largest women's organization in the world. Under Willard's leadership the membership quadrupled in the next decade, and the WCTU became "not only the largest but also the most efficient and effective women's organization in the nineteenth century. It was in the WCTU that the leadership was trained that would give birth to the Nineteenth Amendment in 1920" (Hardesty, 1984, p. 22).

In linking world peace and suffrage issues to the WCTU platform of temperance and protection of the home, Willard saw the WCTU as "a world republic of women—without distinction of race or color—who recognize no sectarianism in religion, no sectionalism in politics, no sex in citizenship. Each of us is as much a part of the world's union as is any other woman; it is our great, growing, wonderful home" (Harwood, 1991, p. 81).

In 1914, fifteen hundred women paraded in New York City to protest the war in Europe. The *New York Times* editorialized that this event marked "a definite determination on the part of a considerable number of women to exert a practical influence on a field of public action from which in the past they had been almost fully withdrawn" (Harwood, 1991, p. 81).

Many of these women represented the Women's Peace Party. The party's preamble stated: "As Women, we feel a particular moral passion of revolt against both the cruelty and waste of war. As women we are especially the custodians of the life of the ages. We will no longer consent to reckless destruction. . . . We demand that women be given a share in deciding between war and peace." The party held its first congress at The Hague during the war, with Jane Addams chairing. She had been asked to chair since the United States was at that time still a neutral nation. The congress was attended by fourteen hundred women from twelve countries, who risked traveling during wartime to attend.

In her opening address to the women gathered there, Arletta Jacobs said, "Those of us who have convened this Congress . . . have never called it a Peace Congress, but an International Congress of Women assembled to protest against war and to suggest steps which may lead to warfare becoming an impossibility" (Bussey and Tims, 1980, p. 19). Of the twenty resolutions adopted by the Congress, these three are especially important:

Continuous Mediation

> This Congress of Women resolves to ask neutral countries to take immediate steps to create a conference of neutral nations which shall without delay offer continuous mediation. The Conference shall invite suggestions for settlement from each of the belligerent nations and in any case shall submit to all of them simultaneously reasonable proposals as a basis of peace.

Women's Voice in the Peace Settlement

> An International meeting of women shall be held in the same place and at the same time as the Conference of Powers which shall frame the

terms of the peace settlement after the war, for the purpose of presenting practical proposals to that Conference.

Envoys to Governments

That envoys shall carry the message expressed in the Congress Resolutions to the rulers of the belligerent and neutral nations of Europe and to the President of the United States.

Returning from the Congress, Jane Addams met with President Woodrow Wilson in August. In President Wilson's 1917 "Peace Without Victory" speech, many of his points came from the Hague Congress. With the U.S. entry into the war, plans for a conference on mediation were put on hold. The women then turned their attention to studies of conditions for a just-peace settlement and the creation of a League of Nations. In 1919 they adopted the name Women's International League for Peace and Freedom (WILPF) and moved from The Hague to Geneva in order to be close to the headquarters of the fledgling League of Nations.

Emily Greene Balch (whose twenty-five–year professorship at Wellesley College had been terminated in 1918 for her antiwar activities) became the first International Secretary in Geneva. In the aftermath of World War I, Balch made a strategically important distinction in declaring that WILPF was not primarily a humanitarian organization: it was striving to remove the causes of war rather than allaying the suffering that resulted from it. WILPF monitored the first assembly of the League of Nations very closely, circulated position papers, suggested structural and procedural changes, and continued to push for disarmament. (In 1931 Jane Addams was awarded the Nobel Peace Prize for her work, and in 1946, Emily Greene Balch was awarded the same prize.)

In 1924, the Fourth International Congress of WILPF was held in Washington, D.C., with the theme "A New International Order." To construct such an order, said Anita Augspurg, the most important factor was "the bringing into equilibrium of the influence of men and women. Women must cease to admire a man with a gun in his hand and must seek to counteract the destructive tendencies of the masculine mentality by what is called inner devotion to the right" (Bussey & Tims, 1980, p. 47). Thirty-nine nations were represented at the conference, and many delegates were harassed by the Daughters of the American Revolution and the American Legion, and were accused of being "foreign spies."

A major effort of the early 1930s was the collection of eight million signatures presented to the 1932 League of Nations

Disarmament Conference. In the mid-1930s Dorothy Detzer, then executive secretary of the U.S. section of WILPF, was credited with persuading Senator Nye to hold hearings on the role of the arms industry in promoting and profiting from arms trading. In her autobiography, *Appointment on the Hill,* which chronicles her twenty years of lobbying on behalf of WILPF, Detzer remarked, "Surely no Senate Committee ever rendered to the American people a more intelligent or important service. It was the nation's loss that it did not comprehend it" (quoted in Bussey and Tims, 1980, p. 131).

Another important WILPF member during the 1930s and 1940s was Jeannette Rankin. She had attended the Hague conference in 1915 as the first female member of the Congress of the United States. She later cast her vote against entering World War I and was "banished" from Congress. Later reelected, she cast the only dissenting vote against entering World War II. Rankin once said that "the work of educating the world to peace is a woman's job, because men have a natural fear of being classed as cowards if they oppose war." She also spoke out against munitions manufacturers and implored people to "insist on having information regarding our own American patriots who are willing to give the life of your son for their profit" (Harwood, 1991, p. 94).

With America's entry into World War II, WILPF was to see its membership slip from fifteen thousand to five thousand. Those who stayed remained pacifist. Dorothy Detzer declared, "We can never yield our inalienable right to affirm and declare that war between nations or classes or races cannot permanently settle conflicts or heal the wounds that brought them into being" (Harwood, 1991, p. 97). Once again the distinction between war and justice had become important.

During the patriotic fervor of World War II, peace activists were increasingly regarded as subversive. This mood continued after the war into the 1950s. Yet there were signs of hope, one of which was the awarding of the Nobel Peace Prize to Emily Greene Balch in 1946. In making the presentation, Gunnar Jahn stated:

> She has shown us that the reality we seek must be won through hard work in the world in which we live, but she has shown us more than this; that one does not become exhausted and that defeat gives new courage to those who have within them the holy fire. . . . I can't repeat to you all the resolutions passed as amendments for the Peace Treaty from the (WILPF) Congress of 1919, but I want to say this: it would have been wise if the statesmen of the world had listened to the proposals from the women. But in a men's society in which we are living proposals from women are not usually taken seriously (Bussey and Tims, 1980, p. 189).

Just as WILPF had affected the League of Nations, it began its work with the United Nations by requesting status as a nongovernmental organization to consult with the Economic and Social Council. This request was granted in 1948. Consultative status with other NGOs followed. The role of international NGOs is a significant one, but often overlooked in the public policy discussion. Elise Boulding has written extensively about their importance, pointing out that there are over 18,000 INGOs, and states that "Since a major INGO goal is international understanding, peace and security for the whole world, not just one block of nations, they work with more multidimensional concepts of security than do governments" (Boulding, 1988, p. 37). One example of such a group is the International Peace Research Association, which was one result of WILPF consultation. The two United Nations special sessions on disarmament were also INGO-initiated.

Parallel to this work is the emergence of what Boulding calls newer "people's associations," which tend to focus on grassroots organizing. She writes:

> Much of the new organizational energy for peace and environmental work comes from women. The rise of feminism and the entry of women into public life has meant that a whole new set of questions has been asked of the social order. Like the peoples of the Third World countries, women feel they are being asked to maintain an order they did not help create. If they are going to be participants in the international arena, they want it known that the old patriarchal order, which for centuries has meant the domination of women by men, has to go. They see patriarchy and militarism as closely linked. By introducing more participatory processes, more dialogue, and more listening in every setting in which they work, they are laying' the groundwork for the replacement of power politics by the politics of mutual aid (1988, pp. 45–46).

Clearly, WILPF has been functioning in this way for more than seventy-five years, and its role as an INGO has provided a model for other women's peace groups.

Women and the Nuclear Arms Race

With the advent of the nuclear era, women became increasingly strident in protesting the militarism that seemed to dominate our society, even in post–World War II prosperity. The cry of the Women's Strike for Peace (WSP) was, "End the Arms Race, Not the Human Race!" Dagmar Wilson initially envisioned a one-day strike by women to counter the male status quo. "You know how men are.

. . . They talk in abstractions about the technicalities of the bomb, almost as if this were all a game of chess. Well, it isn't. There are times, it seems to me, when the only thing to do is to let out a loud scream" (McAllister, 1991, p. 55).

On November 1, 1961, fifty thousand women in cities and towns throughout the United States went on strike for a day. Although the strike was originally to be a single event, WSP continued to mobilize women, suggesting that they join already existing peace groups. This activity attracted the attention of Senator Joseph McCarthy and his House Un-American Affairs Committee (HUAC). McCarthy saw WSP as a sinister and subversive organization and was determined to rid the country of the group. He summoned Dagmar Wilson to appear before the committee. Outraged WSP members began to inundate the committee with telegrams demanding that they too be included in the "inquisition." Eighty-six women volunteered to testify.

On the day the hearing began five hundred women deluged the hearing room, many of them with children in tow. As each witness was called to testify, five hundred women would stand as a body of solidarity and present the witness with bouquets of flowers. Children crawled in the aisles, and their mothers cheered as Dagmar Wilson and others fielded questions. The committee seemed confused at the difference between a movement and an organization. Alfred Nittle, counsel for the committee, asked, "If a group isn't an organization and has no members, how on earth does it function?"

The questioning began to disintegrate, and at one point a frustrated committee member was heard to ask, "Did you then or have you recently operated a mimeograph machine?" (Deming as quoted in McAllister, 1991, p. 113). A Herblock cartoon showed an anxious congressman asking another, "I came in late. Which was it that was Un-American—women or peace?"

The 1960s and 1970s seemed to many to be characterized by increasing levels of violence against people working for peace and justice. Within a single decade key political leaders were assassinated, schools were shut down, cities were burned, and student protesters were shot on college campuses. In addition to the escalation of the Vietnam War and the political chaos of the period, many women were becoming more aware of the threat of the "nuclear shadow." As the decade of the 1980s began, women involved in the peace movement began to lead in new ways and to form themselves into women-specific groups. The leadership of women such as Randall Forsberg, Helen Caldicott, Betty Bumpers, and Justine Merritt transformed the peace movement.

Women's Motivations for Peace Activities

Why do people make the choices that motivate their actions? What are the values undergirding those motivations? What is the glue that keeps people involved? In the 1970s, many women became active in the peace movement, having first been social activists during the civil rights struggle.

According to Ginger Hanks-Harwood (1991, p. 260), "For ethicists, the women's peace movement of the 1980s holds particular interest because it is a project in applied social ethics." Having found Carol Gilligan's (1982) argument that women have a different style of moral reasoning to be persuasive, my colleague, Robert Gribbon, and I decided to test the theory with some of the people with whom I had worked in the peace movement. We distributed a questionnaire to approximately three hundred men and women who had been active in the National Peace Academy Campaign, as well as to some who had attended peace conferences and actions in Washington, D.C., in the early 1980s. In evaluating the responses, we concluded that women tended to be motivated by three distinct elements: Community (relationship), Context, and Concreteness.

• *Community.* In the interviews, respondents were asked why they chose to become involved in the peace movement. Women spoke of relationships and community as significant factors. A staff member at Women's Action for Nuclear Disarmament (WAND) said, "In describing their reasons for being involved with the issue, the first words from each person . . . referred not to the devastation that would be wrought in a nuclear war, nor to the current waste of federal monies, but what they cared about saving and nurturing. . . . I found that the answers to these questions reflected a deep love of living relationships . . . to children, grandparents, the earth, to friends and even strangers. The answers gave an acute, often painful awareness of the preciousness of life, and what it is to care for and love someone . . . of concrete, tangible relationships" (Washburn and Gribbon, 1985, p. 49).

• *Context.* The word "context" comes from *contextere*, which means "to weave together." Dorothy Austin, of the Nuclear Education Project at Harvard Medical School, said, in reflecting on the work of Carol Gilligan, "No longer is woman's style of moral reasoning and the desire to preserve context perceived as less developed. It has become a political necessity for the preservation of the world" (Washburn and Gribbon, 1985, p. 49). One of the most moving examples of relating peacemaking to a specific context was the "Ribbon Project," conceived by Justine Merritt. Thousands of people made 36" x 36" needlework squares representing things they did not want to lose in a nuclear war. The squares were connected to form a ribbon several miles long, which was then used to encircle the Pentagon.

• *Concreteness.* In the responses to the questionnaire, it became apparent that women wanted to deal with issues "close to home." In her work with Peace Links, Betty Bumpers used this concept strategically. For example, one of the resources women found most helpful was a nuclear grid overlaid on a particular community that showed the extent of radiation damage from a nuclear detonation. When women could see their own neighborhoods, schools, and residences in this concrete visual way, it was more meaningful than discussing throw weights and other theoretical examples of nuclear war. Nell Noddings has pointed out that "Women . . . give reasons for their acts, but the reasons point to feelings, needs, situational conditions, and their sense of personal ideal rather than universal principles and their applications. . . . Moral decisions, after all, are made in situations. They are quantitatively different from the solution to geometry problems" (Washburn and Gribbon, 1985, p. 50).

Harwood personally interviewed one hundred women and found that a cluster of thematic concerns motivated them. These major themes are the following.

• *Motherhood.* Although not all of the women interviewed were mothers, "concern for children emerged as a prominent and critical factor in the motivation for sustained activism in cases where another concern was designated as the prime reason for participation" (Harwood, 1991, p. 177). When we look at several of the women-specific groups that emerged during this period, we see a focus on children. Helen Caldicott's organization, WAND, has as its logo a woman with a child on her lap holding a globe, and the caption is, "Children ask the world of us." Many of the segments of Justine Merritt's Ribbon Project reflected a concern for children, and Betty Bumpers says that her "conversion" came in a conversation with her daughter.

I recall asking my own twelve-year-old daughter whether she ever thought about the bomb. Her eyes filled with tears, and she answered, "I think about the bomb every day, Mom." One of the women interviewed by Harwood said, "We are the creators, really, the caretakers of the creation of life. And it's stupid to pour all this energy into giving birth and rearing healthy children and then stand around and let some fool maniac, because he is hungry for power, destroy them" (Harwood, 1991, p. 178).

• *Humanity.* Harwood found that many women speak of being citizens of the world and see nuclear war as a crime against humanity. Women felt themselves a part of one family, members of a global village. The World Council of Churches has named the 1990s the Decade of Women in Solidarity. Experience shows that women are increasingly seeing themselves as "sisters" of those marginalized by militarism. Linked to this sense of global awareness is a concern for justice. Often women of color tend to see the arms race as one of misplaced priorities. One of their slogans reads: "Peace begins when everybody is fed."

• *Earth.* Harwood noted that increasing awareness of the "fate of the earth" emerged in the 1980s and was the motivator for some women. Ecology, stewardship, and pollution became prominent themes for organizations like Greenpeace and Earth Watch. As one woman said, "It is saving the earth that is really important. It's not just humanity or our country, it's the whole web of life" (Harwood, 1991, p. 183). For some women, nurturing the earth was linked to their self-understanding, and images of Mother Earth were prominent in their stories. Violence against women and against the earth were linked.

• *Feminism.* Almost 90 percent of the women Harwood interviewed identified themselves as feminist/womanist, but for some women feminism was the chief motivator. (For an interesting treatment of this topic see Reardon, 1985.) For them dismantling the patriarchy was a central task. One apparent tactic to accomplish that was nonviolent resistance. As Barbara Deming remarked, "By our refusal to cooperate, we keep reminding them [the patriarchy] of our dissent, refusing to allow them the godlike sense that their will alone exists" (Harwood, 1991, p. 188).

• *Spirituality.* Harwood says, "Spirituality is the core of the person, the center from which meaning, self and understanding are generated . . . over half the women claimed a spiritual or religious basis for their activism. . . . Spiritual concerns appeared as a theme woven throughout 80 percent of the interviews" (1991, p. 190). One of the factors that distinguished people in this group was the degree of radicalism in their witness, which was not necessarily correlated with any denomination. The statement of one religious community, the Sisters of Saint Joseph, states: "We all need vision. Without a vision the people perish as the book of Proverbs warns. Faith's contribution to this vision is the assurance that peace is possible. That is our starting point" (Harwood, 1991, p. 194).

One current form of witness is military-tax resistance. For many people there is a clear link between religious conviction and resistance.

> I am a mother and a grandmother. I stand in prayer and solidarity with my sisters in the Middle East. Therefore, as an act of conscience and repentance for the policy of the United States, I respectfully choose to withhold . . . the portion projected for military expenditures. I pray for all mothers and children as I make this witness. . . . Mother Teresa wrote that "goodness does not derive from our capacity to think but to love." I pray that my witness is done in love, and that it will help build a bridge across a chasm of violence and fear (Washburn, 1990).

• *Caregiving and Consciousness.* In 1984, the "First Women's Conference to Prevent Nuclear War" was held in Washington, D.C. Rosalynn Carter challenged the group by saying, "I always felt that if we were going to have a world free from war, violence and hatred; if we are going to have a more humane and sane world, then women were going to have to become more involved in the policies of our country" (quoted in Harwood, 1991, p. 201). The issue of gender as a motivator was very clear in this conference and to many women interviewed by Harwood.

Harwood writes, "The women interviewed expressed strong convictions that their lives and experiences as women had prepared them to understand what was wrong with the current defense model and to speak for the establishment of an enduring peace. Ninety-six out of the one hundred women interviewed said that they believed that women had a particular contribution to make to the peacemaking project as WOMEN" (1991, p. 203). Harwood summarizes, "Activist women in the 1980s challenged other women who took their gender and socially imparted gender tasks and values seriously, to ask what it meant to be a woman in the nuclear age" (1991, p. 209).

Risks and the Role of Women in the Peace Movement

Last, it is important to address the issue of risk-taking and courage. Pam McAllister's moving stories about women and courage ask the questions, "What is the shape of courage? Where is it fashioned?" (1991, p. 187). In sharing the stories, she in turn gives us models to claim as our own. She says, "Courage is sometimes required in life's cracks and crevices. When the reporters and historians are at lunch, and no one will notice, the courage to do the right thing becomes the measure of a life" (p. 195).

Sharon Welch, asking the same questions (1990), describes what she calls an "ethic of risk," a new paradigm of resistance to the madness of our nuclear arms race.

> An ethic of risk is characterized by three elements, each of which is essential to maintain resistance in the face of overwhelming odds: a redefinition of responsible action, grounding in community, and strategic risk-taking. Responsible action does not mean the certain achievement of desired ends, but the creation of a matrix in which further actions are possible, the creation of the conditions of possibility for desired changes. . . . We can prevent our own capitulation to structural evil. We can participate in a long heritage of resistance, standing with those who have worked for change in the past. We can also take risks, trying to create the conditions that will evoke and sustain further resistance. We can help create the conditions necessary for peace and justice, realizing that the choices of others can only be influenced and responded to, never controlled . . . we can only provide a heritage of persistence, imagination and solidarity (1990, p. 22).

Conclusions

Evidence presented in other chapters in this volume indicates that women who assume leadership roles in the uniformed military service or in those agencies that command its use perform and think much the same as their male counterparts. The women described in this chapter clearly perceive themselves as distinctly different from their male counterparts. This historical examination of the organization of the peace movement in the United States documents not only its dependence on women and the leadership role of women in the movement, but clearly demonstrates a very different organizational style from the more traditional political and military structures dominated by men. Peace groups have consistently stressed local grassroots activism based in the community, and leadership has been diffused to individual communities. While the data are too limited to argue that the characteristic leadership style of the peace movement is caused by its large numbers of female participants and leaders, the movement clearly reflects the organizational style associated with all-female groups, and the values of the peace movement are those associated with women in the "gender gap" polling data.

chapter 11

How Three Female National Leaders Have Used the Military

Jo A. Richardson, Ruth H. Howes

The three women discussed in this chapter were national leaders and military decisionmakers. Each held the office of commander-in-chief, the most powerful of all political roles. This role is politically unique with regard to national security, because it is one in which authority is unchallenged (Rose, 1977). It is the executive who can, almost singlehandedly, plunge a nation into war (Hyman, 1954).

The most formidable criticisms of the executive office have centered on its military power, perceived as expansive and encroaching, because the executive is a maker of decisions that can be costly, hazardous, and in the nuclear age horrendous. "I make foreign policy," Harry S Truman said to a visiting body of Jewish war veterans while discoursing on his office (Rossiter, 1960, p. 10). In 1800, Congressman John Marshall stated that the executive is "the sole organ of the nation in its external relations, and its sole representative with foreign nations" (Tatalovich and Daynes, 1984, p. 260).

Prime Ministers Margaret Thatcher, Golda Meir, and Indira Gandhi have performed as commanders-in-chief in foreign and domestic crises. They have committed armed forces into battle, negotiated peace settlements, and extended civilian control over devastating weaponry in states that are at least capable of producing nuclear weapons. A new generation of female prime ministers currently hold office in nations as diverse as Nicaragua and Norway. Their attitudes toward the use of force may well differ from those of the three women discussed in this book. However, none of them has been tested in an actual war, nor do any of them control a military armed with nuclear weapons.

Meir, Gandhi and Thatcher all served democratic political systems and therefore faced a major paradox. Democracies, like other states, must be capable of defending themselves and assuring their survival. Commanders-in-chief of democratic systems must perform at the helm of military agencies whose structures and organizations are antithetical to democracy, stressing obedience to authority, hierarchy, and command (Koenig, 1986).

The U.S. presidential system has not produced a female chief executive. Women's access to political office in the United States is hampered most seriously by the stereotyped belief that a woman cannot hold a difficult job:

> One study of senior-level women business executives found that they frequently encounter myths about a woman's ability to travel, take criticism, work with numbers, or work as a manager. As long as these prejudicial attitudes remain, women who seek political office will have to overcome the hurdle of convincing voters they can do the job (Conway et al., 1992, p. 25).

Meir, Gandhi, and Thatcher were commanders-in-chief in parliamentary systems, specifically European and Asian ones. Political institutional differences explain the rise of female chief executives in parliamentary systems. The chief executive in this kind of system is elected from among the ranks of the majority political party. This selection is an internal, party affair and favors a party member with experience and seniority. The U.S. president is elected by the public, and party support can be sidestepped by a popular personality backed by political action committee funding. Female stereotypes damage female candidates more in this context than they do in the parliamentary system, where individuals are personally acquainted with candidates and their records. The Bush-Ferraro television debates of the 1980 presidential election clearly illustrate this point.

Conway et al. also suggest that it is easier in the parliamentary systems of Europe and Asia than in the presidential system of the United States for women to become politicians because

> the historical tradition of Joan of Arc or Eve Curie, the tradition of the woman in her own right pursuing her own career, does not really exist in America . . . it is more common to find women in high places in Europe and Asia than in America. I think this is largely because women have enjoyed such power for a long time, for instance, in Britain ever since the time that they presided over religious communities as prioresses, having their own role, a role that entailed the right to command (1992, p. 27).

The British Parliamentary system has also produced powerful female monarchs such as Elizabeth I, Anne, Victoria, and Elizabeth II.

Golda Meir and Her Government

When Golda Meir became prime minister in March 1969, after the death of Levi Eshkol, there were many who doubted the wisdom of appointing a woman already over seventy whose health was suspect and who—although she had been foreign minister before retiring in 1965—was hardly a national figure. The doubters were rapidly silenced by her taking firm control of a centrifugal Cabinet and by her flair for personal negotiation with world leaders. The standard joke about "Mrs. Meir" being "the strongest man in the Cabinet" had a core of seriousness. She spoke in a low growl, and her large head and shoulders—all that most people saw of her on the television screen—gave an impression of natural authority (Insight Team, 1974).

Meir saw no contradiction in the fact that a female commander-in-chief should head a nation that was in a constant state of readiness for war. She was as much concerned with security as any man in the military establishment, believing that a strong and independent Israel was the only guarantee of the Jews' survival. "When people ask me," she once said, "if I am afraid, because of Israel's need for defense, that the country may become militaristic, I can only answer that I don't want a fine, liberal, anticolonial, antimilitaristic, dead Jewish people" (Insight Team, 1974, p. 389).

She was born Golda Mabovitch, daughter of a carpenter in Kiev, in May 1898. The family emigrated to the United States and settled in Milwaukee when Golda was eight years old (she spoke English with a strong U.S. accent). In 1921, after marrying Morris Myerson, she left with her husband for Palestine. Both of her children were born on a kibbutz (Adler, 1984).

Meir's style of government was democratic but intensely personal. According to one close student of her method, "She listens carefully to what her colleagues have to say, then presents as a consensus what she had decided beforehand" (Insight Team, 1974, p. 389). As likely as not, the decision had been made over the coffee cups at her "Kitchen Cabinet"—Meir's Saturday-evening sessions at home for a few senior ministers (Perlmutter, 1978). (The regulars at those sessions included Yigal Allon; Moshe Dayan; the minister without portfolio, Israel Galili; and Pinhas Sapir, the finance minister.) Between 1969 and 1973, this small informal group conceived, designed, and formulated Israel's national security and military policies.

Between 1969 and 1974, the national security inner circle was composed of three layers. At the top, national security was the business of the triumvirate: Meir, Dayan, and Galili. Deputy Prime Minister Yigal Allon and Minister of Justice Yaacov S. Shapira played key roles in the Kitchen Cabinet. In defense policy, however, Dayan was preeminent, and Meir left him to conduct defense policy and policy over the occupied territories. In 1971, when Chief of Staff General Chaim Bar-Lev retired from the army and entered politics to become minister of commerce, he also joined this group.

Thus, national security policy and military strategy were divided between the political and military inner circle that governed Israel. This inner circle became a powerful instrument over and beyond its constitutional role. The upper trio ruled supreme since the formation of the Labor Alignment in 1969, when the latter became the most powerful political structure in Israel (Perlmutter, 1978). The members of the inner circle were also the leading politicians of the Labor Alignment government.

The Arab-Israeli Yom Kippur War

The Yom Kippur War broke out on the holiest day of the Jewish calendar and on the first day of the Arabic Ramadan fast, October 6, 1973. Egyptian and Syrian troops initiated a surprise attack on Israel and were able to dictate the conditions of battle for the first few days (Safran, 1974). The extent of "surprise" was based on the Israeli leaders' belief that the Arabs were incapable of waging a coordinated, modern war. A former director of Israeli military intelligence observed, "a mixture of conceit and complacency tended to color the evaluation of future developments in the area. Moshe Dayan was particularly instrumental in propagating the view that war was not to be expected for another ten years" (Shlaim, 1976, p. 380).

Despite the success of the initial Egyptian and Syrian strikes into Israeli-occupied territory, Israeli forces subsequently succeeded in breaking through the Egyptian lines to the western bank of the Suez Canal and advanced to within twenty miles of the Syrian capital of Damascus (O'Connor, 1979). When the Egyptians realized that the road to Cairo was virtually open and that the Israeli forces were close to their capital, they lost their nerve (Sella, 1981).

The Superpower-Israeli War

To avoid total defeat and humiliation of the Arabs, the United States and the Soviet Union joined in pressing for an end to the fighting.

Together, the two superpowers secured a cease-fire resolution on October 22, 1973. Between October 16 and 19, the possibility of a global crisis loomed. Brezhnev's threat to take steps unilaterally represented "the most serious threat to U.S.-Soviet relations since the Cuban missile crisis" (Sella, 1981, p. 101). Either from realizing how dangerous their military situation was or from panic, the Egyptians reached agreement with the Soviets on the possibility of Soviet entry into the war (Sella, 1981), and it was under these conditions that President Sadat agreed to a cease-fire. Meir found herself not only fighting the Arab states, but also protecting Israel against sacrifice on the altar of superpower agreements.

The cease-fire ultimatum had, at a stroke, overturned Israeli confidence in the United States. Kissinger's stalling over supplies to Israel in the vital first week had outraged Meir. Now she was learning that to the superpowers, détente was more important than the advancement of their client states' political aims (Insight Team, 1974). Israel would not be permitted, in Meir's words, "to hit back with seven blows for each one she receives" (Whetton, 1974, p. 84).

Militarily, Israel was a medium-size power, but its demographic, political, and economic basis was that of a small country. The Yom Kippur War brought home to Israelis their vulnerability to U.S. pressure (Laqueur, 1974). Even in the face of this dependency, Meir adamantly stated, "We have the right to demand that United States policy should not be conducted at the expense of our vital interests" (Whetton, 1974, p. 81). She insisted that the great powers were obliged only to bring the warring parties together, not to impose independent solutions.

Israeli reactions were largely a response to genuine fears that the United States might again impose a "solution" that it would later fail to honor (as had happened with the 1957 agreement) and that the United States was likely to place such a high priority on preserving its Soviet dialogue that Israeli interests might be jeopardized. This war would have ended with an Israeli military victory had it lasted a few days longer. The superpowers prevented that (Laqueur, 1974).

The Internal Israeli Wars

In addition to the war with the Arab states and the "war" with the United States, Prime Minister Meir was facing internal unrest. The debacle of the first two days accelerated the war of the generals, especially the rivalry between Bar-Lev and Sharon over strategy. The freeing of the Egyptian army, the harried and confused Egyptian-Israeli disarmament, and, above all, the pressures of the Kissingerian step-by-step troop disengagement—all results of monumental U.S. pressure—were accompanied by the nation's desire to have the troops back home. The loss of nearly 4,000 dead and some 6,000 wounded left the country confused, bitter, and frustrated. Demonstrations were launched against the Golda-Dayan-Sapir party and government (Perlmutter, 1978).

O'Ballance offers some insight into the prime minister's difficulties with her Cabinet:

> Of the more prominent personalities who had influence or control over events during this October War, the staunchest figure was that of the premier, Golda Meir, who remained calm throughout and overshadowed her defense minister, Dayan. The hero of two previous wars against the Arabs, Dayan, by reason of his past military and political experience and the authority of his appointment, might have been expected to emerge as the strong man of Israel in its hour of need and to be proclaimed as its savior. However, he seems throughout to have been hesitant, indecisive, and pessimistic. The top Israeli generals—Elazar, Eytan, Peled, Mandler, Gonen, and Adan—formed a team of only average ability and a team that did not always pull together . . . a team that could not rise above their petty promotion prospects, prestige precedent complexes, and personal intrigues (1978, p. 350).

Golda Meir's resignation on April 11, 1974, was linked directly to the October War. The crucial question is whether the internal wars forced her resignation, or more precisely, to what extent they influenced her to resign. According to her own testimony, her decision was based on three factors: "I was beginning to feel the physical and psychological effects of the strain of the past few months. I was dead tired and not at all sure that in this kind of situation I could ever succeed in forming a government—or even whether I should go on trying to do so" (Meir, 1975, p. 455).

Her fatigue was hardly surprising when one considers her age, her precarious state of health, and her own Labor Party, which was torn by dissent. Golda Meir recorded her deep distress at "the breaking down of solidarity within the inner circle of the party." She wrote, "People who had been ministers in my government, my colleagues with whom I worked closely all through the years and who had been full partners in the formation of government policy now appeared unwilling to stand up to the barrage of unjust criticism" (1975, p. 455). It was the waning comradeship and the weakening of shared responsibility that hurt the prime minister the most. The third reason for her resignation was that she in fact succumbed to public pressure. She conceded, "In the parties as well as in other sections of the public there is a ferment that cannot be ignored" (Sella and Yishai, 1986, p. 97).

Meir's Leadership

The main source of Golda Meir's impact as wartime prime minister was her personality—a synthesis of iron will, courage, and warm sensitivity to human and social prob-lems. Veteran diplomat Gideon Rafael, who knew Meir well, provides an astute evaluation: "Golda's perception of leadership endowed her with a singular strength of resistance—a quality much needed by an embattled people" (Sachar, 1987, p. 158).

Herzog has described the prime minister as having been very much the overbearing mother who ruled the roost with an iron hand. She had little idea of orderly administration and preferred to work closely with her ad hoc system of government. But once war had broken out, these very traits proved to be assets. She was strong and adamant and gave the country the powerful leadership it required both in time of war and during the involved postwar political negotiations. On many occasions, she found herself thrust into a position where she had to decide between differing military options proposed by professionals. She decided, and invariably decided well, drawing on a large measure of common sense (Herzog, 1975).

The prime minister described her role:

> I honestly didn't want the responsibility, the awful stress and strain of being prime minister. But, when the party began to press me, for the sake of the party, recently unified and for the sake of country, which was still in peril, to perform this last service and said, "Ima, we know it will be terribly hard for you, harder than anyone will ever guess. But there is simply no way out—you must say yes." So I did. Today, when I can take time for those reflections, I find I have no appetite for them. I became prime minister because that was how it was, in the same way that my milkman became an officer in command of an outpost on Mount Hermon. Neither of us had any particular r elish for the job, but we both did it as well as we could (1975, p. 378).

Indira Gandhi

Indira Gandhi dominated the political system in India for more than a decade while serving as prime minister. She led the nation not only through the periodic outbreaks of religious and linguistic violence that characterize India but also through a war with Pakistan, the successful development of an Indian nuclear explosive, and the declaration of a state of emergency during which she exercised almost dictatorial power. Her actions and policies were highly controversial. Her personality and motivations are never described as straightforward or simple. However, all authors agree that Indira Gandhi, with the aid of a limited group of advisers, ran the national government of India. She wielded great personal power and did not hesitate to apply political or military force when, in her opinion, it served India.

On November 19, 1917, Indira Gandhi was born to Jawaharlal Nehru and his wife, Kamala. Throughout her childhood, her father, grandfather, and even she and her mother were in and out of jail. Despite the fact that she received love, attention, and a good education, Indira Gandhi's childhood was turbulent and far from typical.

In 1942, against the wishes of her father, Indira cut short her Oxford education to return to India and marry Feroze Gandhi, who not only came from a background of small tradespeople but also was a Parsi. She bore two sons and seemed content to be a traditional wife and mother. However, her father, the prime minister, needed her assistance. She gradually moved into the prime minister's residence along with her children and became her father's official hostess and increasingly his confidante on matters of state. She held no official title and expressed little public interest in politics. (The material here is summarized from biographies by Moraes, 1980, and Sahgal, 1982.)

Following her husband's death in 1960, Indira Gandhi devoted herself to raising her sons and supporting her father, particularly during the sudden invasion of India by China in 1962. Fortunately for India, the militarily dominant Chinese withdrew spontaneously from Indian territory having humiliated the Indian army. Despite the opposition of the military, Gandhi flew to visit the front lines, where she was effective in calming the panicked civilians (Gandhi, 1980).

Nehru died in 1964 and was succeeded by Lal Bahadur Shastri, a veteran Congress Party politician. Gandhi accepted a post in his Cabinet as minister of broadcasting and information. The Cabinet post seems to have been offered more as an honor to Nehru's memory than as a tribute to Indira Gandhi's political skills. She once again kept a comparatively low profile, with two notable exceptions. The Indian constitution established English as the official language of India until it could be replaced by Hindi, the language of northern India. As the deadline for conversion approached, violence broke out in southern India, which has a different linguistic heritage. Shastri attempted to reassure the South that no immediate conversion would occur, but the rioting and killing continued until Gandhi traveled through the fighting in Madras to contact leaders in person and calm the situation.

In 1965, Gandhi, having travelled to Kashmir for a vacation, encountered an attack by Pakistani forces disguised as tribesmen. She phoned Delhi and helped establish military resistance to the unexpected assault. During the conflict she visited the front lines, encouraged civilians, and attempted to keep Kashmiri Moslems from joining forces with the invaders. She warned that the guerrilla assault could well turn into a full-blown war, a considerably more militant position than the Shastri government took. As the war escalated, the Indian army pushed the invaders back into Pakistan. In early January 1966, Shastri signed a peace treaty consolidating his victory (but not humiliating Pakistan), and died of a heart attack within twenty-four hours.

The powerful political leaders of the Congress Party had grown impatient with Shastri because he proved too independent to follow their instructions. In search of a more malleable prime minister, they selected Indira Gandhi, believing that Nehru's daughter was a shy, quiet, traditional wife and mother, uninterested in power or politics but carrying the magic of the Nehru name. By 1969, she had seized control of the Congress Party and appealed directly for support to the people on a platform calling for the end of poverty. The older leaders were banished to a splinter group of the Congress Party, and Indira Gandhi took firm control of the reigns of power. Thus, Gandhi served as commander-in-chief of the Indian army during the 1971 war with Pakistan.

War with Pakistan

In 1971, the region that today is Bangladesh was known as East Pakistan. Despite historical differences, the people of East Pakistan were Moslems and were therefore grouped with modern Pakistan during the partition of India following independence. Desperately poor, the Eastern Pakistanis objected to exploitation by West Pakistan. In 1970, elections were held in East Pakistan giving a mandate for greater independence from West Pakistan. On March 25, 1971, Yahya Khan, ruler of West Pakistan, ordered troops into East Pakistan, where they proceeded to crush resistance brutally.

Refugees flooded into India from East Pakistan. India housed and fed them, but the country's food supplies were increasingly stressed. Refugee units operated as guerrillas in East Pakistan. The Nixon administration and China moved openly in support of Yahya Khan, although the U.S. public was outraged by the brutality of the Pakistani troops. On August 9, Gandhi suddenly signed a treaty of peace, cooperation, and friendship with the Soviet Union. The slaughter in East Pakistan continued, and eventually 10 million refugees reached India, a number far too large for support by the fragile Indian economy. Gandhi traveled to other nations, seeking support for the East Pakistanis. By November, Pakistani forces were shelling Indian towns along the border, and Yahya Khan openly threatened war with India.

Gandhi remained calm, bringing her forces to alert and preparing for war. On December 4, 1971, the Pakistani air force attacked India. India declared war, and Gandhi's troops demonstrated that they had prepared well to fight a war in the low, wet countryside of Pakistan. They quickly overcame the Pakistani resistance and ended the war in victory within two weeks. Gandhi defied both China and the United States in launching the invasion. She refused to be intimidated by the U.S. Seventh Fleet, which steamed into the Indian Ocean ostensibly to rescue U.S. citizens stranded in East Pakistan (Moraes, 1980).

Throughout the war, Gandhi listened to a wide variety of advisers but kept her own counsel. Her silence and patience made her appear inactive, but her sudden counterattack belied her apparent paralysis. Like Meir, she was then described as "the only man in the Cabinet." At the end of the war, she listened to the advice of the Cabinet and announced her decision to sign a peace treaty, just as she had surprised most of her advisers by the sudden signature of the treaty with the Soviets. The credit and the blame for the handling of the war with Pakistan rested squarely with Gandhi in the minds of both the government and the Indian people (Tharoor, 1982).

Development of a Nuclear Explosive

Unlike the events of the war with Pakistan and the declaration of a state of emergency, the details of the Indian nuclear weapons program remain shrouded in secrecy. In 1974, India tested a nuclear explosive that was officially declared to be for peaceful purposes (Carras, 1979). Under Gandhi's leadership, India consistently refused to sign the Nuclear Nonproliferation Treaty. The Indian military has become the fourth largest army in the world, and is recognized as the dominant military power in Southeast Asia (Baxter et al., 1987).

Indira Gandhi came from the tradition of nonviolent protest espoused by Mahatma Gandhi and her father. Nehru always strove to make India a force in world politics by virtue of moral superiority and by a position of neutrality in world conflicts. Gandhi, however, writes:

> Arms used by people without conviction cannot provide any credible backing for foreign policy. While we must have arms to defend our country from any aggression, military strength must be supported by conviction in our ideals and confidence in ourselves. Both are equally potent weapons and, without them, other weapons can be dangerous to ourselves and also useless to our defence. This is the essence of our foreign policy (1980, p. 146).

It is clear that she placed a high value on military strength, and the Indian nuclear weapons program probably enjoyed her support because possession of a nuclear weapon would situate India as a regional if not a world power.

The State of Emergency

On June 27, 1975, Gandhi declared a state of internal emergency, which gave her virtually unlimited power in India. She arrested her major political opponents and clamped strict censorship rules on the press. Gandhi claimed that she acted because a climate of violence had resulted in the assassination of a Cabinet minister (Gandhi, 1980). The state of emergency remained in effect until March 1977, when Gandhi called for parliamentary elections. She was soundly defeated at the polls and left government until 1980, when she was reelected. She served as prime minister until her assassination on October 31, 1984 (Baxter et al., 1987).

Gandhi's decision to declare a state of emergency was clearly her own. She accepted little advice and moved so suddenly she took opposition leaders completely by surprise. Her stated reasons for declaring the emergency seemed inadequate. Rumors abounded that she took this drastic step to maintain her own political power because a court had just ruled that, because she had used corrupt election practices in 1971, she must leave her office for five years.

Alternatively she was suspected of declaring the emergency to protect her younger son, Sanjay, from charges of corruption. Her decision to end the emergency and call elections was equally unexpected, particularly because she and Sanjay were immediately accused of a variety of crimes associated with the imposition of the emergency. Her subsequent return to power proved both her political durability and the inability of the opposition parties to maintain a unified political position.

As a leader, Indira Gandhi strove to increase Indian influence on international events. Although she professed nonviolent ideals, she demonstrated repeatedly that she would willingly employ legal force and utilize the military to establish India's position in the international community. Although she did not personally lead troops, she repeatedly demonstrated her own personal courage on front lines. Her approach to the use of military force must be characterized as traditionally masculine despite her personal femininity.

Margaret H. Thatcher

The general election of May 1979 was historic: Margaret Thatcher became the first female prime minister (the Conservative Party had elected her as leader in February 1975) of the United Kingdom of Great Britain and Northern Ireland. Her election victory initially attracted such unflattering nicknames as "Attila the Hen," "The Immaculate Misconception," and worse (King, 1985, p. 101).

Margaret Hilda Roberts was born on October 13, 1925, in the small provincial town of Grantham. Her father was a grocer who had left school at age twelve, and her mother had been a dressmaker. She graduated from Sommerville College in Oxford and married Dennis Thatcher, managing director of a family paint firm. He was ten years her senior, established and devoted. Two years after their marriage in 1951, Margaret Thatcher bore twins, Carol and Mark.

Thatcher was called to the Bar in 1953 and first won election to Parliament in 1959. Her secret for combining a career and a family with two homes required self-discipline, remarkable energy, and intelligent organization. A colleague wrote:

> She makes lists of things to be done and ticks them off as she does them—what management consultants grandly call "linear program-

ming." She rarely gets to bed before 1:30 A.M. and gets up around seven to make early morning tea and a hearty breakfast for the family. Until recently, she did the shopping and took her dirty washing to the launderette (Lewis, 1975, p. 146).

At the end of 1981, Margaret Thatcher, although having made progress in getting her economic policy accepted, was still a prime minister on trial. On April 2, 1982, Argentina invaded the Falkland Islands, overwhelmed the small contingent of British royal marines stationed there, and installed an Argentine military governor. Argentina then occupied the South Georgia Islands, part of the Falklands dependencies, on April 3. It was the Falklands War that displayed the prime minister's qualities of decisionmaking and fortitude (Young, 1989).

The Empire Strikes Back

When Thatcher met the Commons on April 3, a rare Saturday sitting, preparations for war were already well advanced. Before Parliament had been consulted, a naval task force was being assembled. The assembling of a war machine presented the prime minister with great risks. "She would be damned if she did not get the Falklands back. But she would be double-damned and destroyed, probably alongside her government, if she tried and failed" (Young, 1989, p. 264). After hearing incredulously that British territory had been occupied, the Commons met in a mood of bulldog outrage. The Conservative Party snarled and fumed its way through a three-hour debate; the Labour Party was almost as militant. Margaret Thatcher was, by comparison, unexultant. Apart from two backbenchers, one on either side, who dared to puncture the balloon of warmongering hysteria, hers was the most moderate voice in the house.

She had a nation to keep on her side, as well as a cabinet and a party, and she had to preserve the appearance of balance. The search for peace had to be seen as a priority as high as the voyage to war. Sobriety and seriousness, neither of them contrived, were therefore the hallmark of her parliamentary appearances. But to the wider public, and especially when the cameras were in evidence, she issued more resonant summonses to arms. "Failure? The possibilities do not exist," Margaret Thatcher, borrowing from Queen Victoria, stated to the press (Kempe, 1982, p. 29).

First Sea Lord Sir Henry Leach and his fellow officers agreed that, as a leader of the warrior class, Margaret Thatcher could not have been improved upon. They liked her, first of all, because she was decisive. She didn't hesitate to send the task force, but she also didn't shrink from any of the implications of this: the resources it would consume, the massive mobilization, the exceptional powers of requisition, the huge distortion of the defense budget. Leach thought that if the task force had not sailed, "we would have woken up in a different country" (Young, 1989, p. 276). Thatcher, the military were pleased to note, thought the same. They were quite unused to such clarity in a politician. Because they warmed to her decisive mien (King, 1985), she was able to rebuke them over details. At the first breath of interservice rivalry, over the use of Vulcan bombers to incapacitate the Port Stanley airfield, she squelched the air marshals.

The commander-in-chief's officer corps liked her, second, for her executive courage. On May 2, when the *General Belgrano* was sunk by the British submarine *Conqueror* and 368 sailors drowned, she quickly ordered escalation of the war, which, until then, had been almost without casualties save those lost in helicopter accidents. In a lecture after the war, Rear Admiral J. F. Woodward, commander of the task force, described her decision: "I sought a major change in the Rules of Engagement to enable the *Conqueror* to attack *Belgrano* outside the exclusion zone. This was achieved in remarkable short order, reputedly in the entrance porch at Chequers" (Jenkins, 1983, p. 14).

Two days after the *Belgrano* was sunk, HMS *Sheffield* became the first major British casualty of the war. The destroyer was hit by an Exocet missile, with the loss of twenty-one lives and many more sailors grievously injured. Until then, after the exhilarating launch of the task force and the slow build-up as its vanguard reached the South Atlantic, all that the British knew of this unfamiliar business of war was a series of successes.

Nothing had prepared Thatcher for the loss of young British lives, nor for the apprehension this drove home of how close the entire fleet was always going to be to similar disasters. The prime minister did not conceal her feelings or her tears. But neither did she wilt. Throughout the entire episode, an awareness of the possibility of her political destruction was never far away. Her fate was absolutely bound up with the need for a victory that no one could doubt.

But she remained patient. Riddell (1989) states that until May 21, when troop landings finally commenced at San Carlos, cabinet deliberations took place in an atmosphere of feverish anxiety. The peace process continued, but as the large troop carriers bore down upon the Falklands, their deployment became inevitable. What would then happen was, as seen in London, imponderable. Quite apart from the running danger of either aircraft carrier, *Hermes* or *Invincible,* being hit, or the troop carriers *Canberra* and the *Queen Elizabeth II* going down with all hands, nobody was sure how a landing could be safely effected.

Young describes this period:

> Through weeks of turbulence and political fear, Mrs. Thatcher behaved like the best kind of soldier. She was calm and, having identified her objective, clear-sighted in separating the risks she was prepared to run from those which she rejected. The acceptable risks were always, in the end, those of military action, the unacceptable those that might flow from a settlement which fell short of a complete Argentinian surrender. . . . She maintained her patience and nerve to the end. The three weeks of fighting on the island imposed, at times, severe strains. But the Prime Minister, as ever, supported the military judgment that delay was necessary for the preparation to be complete. Whatever the rank and file might feel about the point of the war they were fighting or the political incompetence that had preceded it, to the admirals and generals at the top, who can never have expected to be running such a tremendous operation, Margaret Thatcher had proved herself to possess every quality they least expected in a politician (pp. 278–279).

After twenty-five days of fighting on land, the British recaptured Port Stanley and obliged all the Argentine troops in the islands to surrender on June 14, 1982.

Confidence and Success

Unlike any other postwar British politician, Thatcher left her personal mark upon Britain. "Partly because she was the first woman political leader of a leading western country, partly because of her uncompromising style, and notably because of her determination and success during the Falkland War in 1982, she has become a symbol of a revived Britain—Boadicea with a handbag" (Riddell, 1989, p. 185).

Following the successful conclusion of the Falklands War, Thatcher's approach to leadership and assertion of prime-ministerial influence were matched by an air of confidence and success. By mid-1982 her Cabinet members were supportive of her central economic policy. The situation was analogous to a medium-sized business with the boss firmly in charge (Burch, 1983). That Britain should have stood up for a principle so far from home, and returned victorious, gave Thatcher a special standing in the club of nations. Thatcher's very strength and long political life drew the admiration of other national leaders (Prior, 1986). In many of the countries she visited, she fascinated the people as much as she mesmerized the politicians. She acquired, therefore, a reputation that any other British leader would find hard to replicate.

At home, a quality often attributed to the prime minister was dominance. One had only to cast an eye over the newspapers any day of the week of any year to understand the measure of her domination. "There was no corner of British society to which 'Maggie' could not sooner or later turn her hand; no problem which she could not solve, no governmental triumph that failed to be peculiarly hers" (Prior, 1986, p. 42).

On the world stage, "Maggie" would order Europe, instruct Reagan, see off the Russians, direct the Commonwealth. On the local level, she took charge of problems large and small, from football hooliganism to the drug crisis, from a detailed subclause in the Law of the Sea treaty to the precise configuration of the customs hall at the British end of the Channel Tunnel. She was portrayed as the person without whom nothing could be decided and nothing *was* decided.

A decade of Thatcherism appeared to have controlled inflation and enhanced industrial productivity. Although continuing to run above historic levels, unemployment was declining. As Thatcher began her second decade, however, inflation started to rise and the growth of the GNP to decline. Unemployment, while considerably lower, clearly was not going to reach the low level common during Britain's prosperous 1950s (Dragnich, et al., 1991). Some observers were predicting a major economic crisis. The crisis that ensued, however, in late 1990, was political: Margaret Thatcher's domination of British politics for more than a decade ended.

The term served by prime ministers in Great Britain has averaged little more than four years. Thatcher was exceptional in having served an unprecedented, unbroken term of more than a decade. Margaret Thatcher was the only prime minister in Britain's entire history to shape government policy so completely to her own values and goals that her name became an "ism" (Dragnich, et al., 1991). Margaret Thatcher is proof that the political virtues of competitiveness, toughness, and determination required of commanders-in-chief are neither the innate preserves of the male nor unacquirable by the diligent female aspirant. In 1975, Margaret Thatcher took an opportunity offered her by the events of the leadership battle in the Conservative Party and went for the top. As she herself said at that time, "You cannot go so far up the ladder and then not go the limit just because you are a woman" (Vallance, 1979, p. 81).

Conclusions

These case studies of three women who served as commanders-in-chief of powerful modern military machines during wartime indicate that all used force decisively to achieve their international aims and to protect their countries. In Meir's case, the danger was actual invasion; in Gandhi's, it was economic harm; and in Thatcher's, the danger was loss of national pride. Each woman was willing to build a strong military and was capable of devising and implementing effective aggressive military strategy.

Although these female prime ministers used the military primarily for defense against clearly perceived external aggression, none of them showed a particularly pacifist or conciliatory attitude toward their enemies. Each became known for taking the lead in calling for the use of force. Once they found themselves in a position where the use of military force was required to preserve their nations, each unhesitatingly used it. Each also showed herself aggressive in seizing control of other aspects of national life. There is little doubt that each woman could and did control the military of her nation and personally make decisions involving the sacrifice of lives. Thatcher and Gandhi made peace only after a clear military victory, and Meir stopped short of total victory only because of external pressure from the United States.

All three women were wives and mothers. None of them lacked feminine attributes, and there are no accusations in the literature that any of them was inferior as a woman per se, although their enemies frequently found them significantly lacking in feminine charm. Thus, their military response to military aggression cannot be attributed to their being something other than female. On the other hand, they rose to power in male-dominated systems, and their management styles and responses to force were probably shaped by the environment in which they worked. Certainly none exhibited a management style that is characteristic of those used by women.

Each woman came to power through a parliamentary system and was faced with military aggression rather than acting as the aggressor. It may be that other political systems where women are more numerous will be less willing to respond to military threat with military force. Female leaders in Nicaragua and the Philippines have been used as symbols of peace and national healing. In these cases, it is not clear that the women control their own militaries or what their direct response to aggression would be.

The data on Meir, Gandhi, and Thatcher demonstrate that women as leaders are willing and able to order the use of military force on a massive scale. Perhaps Thatcher best links a woman's traditional role to the business of governing:

> I know what it is to run a home and a job. . . . It may just be that many, many women make naturally good managers and organizers. You may not think of it that way . . . but each woman who runs a house is a manager and an organizer. We thought forward each day, and we did it in a routine way and we were on the job twenty-four hours a day (quoted in Fraser, 1989, pp. 320–321).

chapter 12

No Going Back: Women's Participation in the Nicaraguan Revolution and in Postrevolutionary Movements

Barbara Seitz, Linda Lobao, Ellen Treadway

Women lose and gain during periods of revolution and political upheaval. On the one hand, women and their children tend to bear the brunt of economic dislocation caused by political strife, and children just reaching young adulthood often become targets of state violence and repression. On the other hand, revolutions by definition alter existing social structural arrangements. Traditional gender roles may be suspended while basic survival strategies take precedence and gender ideologies may be realigned to reflect new sociopolitical realities. Women who once "knew their place" may take up arms against a government trying to keep them there.

A decade ago there were little more than sporadic accounts of women's contributions to revolutionary struggles and other forms of collective action. There is now a growing literature on the topic. Sources include books and edited volumes (Bourque and Divine, 1985; Ridd and Callaway, 1987; West and Blumberg, 1990; Rowbotham 1974); journal articles (Acosta-Belen and Bose, 1990; Jaquette, 1973; Safa, 1990; Chinchilla, 1977, 1990; Reif, 1986); and biographies of individual women.

Although we know increasingly about the extent and forms of women's participation, the issues that draw them into struggle, and the barriers they face, we know relatively little about how women's activism affects their status and consciousness after victory has been assured. In part this lack of knowledge is attributable to the failure, until recently, to consider seriously women's roles in revolutionary struggles. In addition, it stems from a sparsity of documented examples of women's mass participation in the framework of successful revolutions. This chapter will present a case study of women's involvement in the Nicaraguan revolution and its aftermath. Through personal interviews with Nicaraguan women and use of secondary data, we trace changes in the objective conditions of women's lives and in their subjective experiences and consciousness. We focus particularly on the recent transition to the post-Sandinista National Opposition Union (UNO) government, a period that portends enormous changes for women.

Our discussion is organized in four parts. First, we summarize some of the broad conclusions from the last decade's literature regarding women's contributions to revolutionary struggle. Second, we describe the context of the Sandinista revolution, which held the promise of building a new society compatible with both class- and feminist-based goals. Similarities and differences from past and ongoing struggles in Latin America are delineated. The next section describes how many of these goals were thwarted by the contra war and the subsequent election of Chamorro and her UNO government. We examine how women have fared economically, socially, and politically under the new government, focusing on several questions: How do women assess the changes brought about by the new government? How embedded are the feminist ideologies put forth by revolutionary women? And conversely, to what extent has machismo remained dominant? How have women responded politically to attempts to roll back their gains? Finally, we examine the factors that will lead to Nicaraguan women's continued resistance and future empowerment.

Women and Revolutionary Struggle

Several points made by feminist and other critical scholars in the past decade are particularly relevant for understanding women's involvement in revolutions and related forms of social protest. First, scholars challenged conventional social science views that confine political struggles to the arena of formal-legal institutions and the public sphere. Scholars now recognize that much of the meaningful political action in the developed and developing world is taking place outside formal electoral channels. With the rise of "new social movements," they see women acting in major roles, dealing with environmental, feminist, human rights, and tenant and welfare rights issues. Taking a closer look, they discovered that the household, or "domestic," sphere constitutes a politically significant arena where gender roles are negotiated and the socialization of future political generations takes place. Difficulties related to household survival precipitate political mobilization. When faced with an insufficient or unsafe food supply, inadequate physical housing, or unsafe conditions for raising their children, women are moved to action. As new social movements focus on the quality and quantity of consumption and span issues beyond those of interest to the working class, classical Marxist assumptions about struggle taking place at the point of production are called into question.

Not surprisingly, with this recent redefinition of politics, women's invisibility as political actors is diminishing. Studies of modern revolutions pay increased attention to the extent and forms of women's participation and attribute greater value to traditional noncombatant roles in family support, neighborhood networking, and public protest. Lacking, however, is a broad understanding of how and to what extent women contributed to early revolutionary struggles, particularly those before the first half of the twentieth century that are now beyond the range of oral history. For example, is women's widespread mobilization and use of traditional male forms of force, as in the Nicaraguan guerrilla army, the new phenomenon in Latin America, or did historians write women (and children) out of earlier accounts?

Second, we know that women the world over face different sets of barriers to political participation than do men. Women's subordinate social structural position locates them in a narrow range of generally low-paying, unstable jobs. These jobs, such as domestics and market women, make it generally more difficult for women to organize in collective protest. Women also have nearly total responsibility for household operation, leaving them with less time and fewer financial and organizational resources than men of their class. Sexist ideology both within and outside the movement is a further barrier (West and Blumberg, 1990).

A related point is that women's political struggles often take place in different arenas than those of men. In addition to opposing the forces and ideologies of the state, women confront patriarchy in the family and in movement organizations (West and Blumberg, 1990). Sexism pervades national liberation movements, varying in intensity by time and place. For instance, publications by the Latin American left before the 1970s laud guerrilla women for their cooking, "housekeeping," and other domestic duties, noting that they perform work their male comrades "scorn" (Lobao, 1990). While women have always occupied support positions in guerrilla armies, such as running messages and operating safe houses, and acted in relief capacities as substitutes for men, women's acceptance in combat and leadership positions has been much more tenuous. In Latin America, a high proportion of women do not seem to have been routine combatants until the 1970s, as evidenced by the dramatic escapades of Tupamaro women in Uruguay (Lobao, 1990). And women were not visible in a high proportion of leadership positions until the Sandinista revolution.

Third, the factors that draw women into struggle may differ from those that affect men. Obviously women and men share similar interests in the overriding goals of social movements; however, women may participate for additional reasons. Molyneux (1985) has described two major types of gender interests—strategic and practical—for which women may struggle. Strategic gender interests involve long-term, clearly feminist objectives directed toward ending women's subordination, such as abolishing the sexual division of labor, institutionalized gender discrimination, and other forms of patriarchy. Practical gender interests arise from everyday experiences associated with women's position in the gender division of labor. These interests usually arise in response to an immediate need or crisis connected to family survival, such as lack of material goods or support for public welfare, and do not generally involve strategic goals of emancipating women. Economic crisis affects poor women more deeply than rich women. Consequently, practical gender interests are closely related to those of class. According to Molyneux (1985), movements advocating strategic gender interests must be perceived as addressing practical gender interests first before most women will join. Recent revolutionary movements in Central America have gained widespread female support, in part, because they have addressed seriously practical gender interests while sponsoring some strategic objectives (Lobao, 1990).

Less studied is the long-term impact of women's participation in revolutionary struggle and other types of collective action. West and Blumberg (1990) note the need to distinguish between short- and long-term consequences of women's involvement in social protest. Most research has focused on short-term consequences, during or shortly after protest, such as state violence, sanctions by husbands and other family members, and changes in women's political consciousness and family roles. Less is known about longer-term consequences for women's interests and whether consciousness raised during struggle is enduring or temporary.

These consequences seem to vary depending upon whether individual women or women as a group are considered. Some U.S. analysts claim individual female activists gain valuable skills through social movement experience, for example, in the civil rights, welfare rights, or feminist movements. These organizational and management skills prove useful in future organizing, in electoral politics, and in employment. Women acquire a sense of personal empowerment and self-esteem. Subsequently, this personal growth may cause new tensions or renegotiations of gender roles in the family (West and Blumberg, 1990). Similar consequences have been described for women in national liberation movements, particularly in biographical accounts (Randall, 1978, 1981; Marin, 1991).

Because social movements challenge the existing sociopolitical order, they may benefit women as a group in limited and indirect ways, even if their agenda does not specifically concern women. For example, West and Blumberg (1990) point out that there is little dispute that the U.S. abolitionist and civil rights movements had some positive consequences for women. They gave women greater visibility as political actors and provided organizational networks and a training ground for the suffrage and feminist movements to come. In the case of revolutionary movements that have even greater potential to advance women's interests, O'Barr (1985) has noted only limited gains. Summarizing the outcomes of various African revolutions, she argues that despite women's participation, in most cases their positions in work and politics changed little after independence.

How women have fared as a group in the aftermath of revolution seems to depend on several factors, including sociohistorical context; revolutionary leadership, goals, and ideology; and the potential for continued grassroots activism. In rigid, patriarchal social systems, such as in Cyprus during the 1974 war, women's subordination was deepened (Ridd and Callaway, 1987). A revolutionary leadership willing to confront sexism and an accompanying feminist ideology to support change are factors that O'Barr (1985) and Chinchilla (1990) consider crucial for bettering women's position. O'Barr (1985) argues that despite women's strong participation in the Mau Mau movement, the absence of these factors in the subsequent period limited gains for Kenyan women. In contrast, the Sandinista leadership confronted sexism ideologically and in practice. This, coupled with women's sustained activism both within and outside the Sandinista party, allowed some feminist goals to be supported even under the crisis conditions of the contra invasion and economic decline.

It should be noted that women's visibility in revolutionary movements does not guarantee their subsequent status will improve, as was shown in the cases of women in the Mau Mau movement and the activists against the Shah of Iran. The Cuban revolution is another example (Lobao, 1990). Only an estimated 5 percent of Fidel's troops were women. Yet, the revolutionary leadership supported women's interests, mobilizing women in the Cuban Women's Federation in 1960 and addressing practical as well as strategic gender interests in legislation culminating in the far-reaching Family Code.

In sum, although much is now known about women's place in and contribution to revolutionary struggle, the outcomes of struggle are less apparent. The Sandinista revolution provides a case where widespread women's mobilization resulted in some real inroads against sexist ideology and practice. How women respond to attempts to roll back these gains highlights the extent to which changes in consciousness remain ingrained and enduring. The implications extend not only to the potential for future women's struggles in Nicaragua but to other revolutions that seek to create rapid and profound changes in consciousness.

The Sandinista Years: Revolution and Its Aftermath

Women and the Insurgency Period

Just as it has often been considered remarkable that the emergence of socialism occurred first in a barely capitalist Russia, it was likewise unanticipated that a revolution confronting sexism would emerge from a country steeped in machismo where women were unable to vote until 1956. The widespread mobilization of Nicaraguan women in the late 1970s in the Sandinista National Liberation Front (FSLN) against the Somoza dictatorship is regarded as an unparalleled achievement and milestone in Latin American history. By the end of the revolution, about 30 percent of Sandinistas were women. They were visible at all leadership levels and came from all socioeconomic classes. They violated traditional norms, and "women of all ages broke the taboo . . . to take up their spot in the combat trenches" (FSLN, 1987, p. 17).

Already in 1965, women had been imprisoned for political mobilization. Beginning in 1967, they entered the guerrilla forces in the mountains. They were combatants and leaders. They made bombs, gathered medicines, and provided first aid. They organized city and rural safe houses to assist other combatants and political leaders. They organized strikes and demonstrated in the streets. They served as spies and messengers, carrying food and information over long distances, often risking their lives and families. Some were tortured and killed. The names of numerous female heroines of the revolution are well known, including Nora Astorga, Luisa Amanda Espinoza, Arlen Siú, Doris Tijerino, Gladys Baez, and the women of El Cuá who were tortured to death for refusing to divulge information. Women like Dora Maria Téllez, leader of the extremely important western front, commanded units and led major military offensives like León, where four of seven commanders were women.

Several aspects of the Nicaraguan revolution distinguish it from earlier struggles like those in Colombia and Cuba, which did not include such high proportions of women (Chinchilla, 1982). First, it occurred in the historical context of the rise of feminism throughout Latin America. Although feminist ideology diffused from the developed West, its Latin American variant emphasized the intersection of class and gender, in a form of socialist feminism (Flora, 1984).

Second, the mobilization strategy employed by the FSLN represented a significant shift from earlier armed struggles. Unlike the *foquista* strategy followed in Cuba (but seen as responsible for Che Guevara's failure in Bolivia), in which a small group of guerrilla cadre used rapid military action to shatter the dictatorship, the Sandinistas emphasized gradual establishment of mass-based support. This popular mobilization strategy transcended class and gender boundaries in that it united all those opposed to Somoza.

A final difference was that the FSLN created organizational conditions responsive to women (Chinchilla, 1982; Lobao, 1990). FSLN cadre established a separate women's organization, Association of Women Confronting the National Problem (AMPRONAC), renamed the Luisa Amanda Espinoza Association of Nicaraguan Women (AMNLAE) after the 1979 victory. This organization helped articulate both practical and strategic gender interests and pressed their incorporation into the broader FSLN revolutionary platform. Sexism within the FSLN was confronted, and an organizational climate of support for women was fostered. Subsequent revolutionary struggles like those in El Salvador, Guatemala, and to some extent Peru have followed the Sandinista model of mass-based mobilization of women and the targeting of platforms that address women's interests.

The Context of Women's Lives

In order to understand Nicaraguan women's struggles, it is important to recognize the social structural context that shapes their lives. Three aspects of this context have a continuing and powerful influence: the ideology of machismo, the economic insecurity most women face, and a family structure in which a high proportion of women raise their children alone.

In Nicaragua, education, family relations, church hierarchies, commercial interactions, and advertising have promoted machismo for centuries as a valued norm thought to reflect the basic character of human nature. In everyday life for women, machismo has meant "being an instrument of men": for poor men, women produced children and provided domestic labor; some men profited by selling women's services as prostitutes for other men's pleasure; wealthy women became luxurious objects, their husband's "prized possession" in his home (interview with Orbelina Soza Meirena).

Machismo takes many forms. Often it surfaces in automatic responses triggered by force of habit, based on beliefs and behaviors largely acquired through life experience. Even if one has the conscious intention to change them, the customs and patterns established in early childhood remain difficult to change (Seitz, 1991).

Under the Sandinista government, machismo was transformed from an often unconscious belief system circumscribing women's and men's lives to a recognizable force that could be confronted and finally overcome. This is evidenced in one peasant woman's comment that machismo has not ended and in criticism of the "protectionism" of men who refuse to let their wives work (interview with Elba Aguilera). Gladys Baez, executive director of AMNLAE, stressed the need to eradicate machismo from the mindsets of both men and women (interview).

Gender differences in freedom and accountability constitute important aspects of Nicaraguan machismo (Seitz, 1991). Before the revolution, the norm was that women lived under the authority of their husbands, even having to ask permission to go out in the evening. According to the old system, only if economic pressures make it impossible to stay home ought women to work outside the home, and then only to supplement the family income.

The traditional ideal that women should be confined to the domestic sphere has always been at odds with the reality of most Nicaraguan women's lives. Economic insecurity coupled with a legacy of high seasonal male migration for agricultural work resulted in the lack of a stable, monogamous family life (Collinson, 1990; Seitz, 1991). In addition, the country has one of the highest birthrates in Latin America (*Envio,* 1991). Consequently, more women in Nicaragua have participated in the labor force than in other Latin American countries (Buttari, 1979). Forced self-reliance, independence, and participation in the labor sector ripened Nicaragua for a strong women's movement (Seitz, 1992).

The Revolutionary Government

The successes and failures of the revolution in addressing women's issues and in improving their status have been documented recently by a number of analysts (Chinchilla, 1990; Collinson, 1990; *Envio*, 1991). The initial FSLN platform in 1969 recognized women's emancipation as largely an issue of their full participation in the work force (*Envio*, 1991). Later platforms encouraged by AMNLAE addressed domestic issues, making the FSLN increasingly progressive with regard to women's interests through the first years after the insurgency. New laws were passed in 1981 and 1982 regulating the relations between family members. The traditional delineation of the male as head of household was abolished; mothers and fathers were to share equal responsibility in childrearing, and everyone, including men and boys, should assist with household tasks.

AMNLAE's defense of women's role in the military failed. After their victory in July 1979, most women were demobilized, and the rest were placed in all-female battalions. The government encouraged educated women to enter the administrative sector. Pressure from parents and the church motivated the separation of troops by sex and the decision not to draft women, who could still volunteer but were only called into active service in 1986. Women, however, made up 50 percent of the popular militia units (Collinson, 1990).

The contra war, which intensified by 1982, devastated the Nicaraguan economy and people. By the late 1980s, estimates counted more than 7,000 kidnapped; 250,000 (8 percent of the population) displaced; and 46,000 dead (Collinson, 1990). Material shortages forced the government to abandon many social and political programs to cope with the war.

The FSLN empowered women by recognizing their political voice, officially represented by the women's organization AMNLAE, which introduced many pieces of legislation, and by the Office on Women established in the presidential office building. Women became integrated into leadership positions at all levels. Alimony and child support became newly legislated rights. Common law marriage was recognized, providing the majority of women and children protection under the law. A new Nicaraguan constitution includes more than ten articles on women's rights and guarantees equality between the sexes. Through their military and political participation in the revolution and its new government, women came to see themselves as having rights and political force.

Women and the UNO Government

In the 1990 elections, Violeta Barrios de Chamorro, widow of Pedro Joaquim Chamorro, a hero of the revolution, ran for the National Opposition Union, a coalition of fourteen parties. She received 55 percent of the vote, compared to 40.9 percent received by Daniel Ortega of the FSLN. The deteriorating national economy and contra war are the major factors cited by analysts as responsible for the FSLN overturn. Even women who supported the revolution and its ideals voted for UNO, hoping for no more deaths of their children in war and for an improved economy allowing them to feed their families (Callejas, 1990).

Other factors that may have influenced voters include the style of campaign waged by the FSLN, which featured macho symbolism (e.g., female cheerleaders and sexually suggestive posters) and a lack of attention to women's issues (Chinchilla, 1990; *Envio*, 1991). Meanwhile, Violeta Chamorro invoked images of the Virgin Mary like an "all-forgiving mother promising to put Nicaragua's shattered family back together" (*Envio*, 1991, p. 39).

Effects of the UNO Government

The new government has not only taken a more conservative stance toward women but has begun "a major offensive against women's rights" (*Envio*, 1991, p. 39), not only ordering women to return to their homes, but trying to convince them it is "their place" (Callejas, 1990, p. 3). Attempts to roll back women's gains are evident in economics, social organizations, education, health care, and the media. The new government has implemented an economic structural adjustment plan that in other contexts has tended to feminize poverty.

In separate interviews, AMNLAE leader Dora Zeledón and teachers Martha Hernandez and Cristina Picada argued that through its economic program the government is forcing women back into traditional roles (interviews). Supportive daycare centers and children's lunch programs have been discontinued, and women realize they will be among the first to be laid off (interviews with Hernandez and Zeledón). In March 1992, the unemployment rate was estimated at more than 40 percent by the Labor Ministry, more than 58 percent by the National Workers Front (FNT), and more than 61 percent in the capital by FIDEG, a nongovernmental economic research agency (*Barricada International*, March 1992, p.

23). These factors pressure women to elect the Plan of Occupational Conversion (one facet of the adjustment program) that offers a financial reward for agreeing to leave a job for four years. The reward, however, is not enough for one to survive for four years (interview with Zeledón, Seitz, 1991).

A national survey conducted by FIDEG (1991) found about half of all households are headed by women. Those households are significantly poorer (81.8 percent versus 64.8 percent), with 37.5 percent in extreme poverty (unable to meet two or more basic necessities). According to the survey, the quality of women's lives has been dealt a severe blow. Their inability to provide for their families is evident in that 69.9 percent of homes interviewed have abandoned consumption of at least one type of food. During the six months leading up to the March survey, a little more than 60 percent of the families interviewed had eliminated meat from their diet, and 27.4 percent had also given up milk (FIDEG, 1991). Unfortunately, unemployment, hunger, lack of resources, and lack of available credit for the purchase of seeds and fertilizer, complicated by two years of droughts in some areas (*Barricada,* 1992, p. 1), have put the country at the brink of social collapse.

After having experienced an improved and more equitable status in society during the period of the revolutionary government, women are now feeling threatened by the erosion of their ability to participate in organizational activities that potentially empower them to influence events and decisions, the formation of national policy, and ultimately the course of their own lives.

Women are very visible in the UNO organization, but they are upper-class women whose party encourages women to return to traditional domestic roles, leaving only upper-class women with time to pursue political careers. The women in the UNO party have concerned themselves neither with the problems facing women in the lower socioeconomic strata nor with women's issues in general. On the contrary, they have moved to restrict women's rights, as evident in recent legislation; for example, whereas under the Sandinista government a woman who already had a certain number of children could elect to be sterilized, now she must have the signed consent of her husband.

Another set of changes with negative consequences for present and future political generations of women is occurring in health and education. Many daycare centers, health centers, and medical posts have been closed for lack of funds to pay the doctors (Mendiola, 1992). Others close because its doctor elects to participate in the Plan of Occupational Conversion, and no other doctor is available.

Increased educational costs, decreased family resources, loss of access to free transport to and from school, lay-offs of teachers, and the closing of small village schools have now barred many children from the classroom. When surveyed in August 1991, twenty women representing a rural community of sixty-five families in Region II revealed that whereas all of their children attended school before the change of government, now only 20 percent are enrolled, for lack of money to pay for pencils, notebooks, and book fees (interviews).

The new school textbooks emphasize a Catholic moral code. The ten commandments are presented and interpreted as a code of behavior, and the student is instructed to give her first allegiance to God. In a typical sermon, one bishop lauded the model set by the mother of Jesus, who did not go to sit with the guests but instead went humbly to the kitchen where she was content to cook for and serve the attendants at the wedding.

At the universities tuition soared and openings were cut back, sacrificing the futures of "thousands of youths" (Jirón, 1991). When the 1992 school year began, a "state of emergency" was declared (Loáisiga, 1992). Barriers of cost and access will deny many women levels of participation and influence in government they might otherwise have had.

The media is likewise attempting to turn back the clock on its portrayal of women. This is especially evident in the Latin American soap operas (*novelas*) introduced into Nicaragua recently (Seitz, 1992). Novelas are similar to but have a vastly wider appeal than U.S. soap operas. Each day from about 1 P.M. to 9 P.M., they captivate adults and children alike. The novelas present women as sexually alluring and have become the object of controversy for their "pornographic" depictions of women in love scenes.

Women's Political Response

Despite the obstacles, women are continuing to engage in activities intended to influence policymaking on the local, departmental, and national levels. Organizationally, women are attempting to advance their interests in two major ways: through recently established, grassroots social organizations in the community and the workplace and through the continued efforts of AMNLAE and the FSLN. In addition to AMNLAE's dozens of similar facilities, locally organized women's centers and clinics have emerged to help solve current problems facing women and to provide services dealing with economic alternatives, sex education, legal problems, and family planning.

In a way, the path is clearer today for women's activism than it was under the Sandinista government, when the central focus was on defense against U.S.-backed aggression. Everything else was secondary. Amanda Lirios, secretary of the national organization Centro para la investigación, la Promocion y el Desarrollo Rural y Social (CIPRES) argues that today the situation of the Nicaraguan woman has been "unveiled": "the abuse, the vengeance, the maltreatment, the violence. . . . Well, the mask has been removed and everyone knows what it means to be a woman in this society" (interview, Seitz, 1991). As in other Latin American countries undergoing structural adjustment and implementing conservative free-market principles, the government cannot be counted on for any assistance.

Recently adopted, the platform of the FSLN suggests their support of women's rights, focusing on four major goals: eradication of all manifestations of discrimination against women and establishment of equal opportunity for women in all arenas; better conditions for mothers with family responsibilities so that these functions and responsibilities do not become an obstacle to women's personal development; elimination of machismo, which is considered a survival of ideological regression unacceptable to revolutionaries; and abolition of all laws that perpetuate forms of discrimination against women and vigilance that the gains made in women's rights not be reversed through the revision of just laws (*L'Avispa,* 1991).

Women are well represented in the Sandinista party. Although a woman was not named to its directorate, a promise was made that one would be included in the next. Eighteen percent of the National Sandinista Assembly (selected from among locally elected representatives) are women.

Instead of one women's movement, there are now many vital groups, made up almost entirely of Sandinista women, organizing and communicating their concerns. The new groups and AMNLAE accuse each other of lacking sensitivity to the interests of women and of exerting too much control. AMNLAE charges the other groups with "trying to impose their agenda on the women's movement" (Light, 1992, p. 18). While encouraging them to pursue their goals, Benigna Mendiola, a combat leader at El Cuá in the revolution and today head of the women's section of the National Union of Farmers and Cattle-Raisers and FSLN deputy to the National Assembly, warns the independent activists that their "philosophical questions" may not be relevant to the "reality of the countryside [and] . . to force-feed it . . . would be disrespectful" (1992, p. 25).

On the other hand, AMNLAE has been called "a conveyor belt for the party line" that prevented them taking "'radical' feminist positions" (*Envio*, 1991, p. 37). New activists criticize AMNLAE for being "more committed to its membership in the party than to its leadership role for women" and for its vertical structure. They accuse the FSLN of not taking women or women's problems seriously (*Barricada International,* 1992, p. 28). Though impacted by the differences among their various groups, a national meeting of more than eight hundred women from the rank and file of all Nicaraguan women's organizations took place on January 24, 1992, to exchange experiences, to examine the impact of the current economic adjustment policies on women, and to decide upon appropriate responses. They criticized the government for not considering the needs of women and agreed that action must be taken to "put a brake on the adjustments" (*Barricada International,* 1992, pp. 22–23).

Since that meeting, negotiated and military responses to the current socioeconomic crisis have evolved, one with women's input, the other instigated by an all-female group. On March 29, 1992, the Sandinista Assembly voted eighty-one to ten, with three abstentions, to seek a "National Agreement" with the government to maintain national stability while attempting to influence economic policy for the benefit of the masses (Nicaragua Network, 1992).

On the same weekend, near Ocotal, a militant guerrilla group called the Nora Astorga Northern Front (named for a heroine of the revolution) emerged, made up of three hundred armed women undergoing military training in the mountains. Containing former contras, former soldiers, repatriates, and others, the group had begun as a support for the so-called *recompas* (rearmed former members of the Sandinista army) but converted into an independent military unit after all the demands presented by women were seemingly ignored during recent negotiations in Ocotal between the government and an occupying force (made up of armed former contras and former soldiers) that had taken control of the city. The women's demands included a nursery, a birthing clinic, medicines, and the creation of jobs for women. According to a member of the group's high command, they "are ready to do whatever it takes" to force the government to address their needs (Nicaragua Network, 1992). Clearly, Nicaraguan women, whether by peaceful or military means, are determined that their voices be heard and their needs addressed. Recent events show there is no going back to the prerevolutionary society wherein women were passive and submissive.

Conclusions

Nicaragua provides a case study of the typical effects of women's involvement as combatants in military actions. A dramatic movement toward the involvement of women from all sociopolitical spheres in the revolution and then in the business of government followed the overthrow of Somoza. Women advanced toward equality on the job, in politics and at home, and toward independence in controlling their reproductive rights. The Sandinista government achieved legislation guaranteeing child support and mandating that men and young boys accept, at least in principle, shared responsibility for household chores. Strategic and practical gender interests were elevated to national political concerns. Traditional images of woman underwent revision and the ideology of machismo was unveiled.

Certainly there were limitations in the Sandinistas' program. Though women's interests were acknowledged, it is less clear how deeply change was embedded in society at large. It can be argued that whatever real transformations in women's status the FSLN supported, these were incomplete, halted by factors within varying degrees of FSLN control. The contra war and resulting economic crisis diverted material resources away from women and their households and made it more difficult to address strategic gender interests, such as abortion, out of perceived fear of alienating popular support.

The FSLN neglected to address the needs of certain segments of women, such as household workers and marketers. AMNLAE could not function as an autonomous women's organization but was attached to the FSLN from its inception and shared leadership. Initially, this served to advance women's interests within the FSLN and within the new society it would create. After the insurgency stage, however, a revolutionary government must resolve differences among the various political sectors that support it and consolidate power. The contra war and failing economy made this a difficult task within the Sandinistas' democratic framework.

Nevertheless, the revolution had defined new roles and status for women, attacked machismo, and sensitized women to spouse abuse and reproductive rights. In short, it created greater expectations among many women that their interests would be advanced.

With the change of government and the formal end of the contra war, women have been told to return to the home. As a consequence of the government's structural adjustment program, decreased government assistance, and emphasis on free-market strategies, poor women have been forced to occupy themselves with the struggle to survive. All but the wealthiest women have been excluded from formal politics. The government has embraced the traditional Catholic Church and all of its moral teachings, which deny women many rights.

Although the transformations in women's political status and consciousness under the Sandinista government were deep, they were manifest for a relatively short period of time, about one decade. Further, with the UNO victory, nearly 400,000 Nicaraguan emigrants have returned home (*New York Times,* 1991), undoubtedly bearing the imprint of the older, patriarchal culture of the Somoza epoch. It is generally agreed that the most important factor contributing to the UNO victory was that it would return Nicaragua to normalcy, or economic prosperity and an end to war. This theme has been in turn elaborated upon by equating "normalcy" with a return to traditional values.

There are forces working in favor of women's resistance to the reestablishment of a patriarchal society. The economic crisis among developed nations is likely to lead to reduced foreign aid. The end of the cold war also provides less political reason for the United States to bolster the Chamorro government out of strategic necessity. Feminism has blossomed as a political ideology and mobilizing factor throughout the Third World. Opportunities have grown for developing grassroots networks among women and linkages among women from different countries. Likewise, women's struggles have become linked to other popular struggles involving issues such as human rights, deforestation and the environment, and world hunger. These and other new social movements have been a catalyst for political change globally in the face of rigidity of modern political institutions. Finally, there is greater recognition of women's issues, at least in principle, by Third World governments in general and by donor agencies (such as the Agency for International Development). In sum, Nicaraguan women now have the opportunity to organize in a social movement context of cross-national, cross-issue support and with donor agencies that are increasingly sensitive to women's issues.

Factors internal to Nicaragua will also help women resist a

return to their traditional roles and subordination. The fiction of ideal family life where women are confined to the home is clearly at odds with the reality of most Nicaraguan women's lives. It may be the fantasy of soap operas, but it will not serve to guide effective government policy in the long term, particularly in a nation where half of the households are single-parent and most of these impoverished. In view of the extent to which economic development and other national policies are being pursued at the expense of women and the poor, it should not be surprising that there has been a popular mobilization against these strategies.

Throughout the Third World, women have become key political actors and their interests, particularly practical gender ones, have driven the mobilization of other marginalized segments of the population. The active participation of women in the Nicaraguan revolution led to a government at least temporarily concerned with women's rights and a recognition of the worth of women as citizens. Peace and military demobilization sadly coincided with a threatened loss of women's rights and their positions in society. If, however, the present vigor of the Nicaraguan women's movement can be maintained and differences between factions can be resolved, the movement offers the possibility of advancing women's interests while supporting other aims of the revolution.

Note

This article is based in part on field work conducted by Barbara Seitz during ten visits to Nicaragua from 1987, in the midst of the contra war period, to the present. Open-ended interviews were conducted with more than thirty women from a wide range of socioeconomic backgrounds primarily located in Region II and Managua. The women were asked to recount their personal life histories. In addition, they were requested to act as key informants, reporting about their perceptions of the status and roles of Nicaraguan women over time. In particular, women were questioned as to whether or not and how the position of women in Nicaraguan society changed over the course of their lives. Copies of the interviews are housed at the Archives of Traditional Music, Indiana University, Bloomington, Indiana. These data are supported and complemented by personal observations and published sources, including recently issued reports by the government of Nicaragua.

chapter 13

Women, Resistance, and the Use of Force in South Africa

Patricia T. Morris

African women have had a long history of participation in the liberation struggles of their continent. They have organized resistance movements, led peaceful protests, and borne arms to ensure social change. One anthology of the international women's movement (Morgan, 1984) provides a *herstory* of the role of women in the independence movements in Ghana, Kenya, Senegal, and Zimbabwe, where African women led early anticolonial movements and participated in the liberation of their countries. In Ghana, Yaa Asantewaa took her people into battle during the Anglo-Ashanti war in 1900. Many women were also active in the nationalist movement that resulted in Ghanian independence in 1957. In Kenya, Me Katilili led her people in the 1911–1914 uprising against the British. As in Ghana, women in Kenya were involved in the independence struggles of the 1950s. Senegalese women have been chieftains and warriors since before the fifteenth century and participated in protests that resulted in Senegal's independence in 1960. In Zimbabwe, Ambuya Nehanda led her people in the 1896–1897 war of liberation against the British. More than ten thousand female soldiers fought in the war that ended with Zimbabwe's independence in 1980.

Like their sisters across the continent, South African women have resisted oppression and domination. While the activities of their African sisters in Ghana, Kenya, Senegal, and Zimbabwe have led to political independence and the formation of indigenous governments, South African women are just beginning to induce major social change. Female resistance in South Africa has been primarily peaceful, and women have been in the forefront of significant nonviolent demonstrations there. Recently, however, women have taken a more active and forceful role in the political struggle of their country. This chapter focuses on women's part in the antiapartheid movement in South Africa.

The emergence of female use of force in the struggle can be understood best when the antiapartheid activities of women are

185

separated into two periods. The first period extends from the early twentieth century to the mid- to late 1970s, the second from then through the 1980s. In the early to mid-twentieth century, South African women's disenfranchisement resulted in their mobilization against apartheid. South African women conducted two of the most significant nonviolent protests in South Africa, the 1913 Antipass Campaign and the 1959 Antipass Campaign. During the 1980s, a period of increased international isolation of South Africa and internal repression and unrest, women participated in less-organized, more forceful individual protests, much akin to the Palestinian intifada on the West Bank and Gaza Strip. This transition from nonviolence to violence is reflected in the changing activism of Winnie Mandela, who can be viewed as a symbol of the new era of political resistance in South Africa.

Winnie Mandela's trial and its political consequences suggest much about the impact of the use, support, and consequences of female-sponsored violence in resistance movements. Although nonviolent protests like the antipass campaigns are viewed as significant, important, and courageous, more violent protests by women are more likely to be seen as disreputable. Moreover, subsequent improvements in women's social conditions are not entirely assured by either form of protest. Reasons for these differential and ambiguous payoffs are found in the diverse political significance given to these two forms of protests.

The Politics of Violent and Nonviolent Protests

Both violence and nonviolence mark the long history of conflicts that characterize politics worldwide. During the latter part of the twentieth century, revolutionary and resistance movements in the Third World have adopted one or the other means to achieve social change. The politics of the two are, of course, quite different. And the attitudes toward nonviolent and violent means and ends become even more complicated when one considers the role of women. More often than not, women are in the forefront of nonviolent action while simultaneously discouraged from participation in violent protests. The participation of women in both forms of protest raises several questions. What circumstances and conditions lead women toward violent or nonviolent action? What role do women play in these two different types of activism? What impact do both forms of women's activism have on overall social change and the future social condition of women's lives?

Answers to these questions are found in an analysis of the violent and nonviolent antiapartheid protests of South African women. First, hindering women as they attempt to provide for their families' daily needs is a catalyst for female activism. Second, women are more often leaders of nonviolent protests than leaders of violent ones. Finally, although both forms of protest may foster social change, neither ensures any change in women's social condition.

Both revolutionary and resistance movements have adopted strategies of violent and nonviolent protests to counter or reduce the oppressive power of the state. Sharp (1971) argues that although conventional wisdom holds that violent struggle is the only practical counter to state-sponsored oppression, nonviolent methods can be pragmatic and productive countermeasures. Violent methods require the death of people and destruction of property, which tend to encourage further oppression. On the other hand, nonviolent methods "deny the enemy the human assistance and cooperation which are necessary if he [*sic*] is to exercise control over the population" (Sharp, 1971, p. 29). Because the mass's *inaction* (i.e., assistance and cooperation) supports the state's oppressive power and control, it is the mass's *action* that can oppose the state effectively. Sharp further argues that nonviolent action is the more "sophisticated" form of political resistance. The mass's nonviolent action denies and erodes the state's power. Once the people deny power to the state, they weaken the state, cause the erosion of the state's might, and force the state to relinquish the vestiges of power that remain within the government's grasp.

People can deny power to the state in several ways, including (1) nonviolent protests, (2) nonviolent noncooperation, and (3) nonviolent intervention. These methods differ in intensity and level of direct confrontation with the state. Nonviolent protests are symbolic activities aimed at inducing awareness of popular dissent, usually through marches and public meetings. Nonviolent protest is the least direct and least confrontational of the three methods of action. Nonviolent noncooperation includes mass participation in activities that disrupt normal operating practices. Boycotts, strikes, and other forms of civil disobedience are included in this category. The final and most direct category, nonviolent intervention, consists of more direct confrontation with the state and includes sit-ins, obstructions, and invasions. Even though these means are at times confrontational, they are not violent or forceful.

Violent means involve the direct use of force. In revolutionary and resistance movements, force is used to seize, hold, disarm, confine, penetrate, obstruct, hurt, or destroy the state's resources. The use of violent force destroys the state's resources and potential for control over the public and also builds up the opposing group's power. The destruction of the state's resources, human and material, makes it more difficult and costly for the state's oppressive system to remain intact.

There are three types of violent protests that are most often found in the conflict between an oppressive state and its people: (1) turmoil, (2) revolution, and (3) subversion (Rummel, 1963, 1964). Turmoil includes spontaneous conflicts, riots, and other kinds of internal crises. Revolution includes overt organized conflict and general strikes. Subversion involves covert organized conflict and assassinations. Although violence invites further oppression and more direct confrontation with the state, nonviolence cripples the state's ability to engage in retaliation both objectively and morally. Thus nonviolence raises the conflict beyond a physical level to a moral one, where its proponents have the advantage ethically.

Nonviolence is not without physical cost, however. Followers are called upon to make sacrifices. Once a movement engages in nonviolent action, the oppressive state is likely to respond, especially if the resistance constitutes a direct challenge to the state's power. Censorship, psychological pressure, confiscation of literature and funds, economic sanctions, bans and prohibitions, arrests and imprisonments, exceptional restrictions, and direct physical force are all typical state responses to nonviolent action (Sharp, 1971, pp. 537–539). Despite the severity of these responses, the nonviolent activist must be willing to endure them without recourse to violence. Even though this cost can be high, proponents of nonviolence argue that endurance secures an end to an otherwise vicious cycle of retaliatory violence.

Many proponents of nonviolence (Sharp, 1971; Ginsberg, 1990) argue that violence weakens resistance movements. The resort to violence opens the avenue of strength to the state, because the state is usually better equipped with the weapons of force. The strength that was gained by the nonviolent resistance movement is countered by the state's significant power once violence is introduced to the movement. Thus, when a resistance movement uses the same tools as the oppressive state, the advantage lies with the state. The resort to violence also shifts attention away from the state's oppression and to the resistance's use of force, which allows the state to claim it uses violence to excuse counterviolence. Violence also reduces the support base of the nonviolent movement, and in some cases may contribute to its collapse. Sharp suggests that the introduction of violence in support of the nonviolent defiance campaign in South Africa led to the end of the resistance campaign. Retaliatory response on the part of the South African government was seen as "justified" even though the precise causes of the riots were unclear and may have been initiated by agent provocateurs (Sharp, 1971, p. 599).

The perspective of the proponents of nonviolence is clear. The use of violence is immoral, unethical, and unjustified in any circumstance. Violence initiated to counter violence does not work. It weakens and even destroys the gains of a nonviolent movement.

Others argue, however, that sometimes the use of violence is a moral necessity, as when it repels repression, oppression, and victimization. Force used in self-defense and self-protection is ethical and just and has been termed "moral violence." Although some view the notion of moral violence as an oxymoron, the idea has been the cornerstone of many revolutionary movements. Moral violence identifies the innocent and the violator (Ginsberg, 1990 p. 161), allowing for a potential end to the suffering of the innocent through the introduction of fairness in the relations between oppressor and oppressed. In many cases, the hardship of state repression convinces activists that some sort of violence is the only effective answer.

The use of moral violence has been particularly frequent in Third World revolutionary and resistance movements. In Vietnam, Nicaragua, Iran, Afghanistan, Cambodia, and Zimbabwe different levels of moral violence have been adopted with varying success. Moral violence can lead to significant political change, even though it may come at serious physical and moral cost.

Although the two types of protest share a similar end—the dismantling of an oppressive regime—the roles that women and men play in them differ. The most significant differences are found in:

- Who participates
- Who leads
- Who is the target of the activity

Who Participates?

The levels of participation for men and women in revolutionary and resistance movements vary depending on the method of protest used. Even though women have had a prominent role in the violent protests of several Third World revolutions, the overwhelming proportion of soldiers and rebels remains male. Women may serve in supportive roles like food, shelter, and medical facilitators, but men do most of the fighting. In terms of nonviolent protests, however, women are almost always the predominant participants.

There are clear differences between male and female participation in nonviolent protests in South Africa. Women predominated in the antipass and defiance campaigns in the first half of the twentieth century. When various resistance organizations were banned by the government and the African National Congress (ANC) adopted sabotage as a means of resistance, mass female participation in the movement decreased.

Who Leads?

The gender of the leadership in resistance and revolutionary movements also varies depending on the method of protest used. Although women have attained leadership positions in the violent movements of several Third World revolutions, the overwhelming number of leadership positions are held by men. Similarly, even though women are in the forefront of nonviolent movements, they tend to share leadership with, not predominate over, men. Amakosikazi (1975) suggests that it is impossible to separate female from male participation in the innumerable campaigns for national liberation in South Africa. She also indicates that while women played important roles in all these campaigns, "the leadership as a whole was usually male" (1975, p. 40).

Who Is the Target of the Activity?

The different targets of protest activity also suggest varying roles for male and female activists. Revolutionary and resistance movements tend to have two classes of targets: (1) the state and its representatives and (2) the state collaborators, who are almost always recruited members of the oppressed group. Nonviolent protest activities are generally aimed at the first target group, whereas violent protest activity is aimed at both.

In South Africa, both male and female nonviolent protesters target the state. The targets of violent protests, however, seem to differ. During the violent period of protests, male activists have confronted both state representatives and state collaborators, while female activists have generally only targeted state representatives. (Winnie Mandela is one of the few female leaders to embrace violent retaliation against the state collaborators.)

**Third World Women, Resistance
Movements, and Social Change**

Women in the Third World have been active in both violent and
nonviolent revolutionary movements for centuries. Although the
verdict is still out on the effect that female participation in
revolutionary movements has on the subsequent social status of
women, the experiences of Third World women suggest that the
news is not entirely good. Although it is logical to expect that female
participation in revolutionary movements would enhance women's
social status, one study of Third World women in resistance
movements concluded that women's social status in postrevolutionary societies is often unchanged (Davies, 1983).

Interpretations of women's roles in revolutionary and
postrevolutionary societies do differ. Lapchick and Urdang (1982),
for instance, suggest that female participation and leadership in
strikes, protests, and demonstrations against the government of
Zimbabwe, as well as the presence of trained female fighters in the
national army and the Zimbabwe people's revolutionary army, led
African men to accept women as equal participants in the struggle.
In their view, even though women have not reached parity with men,
there is a "new equality" that speaks to progress in this area (1982, p.
166).

This new equality suggests that female participation in resistance
movements, specifically the taking up of arms, may change women's
social condition. Yet, in Mozambique, where African women also
bore arms, the postrevolutionary condition of women remained
unchanged. Four years after Mozambique's independence, a female
activist concluded that it was easier to eliminate colonialism than
traditional patriarchal rites and practices (Davies, 1983, p. 877).
Other authors (Davies, 1983; Molyneux, 1981) argue that while most
postrevolutionary societies are modestly able to address the
economic basis of sexual inequality, they are unable to change (in
fact either deny or are unaware of) the noneconomic basis. Though
it is assumed that sexual inequalities will end with a successful
socialist revolution, eliminating the economic inequalities leaves the
noneconomic inequalities intact (Molyneux, 1981, p. 178).

To overcome this continuing problem, many Third World
feminists have adopted a strategy of "double-militancy," which
involves working both in political parties or national liberation
movements and in women's organizations. The South West African
People's Women's Council, the Omani Women's Organization, and

the Association of El Salvadorean Women are examples of organizations that mobilize women in both struggles. The notion of double-militancy is grounded in the belief that female liberation can occur only after national liberation is achieved (Davies, 1983). This is clearly the perspective that South African women have adopted.

Bernstein (1975) notes that for South African women dismantling apartheid and national liberation are the "absolute conditions for any change in the social status of women" (pp. 59–60). Consequently, women are in the midst of a struggle that goes beyond female oppression. Because the discrimination against South African women is based on both gender and race, these two factors compound and strengthen each other. Both tribal and modern bases of social, cultural, and economic female oppression are exacerbated by apartheid's racism. In an interview on the status of women in the struggle in South Africa, Ruth Mompati, purportedly the most powerful woman in the African National Congress, expressed the logic of double-militancy in the resistance movement:

> If we continue to shy away from this problem, we will not be able to solve it after independence. But if we say that our first priority is the emancipation of women, we will become free as members of an oppressed community. We feel that in order to get our independence as women, the prerequisite is for us to be part of the war for national liberation. When we are free as a nation, we will have created the foundation for the emancipation of women. As we fight side by side with our men in the struggle, men become dependent on us working with them. They begin to lose sight of the fact that we are women. And there's no way that after independence these men can turn around and say, "But now you are a woman" (quoted in Russell, 1989, p. 116).

The Effects of Apartheid on South African Women

South African women have joined the resistance movement primarily because of the unique hardships they have faced under apartheid. The laws of apartheid present distinct legal inequities and other forms of discrimination for African women. Most prominent are (1) internal migration, (2) legal rights, and (3) wages. For the government to achieve and maintain its goal of separateness of the races, it needs to relegate the Africans to second-class citizenship while maintaining a viable economic system. Discriminatory laws ensure an efficient economic system where African women and men provide labor but receive little benefit or power. Instead, they are seriously hindered in their ability to achieve a reasonable quality of life, simply because of their race.

The major tool of this discrimination was the influx control or pass system. Until 1952, African women were not subjected to the pass system and thus were not prevented from going to the towns. When the Native Abolition of Passes and Coordination of Documents Act was passed, however, things changed dramatically. The Act made it illegal for an African woman or man to remain in an urban area for longer than seventy-two hours. Only those who could prove that they had lived in the community continuously since birth, had worked there continuously for ten years, or had lived there for fifteen years before the Act were exempted. The Act extended passes to all African women and men in 1956. Walker (1982) argues that African women were incorporated into the pass system to prevent them from developing a permanent African population in the towns, which would have undermined the labor migration system on which the economy is based.

The restriction on the internal migration of women increased in subsequent years, tying a woman's migration to her husband's. In 1964, the Bantu Laws Amendment Act stated that a woman could only live in an urban area with her husband if his original entry had been legal. Additionally, a woman's right to remain in an urban area could be lost if her husband died or her marriage dissolved. A woman with an independent right to residence in an urban area could forfeit it by leaving the area. In 1950, the government made it illegal to recruit women on the reserves as migrant contract workers. Thus, although one expects labor to migrate to available jobs, female workers in South Africa could not follow this well-established pattern. Instead, they were subject to laws whose aim had nothing to do with fostering fair employment opportunity for African women.

The perpetuation of customary law on the reserves is another example of legal inequity for women under apartheid. In some areas of customary law, women are denied the privileges of legal subjects. In 1943, an amendment to the Native Administration Act declared that if an African had any rights or obligations governed by customary law, he or she would be judged according to that law. For a married woman, this means that she is deemed a minor and her husband is deemed her guardian. She cannot enter into contracts for loan of livestock; her earnings accrue to the house of her husband; she cannot sue or be sued, enforce a claim to custody of her child, or own or inherit land. These legalities are especially problematic for women left on the reserves for months on end while their husbands work in the South African mines.

Labor law, too, discriminates against women in distinctive ways. The Wage Act of 1957 fixed minimum wages and working conditions. Yet, the two areas where most African women work—domestic service and farm labor—were specifically excluded from this Act. In addition, women's wages are lower than men's in the other comparable employment areas. Wages for domestic workers are very low, and African women are considered the lowest-paid of all domestic workers (Davies, 1983, p. 889). This exploitation of the African female labor force allowed the farming and domestic sectors legally to extract extra profits for themselves while maintaining poor working conditions for the women.

Given such legal discriminations, women became entrenched in the resistance movement. Major bread-and-butter issues and issues of survival were affected by the system of apartheid, so women began to organize and protest en masse. Two of the major protest campaigns in the history of the resistance movement were organized and preponderantly supported by women.

Women and Nonviolent Protests in South Africa

South African women have been protesting apartheid for almost a century despite severe state repression. Most of their antiapartheid activities have been nonviolent, a phase that began in the early twentieth century and lasted throughout the mid- to late 1970s. During this phase, women established many organizations that brought to the fore the problem of apartheid and its serious impact on African women.

Walker (1982) provides the most comprehensive description of women's organizations in the antiapartheid movement, documenting the emergence of eighteen women's groups, beginning in 1912 with the Native and Colored Women's Association (NCWA) (see Table 13.1).

1913 Antipass Campaign

The mobilization of South African women occurred around the issue of the extension of passes to the native female population. In 1913, the government attempted to extend the existing pass laws that governed African men in the Orange Free State to African women.

One year earlier, African women had begun to take an active role in the antipass campaigns, which included deputations, press statements, and petitions to the government. On June 6, six hundred women marched in Bloemfontein and eight hundred in Windburg and Jaggerstein, protesting the extension of passes to women. These marches are one of the first known acts of resistance to segregationist policies in South Africa. During this protest, many of the women presenting petitions to the mayor in Bloemfontein refused to carry passes, and thirty-four were arrested. The women forfeited their option of a fine "as a means of bringing their grievances to the notice of the public" (Walker, 1982, p. 34). The incident led to a widespread campaign of passive resistance. In towns such as Kroonstad, Windburg, and Senekal, women defied the pass laws and presented themselves for arrest. As a result of jail overcrowding, the government eventually gave in.

Table 13.1 Chronological Emergence of South African Women's Organizations, 1912–1981

Year	Organization
1912	Native and Colored Women's Association
1931	Women's National Conference of the Communist Party of South Africa
1933	National Council of Women
1933	National Council of African Women
1934	Garment Workers Union
1938	Salt River and Observatory Ladies Welfare Organization
1938	The League for the Enfranchisement of Non-European Women
1943	ANC's Women's League
1946	Women's Food Committee
1947	Transvaal All-Women's Union
1948	Non-European Women's League
1949	Union of South African Women
1954	Federation of South African Women
1955	Congress of Mothers' Committee
1956	The League of Non-European Women
1957	Cape Association to Abolish Passes for African Women
1970	Crossroads Women's Committee
1975	Black Women's Federation
1981	United Women's Organization[a]

Note: a. See Unterhalter (1983) for a description of uwo.

The antipass campaign was spontaneous and informally organized. There was no general strategy and no overwhelming support from any one organization that could direct and sustain the campaign. Nonetheless, the campaign did represent the first large-scale entry of black women into the South African political arena.

1950s Antipass Campaign

In 1952, the South African government replaced passes with "reference books" through the Black Abolition of Passes and Coordination of Documents Act. African women, as well as men, were required to carry these books. This Act, along with many other pieces of legislation, was met with protest by the African population. In 1954, the Federation of South African Women was formed, uniting many women under one umbrella to fight for African women's equality. When the pass laws were extended formally to women, women responded with protests against them and in favor of improved labor legislation and political rights. Two thousand women marched on Pretoria and thousands marched in Durban and Cape Town. In 1956, women burned their passes in an act of civil disobedience, and many female leaders, such as Helen Joseph, Lilian Ngoyi, and Dorothy Nyembe, were arrested. In Johannesburg, some four hundred domestic workers went on strike, while four thousand women in Pretoria blocked city streets. In Venteerpost, five hundred women presented a petition against apartheid signed by ten thousand women, and two thousand women in Evron marched for seven miles to the Native Commissioner's Office (Morgan, 1984). In August 1956, twenty thousand women assembled in Pretoria to meet with the prime minister. Because a formal procession was banned, women walked in groups of three to the capital. The prime minister, however, refused to meet with them.

Even though the demonstration did not achieve its goal, antipass demonstrations by women continued until 1959 in various towns in South Africa. Walker (1982) argues that although the immediate incentive for protest by women was the extension of passes to them, their participation led to more awareness of the wider political-economic context in which the pass laws operated.

Women and Violent Protest in South Africa

More recent protests have been violent. This phase began in the mid- to late 1970s, during which women participated in spontaneous violent protests, often in response to state oppression. Lodge and Nasson (1991) see the late 1970s and the 1980s as a period of mass resistance in South Africa, accompanied by a growing acceptance of the notion of "revolutionary violence" (1991, p. 29). James (1987) argues that violence is at the core of contemporary politics in South Africa, noting that between September 1985 and April 1986 more than fourteen hundred African civilians and thirty-two police died as a result of the intensified conflict. In fact, since the Vaal Triangle incident in August 1984, the conflict in South Africa amounts to an insurrection (Price, 1991; Lodge and Nasson, 1991).

The term "insurrection" refers to the phase of mass opposition that lies between rebellion and revolution. An insurrection differs from a rebellion in that it abrogates the state's power in a portion of the state's territory. In contrast, a rebellion assaults the authority of the state but does not abrogate the state's power. A revolution completely dismantles the state's power throughout the entire territory. Insurrections are made up of two distinct processes—chaos and transformation. Chaos arises through a "seemingly uncontrollable convulsion of mass anger" while transformation is achieved through the liberation of social space, as a "new structure of domination begins to form" in the new social space (Price, 1991, p. 192). Even though most of the conflict and violence in this period was unplanned, unorganized, and spontaneous, the development of an organization in the early phase of the resistance prepared the movement for "multiple forms of mass resistance and protests [that] interacted and reinforced each other" (Price, 1991, p. 193). School boycotts, political strikes, street battles, guerrilla sabotage by the ANC all simultaneously increased, particularly during September 1984 and July 1986. Although the increasing militancy and violence have been attributed to the youth and schoolchildren in the townships, women were also involved in many of these violent clashes with the state.

News reports (Younghusband, 1983) indicate that South African women were in the forefront of the protests and bore the brunt of the state's extreme repression. In the early fall of 1983, women engaged in violent conflict with the police. In what had become a regular practice of destruction and eviction of squatter camps, the police advanced on a crossroads shantytown to evict the inhabitants. The report describes the incident as follows:

> When the police and government officials advanced on their shacks the women wailed, waved their arms and screamed at the police. In

scattered incidents women tried to tear bits of plastic sheeting and corrugated iron from the hands of the demolishers. The result was a scene of struggling groups of women and police engaged in tugs of war over bits of plastic and metal. Several brawls erupted. In one of them a woman fell to the ground and her baby fell off her back and rolled away in the icy mud. Angry policemen swore at the women and fired tear gas pistols directly into their faces. The tear gas finally drove the women back but when police dogs on leashes appeared, snapping at the women and keeping them at bay while the demolition of the shanties went on, the women's anger increased. They began to hurl rocks and debris at the dogs, one of which was hit and collapsed whining in agony (Younghusband, 1983, p. 15).

One of the women present screamed, sobbed, and shouted at the police, "Where do you expect us to go? What do you expect us to do? If you don't let us live here, where else must we go? . . . You are bastards, all of you . . . just bastards" (quoted in Younghusband, 1983, p. 15). The desperation in this woman's plea may explain the growing militancy of many South African women.

From Nonviolent to Violent Protest: Winnie Mandela

Winnie Mandela stands as a symbol of African defiance against apartheid. Not only is she one of the most visible female leaders in the antiapartheid movement, but her transition from nonviolent to violent protests reflects the movement's transition. During the early years of her resistance, Winnie Mandela was a nonviolent activist. After years of incarceration and isolation, she became more militant in her words, and then, tragically, in her deeds. Winnie Mandela's militancy makes her the most notable and outspoken female activist for revolutionary violence. Her position on this issue may have been one of the causes of her recent separation from her husband, Nelson Mandela. And Winnie Mandela's position on the use of force as well as her alleged participation in a number of deaths, although undoubtedly resulting from her experiences under apartheid, is the major reason behind her detachment from the movement. Her recent fall from grace suggests that female leadership may be tenuous in a highly volatile and uncontrollable mass movement.

Winnie Mandela has spent more than thirty-five years of her life in the struggle against apartheid and is admired within and outside of South Africa. She was seen as a symbol of resistance because of the long-term incarceration of her husband, and also as a leader in her own right. She actively participated in numerous nonviolent resistance campaigns. In 1958, just three months after her marriage to Nelson Mandela, she was arrested for participating in the Antipass Campaign (Russell, 1989, p. 96). She was very active with the Federation of South African Women and the Women's League of the ANC. In 1969, Winnie Mandela was arrested under the Terrorism Act, and deprived of sleep for five days and nights while under constant interrogation (Bernstein, 1975, p. 64). She was also held in solitary confinement for seventeen months (Russell, 1989, p. 96). Immediately after being released in 1970, she was banned and placed under house arrest. Several months later, she and twenty others were brought to trial on charges of illegal ANC activities, which were subsequently dismissed (Bernstein, 1975, p. 64). Once discharged, Mandela and the others were rearrested, and she suffered five-and-a-half months of solitary confinement before being brought to trial and acquitted. She was arrested many more times after that and in 1974 served a six-month jail sentence (Russell, 1989, p. 96). Most of Winnie Mandela's arrests were for her defiance of her banning orders, which prohibited her from speaking to groups or individuals. Mandela has described her ordeals as follows:

> Detention means that midnight knock when all about you is quiet . . . it means seizure at dawn, dragged away from little children screaming and climbing your skirt, imploring the man dragging mummy to leave her alone . . . it means, as it was for me, being held in a single cell with the light burning twenty-four hours so that I lost track of time and was unable to tell whether it was day or night. . . . All this is in preparation for the inevitable hell—interrogation. It is meant to crush your individuality completely, to change you into a docile being from whom no resistance can arise, to terrorize you, to intimidate you into silence (quoted in Lipman, 1984, pp. 136–137).

In 1975, Mandela helped found the Black Women's Federation and the Black Parent's Association in Soweto. The government banned her to Bradfort in 1977, where she stayed for eight painful years. She defiantly returned to her home in Soweto in 1985 after her house in Bradfort was fire-bombed (Russell, 1989, p. 96).

Winnie Mandela's suffering at the hands of the South African government gained her national popularity. She became the heroine of the oppressed, the mother of the country. Her courage enabled many to hold fast to the dream of a nonracial South Africa.

As the first African medical social worker in South Africa, Mandela was prepared for the complexities of grassroots work. As she explains it:

> I have really been more engaged in the struggle at the grassroots level. Partly because of my training as a social worker, I have always considered myself as belonging there. I prefer to work with ordinary people and to be part of them. If I had had a choice, I would never have wanted to be in the limelight (quoted in Russell, 1989, p. 97).

In fact, it is from the masses that she received her growing popularity as an antiapartheid leader, and it is also to the masses that her increasingly militant message was targeted.

During the 1984–1988 period of mass insurrection, the United Democratic Front (UDF) played a significant role in channeling the energies of its constituents in the townships into well-organized protests, but it was more difficult to control the protests of the youth in the townships, who were generally intent on ending apartheid by any means necessary. Youth often targeted community conciliators of the state and African police. Their houses and businesses were burned. Their relatives were beaten, and suspected police informers were met with the rebellion's justice of the necklace, which is death by a gasoline-soaked automobile tire placed around a person's neck and then set on fire (Price, 1991). In April 1986, Winnie Mandela publicly endorsed acts of this kind, saying, "With necklaces and our little matches, we shall liberate this country" (quoted in Lodge and Nasson, 1991, p. 91). Endorsement of the necklace brought Mandela into conflict with the leadership of the UDF. Between January and June 1986, some two hundred and twenty people were necklaced (Lodge and Nasson, 1991).

Mandela's outspoken position on the use of force in the antiapartheid movement seemed to evolve into direct participation in the use of force. In 1989 the United Mandela Football Club, Winnie Mandela's bodyguards, were involved in the beating of several youths and the subsequent death of James "Stompie" Moeketsi Seipei. One of the bodyguards was later convicted of this murder. Allegations of Mandela's involvement in the murder reduced her popularity as an antiapartheid leader. Nelson Mandela's release in 1990 restored her position, but only briefly. In May 1991, she was found guilty of kidnapping and assault. She was sentenced to a six-year jail term, which she has appealed. In late spring of 1992, Mandela was alleged to be connected to the death of Soweto physician Abu-Baker Asvant, who was murdered two weeks after he visited her home to examine Stompie Moeketsi Seipei (Battersby, 1992). Nelson Mandela announced their official separation on April 13, 1992, after significant pressure from the ANC and others to rid himself and the ANC of the political liability of Winnie Mandela's militancy.

The persecution of Winnie Mandela has hardened her resolve that apartheid must end. Her view on the best way to accomplish this has changed from an initial acceptance of suffering for the sake of nonviolence to a position that values self-defense, retaliation, and moral or revolutionary violence. For Mandela the necklace and possibly the beatings of these young activists are all part of the process of political change. The unabated violence that continues in the townships, clearly at great social cost, suggests that many other people view violence as part of the political process as well. Violence perpetrated by the Inkatha movement and portions of the South African security forces suggest that the potential political leverage possible from the use of force is deemed worth the cost to some factions. Yet, it seems that Winnie Mandela's perspective actually began to change after her incarceration in solitary confinement. She concedes that this is so:

> Perhaps up to that stage I had not realized the gravity of our struggle and up to that stage, as a mother and as a black woman I wouldn't have known what my reaction would be if I found myself in a violent situation: would I actually take a gun? That was before I went in for solitary confinement. But from that experience I know what I can do in defense of this my country, in defense of what I believe to be a just society. I believe that now (quoted in Lipman, 1984, p. 137).

Thus, for Mandela, the use of force was moral, just, and necessary for a higher cause, the liberation of South Africa.

The Political Significance of Violent and Nonviolent Protests: Lessons from South Africa

The use of violent or nonviolent protests elicits differing responses among potential movement supporters. In South Africa, many antiapartheid groups have a strong tradition of nonviolence and in recent years have been struggling to maintain that legacy amid extreme state repression and increasing black-on-black violence. Although the use of force in some cases is deemed acceptable, in others it is not. The ANC's sabotage campaign has seemed an acceptable use of force, primarily because it has generally been targeted at state facilities and buildings (Lodge and Nasson, 1991). The clashes between state police and African women in the squatter camps are also deemed acceptable uses of force against apartheid, primarily because they are acts of self-defense. On the other hand, some antiapartheid activists are loath to condone the use of violence when it is black on black, specifically the necklacing of state collaborators and the murder of the youth activists. Clearly the line is drawn in terms of who the target is and what is done to the target. When the target is the repressive state, violence seems to be an acceptable recourse, provided the privileged innocent are not in harm's way. When the target is the nonprivileged collaborator, however, violence (though deemed appropriate by the initiators) is seen as unacceptable and reprehensible by many observers.

The ethical and social dilemmas that arise with the use of violence do not arise in the nonviolent protest movement. Female participation in nonviolent and violent protests exacerbates these differences. Clearly, female participants in the nonviolent phase of the antiapartheid movement were viewed as positive, helpful, and courageous. Even the violent clashes that female squatters conducted with the police are deemed courageous. On the other hand, Winnie Mandela's support of the necklace and her alleged involvement in two deaths are viewed as dishonorable acts, worthy of nothing but condemnation.

These differences imply noteworthy patterns in the response to women in protest movements, particularly when the targets of violent activities are differentiated. The case of South Africa suggests that female participation in nonviolent protests is a time-honored role for women. Female resort to force in spontaneous situations is acceptable. Female leadership in the use of force against members of the same race, be they state collaborators or not, is disreputable.

What effect, then, will participation in one or the other of these forms of protest have on the social status of women after the dismantling of apartheid? Evidence from other Third World revolutions is mixed, suggesting that a change in the social status of women is not guaranteed. Women in South Africa, however, view their contributions to the antiapartheid movement as vital to its success and to the attainment of their own liberation as well. In fact, some female activists suggest that women have played a more significant role in the resistance movement than their male counterparts. One activist argues that "women are the people who are most involved and active in the struggle, but that men are in control because of the social structure and because some women are made to feel inferior" (Russell, 1989, p. 340).

Marvivi Manzini, of the ANC's Women's Section (earlier called the Women's League), recalls that "women students actually accused men of being cowards because time and again it was us who had to be in front of the demonstrations facing the guns and the bullets" (quoted in Russell, 1989, p. 132). Clearly, many South African women feel that they have done their share and maybe more for the national liberation movement.

part 3
Conclusion

chapter 14

The Impact of Women's Use of Military Force

Ruth H. Howes, Michael R. Stevenson

Women's roles in the direct use of military force and the decisions to deploy it mirror the changing impact of women on society. Stiehm (1984) has convincingly argued that the modern state reflects a masculine approach to structuring society. With the advent of the women's movement, increasing numbers of women have entered such formerly all-male arenas as the uniformed military and the sectors of government that decide whether or not to use military force. Because military service has long served as one of the methods for defining a "man," women's entry into the military and the effects of women's presence on the military provide a microcosm of some of the likely effects of the presence of numerous women on other power-wielding areas of society—perhaps even on our society as a whole.

The chapters in this volume provide extensive data on women's participation in the use of military force, the reaction of their societies to that participation, and the ways in which the institutions that implement force are likely to change when more women appear within them. Most of the data presented here come from the United States, but the studies of other nations show that conclusions drawn from the United States can probably be extrapolated to other societies.

While the women's movement has flowered during the last quarter of a century, the bastions of military power have resisted women's attempts to enter them. Women who started at the bottom of the system are only now approaching the age and rank where they can be expected to hold positions of real power. The impact of women on these institutions is only beginning to be felt so data on the subject are sparse. Nevertheless, there is enough information to justify a chapter on the probable effects of the participation of substantial numbers of women on the institutions implementing military force.

Participation of Women

Women can and do participate in all aspects of the use of military force and in the institutions that control the application of legitimate violence. Although no woman has ever served as president of the United States, women have served on the staff of the National Security Council and in the upper levels of the Departments of State and Defense. In these positions they have influenced decisions on the use of military force. Women serve increasingly in the uniformed military. Although they are still not formally allowed in units committed to combat, all the services have placed women in positions that are increasingly close to the front lines. Female soldiers certainly were in the line of fire in the Gulf War, and they are demanding and getting positions in active combat units.

Women in other societies have served as commanders-in-chief during wars. They have led troops and committed acts of violence in support of revolutions. No one perceives either Winnie Mandela or Margaret Thatcher as an advocate of nonviolence. Increasing sales of guns to women in the United States demonstrate a growing willingness of women to use lethal violence. Female police officers are common. It is clear that there are no fundamental biological or psychological barriers that inhibit women's use of lethal force more than men's. Women are unquestionably capable of both commanding and implementing military force.

We must qualify this conclusion in two important ways. First, the numbers of women in most arenas that use military force are very small, and women tend to be concentrated in certain specialties. For example, more women serve in the air force than in the marines, probably because the air force applies lethal force remotely, whereas the marines are specialists in hand-to-hand combat. The combat exclusion rule prevents women from obtaining the credentials essential for promotion to the highest military ranks and limits the positions that are open to them.

On the policy level, women also tend to concentrate in certain areas. For example, there are relatively numerous female agency representatives to discussions on the use of both conventional and chemical weapons. Discussions on the control of ICBMs or space-based defense are generally male. The numbers of women in top-level policy positions that influence the use of military force are so small that these women are still considered remarkable.

Second, the evidence from other societies where women have played leadership roles either as prime ministers or as leaders of revolutionary movements shows that women use legitimate violence only to oppose a direct threat to their homes and families. Gun manufacturers in the United States key their sales pitches to women for this purpose. The female prime ministers profiled in this book have used military force to defeat a direct threat to their nations. Women become active in guerrilla movements when their ability to raise children and make a home is threatened by an oppressive regime.

This defensive use of military force arguably differs from aggressive use of force to extend territory or political influence. Women do not seem to need war in order to define themselves. (For an argument supporting this idea, see Stiehm, 1989, pp. 224–227.) Although they are capable of effective use of force, they do not define themselves by its use but utilize it to preserve their homes, families, and nations.

Society's View

Society has traditionally viewed women as out of place both in organizations responsible for the implementation of military force and in applying lethal force as individuals. The use of lethal force is so strongly associated with our ideas of masculinity that the ability to use it is one of the defining traits of manhood.

Because manhood in our society is a criterion for holding leadership positions, women who aspire to positions of political power have had to assume the trappings of the military. In the 1984 vice presidential campaign, George Bush used Geraldine Ferraro's lack of military experience effectively to "kick ass" during their televised debates. Ann Richards, the governor of Texas, who has sometimes been mentioned as a potential candidate for the vice presidency, has taken care to be photographed in aggressive postures with drawn guns.

War is traditionally viewed as a masculine enterprise (Stiehm, 1989). Men have been the main actors of war as well as the primary victims. Preparation for combat has contributed to the construction of hegemonic masculinity (Connell, 1992) at least in part because of the absence of women. Elements of the male role are exaggerated in the military, including misogyny and homophobia (Switzer, 1992). Combat has long been regarded as a test of one's manhood (Borchert, 1989). The armed forces continue to equate soldiering with masculinity, as when "Pentagon officials fret that curbing navy pilots' sexual feistiness will remove the edge they need for battle" (Smolowe, 1992, p. 36).

To the extent that military service is equated with manhood, the mere presence of women is problematic. As Susan Borchert (1989) stated:

> The armed forces continue to use the traditional perspective of masculinity as an integral part of their resocialization process. . . . For many young men historically, entering the military is a means of proving one's status as an adult man. . . . Misogyny is an integral value in this process. Ironically, while the value of male supremacy is being espoused, the recruits are treated as subordinates, "as women." Women are regarded as inferior, subhuman beings. . . . Thus to be a man is to be a soldier, not a woman (p. 10).

Women tend to disappear from historical accounts of military enterprises. Certainly few accounts of the Manhattan Project, which developed the first nuclear weapon, mention the extensive participation of women, and women's presence in revolutionary struggles is often omitted from official histories. At the end of wars, women are expected to give up their military leadership positions and return to the domestic sphere. The aftermath of the revolution in Nicaragua documents this change. Even in the peace movement, where women have been both leaders and majority participants, credit for progress is given to male political leaders and not to the women who actually directed the movement. The Nobel Peace Prize was awarded to male U.S. and Soviet founders of Physicians for Social Responsibility and not to Helen Caldicott, who clearly served as the leading theorist and spokesperson of the physicians movement.

Images of women as soldiers distress our society. The pictures of female soldiers hugging their toddlers as they deployed to the Gulf War graced the covers of national news magazines. Data on differing public attitudes toward women and men who use guns in defense of the home indicate that society condemns females who use lethal force more strongly than males. The case of Winnie Mandela profiles the limits to society's tolerance of the use of force by women.

Because of this large-scale disapproval of their participation in the use of military force, the few women who participate in making policy governing military force and in implementing it tend to protect themselves by adopting the attitudes of their male colleagues. They "go native in order to survive." The attitudes toward the use of military force held by the few women in policy-level positions in the Departments of State and Defense are at least as hawkish as those of their male colleagues, data show. Management styles of such women mirror those of males, and their culture is that of the departments for which they work. Thus, their attitudes present a striking contrast to the attitudes of women in society at large, as reflected in public opinion polls.

The limitations of this survival strategy are clearly underscored by the alleged sexual assaults on female soldiers during the Gulf War and especially by the Tailhook affair, the sexual assaults on women that occurred at the 1991 convention of the Tailhook Association, an organization for retired and active-duty navy aviators. At least twenty-six women, more than half of them navy officers, were forced along a gauntlet of navy fliers who groped, partially stripped, and jeered at them. When the incident was reported to navy command, they attempted to blame the women who complained and to ignore the incident.

Navy Lt. Paula Coughlin, a pilot herself, attended the Tailhook convention as an aide to Rear Admiral Jack Snyder and suffered an assault while men she had assumed were colleagues and friends participated or looked on. Admiral Snyder ignored her complaints. She says, "I've been in the Navy almost eight years, and I've worked my ass off to be one of the guys, to be the best naval officer I can and prove that women can do whatever the job calls for. And what I got, I was treated like trash. I wasn't one of them" (quoted in Lancaster, June 9–July 5, 1992, p. 32).

U.S. Major General (retired) Jeanne M. Holm testified before Congress in part:

> As gross as the conduct of the men in the third floor [Tailhook convention] gauntlet was, the behavior of the admiral on the symposium panel was even more egregious. When asked by a female pilot when women would be allowed to fly combat missions, the male fliers jeered. Instead of taking the situation in hand and giving her the answer she deserved, the admiral apparently ducked his responsibilities by ducking under the table, treating the question as a joke (1992, p. 11).

The aftermath of Tailhook has clearly had an effect. Admirals now apologize for sexist jokes (*New York Times,* July 18, 1992), and military promotions have been withdrawn or delayed because of allegations of sexual harassment (*New York Times,* June 4, 1992). However, few observers doubt that it will take considerable time, as well as leadership at the highest level, to change the attitudes of the navy toward women. The navy is making an effort to change its culture, but few doubt that the process will require time.

Public attitudes toward Tailhook reflect even more extreme views than those of navy personnel. Charley Reese of the *Orlando Sentinel* wrote, "The people who should be booted out of the service are the female officers who complained. If a grown woman can't handle some friendly drunks in a public place, then she's hardly qualified to command men in the much more serious and stressful environment of war" (quoted in Lancaster, July 20–26, 1992, p. 34).

Clearly, the few women who hold positions where they can implement military force face serious problems in being accepted by both their colleagues and the public. Official attitudes change more rapidly than the gut-level reactions of males who feel their jobs and cultures are threatened and the attitudes of the public in general.

Women's Effects on Organizations

Women are present minimally in organizations that make policy concerning the use of military force, and they constitute about 11 percent of the uniformed military services in the United States. It seems likely that their numbers will increase as a result of events such as the court rulings forcing the State Department to promote more women into the political and economic cones and the aging of women who entered the policy establishment during the early phases of the women's movement and who are now eligible for senior positions. Thus, the evidence of women's effects on organizations where they constitute a substantial minority bears on the establishment that controls military force in the United States.

Sociological studies indicate that women's management styles differ significantly from those of men. Women are less hierarcichal. They organize on a broader base and prefer structures that are less like pyramids. Women in groups are less prone to self-assertion and more prone to compromise. The women's organizations that form the backbone of the peace movement reflect this management style. It is worth noting that these characteristics of women's management style are diametrically opposed to the structure of the military, which has little use for compromise and represents the ultimate hierarcichal structure. If women follow the trend shown by the sociological data and become a large minority of military personnel, their presence can be expected to change the organizational structure in which they participate.

Similarly the poll data consistently show that women tend to be less willing to use military force than their male counterparts.

Women who hold leadership positions in organizations that make and implement policy relevant to the use of force do not follow this general trend. It can be argued that their willingness to use military force is necessary for their professional survival and that including more women in the military and policymaking elites will reduce the tendency of the nation to use military force as an instrument of aggressive foreign policy. There is little doubt that women are willing to use force to counter a perceived threat to their homes and families.

Historically there is evidence that using even legitimate violence is a losing proposition for women. Women who use guns in self-defense are punished more severely than men. War has proven costly to civilians in terms of quality of life and has taken the lives of young male soldiers who are sons and husbands to women. Women themselves are regarded as the spoils of war. In reunited Germany, the majority of male-female relationships that cross east-west lines involve western men and eastern women. This peaceful conquest, nonetheless, has involved the taking of the losers' women by the victors (Fisher, 1992, p. 23). Women who use violence to overthrow repressive regimes frequently find little gain in their social and economic status when their societies return to peacetime. Female members of the uniformed military, the police, and the defense policymaking elite are likely to be seen by society as neither male nor female. Certainly the Tailhook scandal provides a violent reminder of the cost to females for participation in the military. Thus, one might expect that women will prove more reluctant to use military force than their male counterparts except in the clearcut case of a domestic threat.

The experience of female police officers bears out this hypothesis. As more women have entered police forces, the style of police work has changed, with less emphasis on the use of overt force to maintain order and more stress on compromise and negotiation to settle civil disorders without a resort to violence. While female police officers continue to experience resentment from their peers and the community at large, they participate in all aspects of police work and are much more accepted than they were a few years ago. Their increasing presence has paralleled a change in the style of policing. It is logical to attribute at least some of the change in style of police work to the increased participation of female officers in the day-to-day operation of the departments.

Women also seem to be changing the uniformed military. In 1984, retiring chair of the Joint Chiefs of Staff, General John W. Vessey, Jr., remarked, "The greatest change that has come about in the United States Forces in the time I've been in the military service has been the extensive use of women. . . . That is even greater than nuclear weapons, I feel, as far as our own forces are concerned" (quoted in Stiehm, 1989, p. 235).

Some observers even attribute the increase in the number of reported incidents of sexual harassment in the military to the increasing influence of women on the services. Major General Jeanne M. Holm says, "I think the recent rise in reports of sexual harassment and assault is, in part, a reflection of trends in our society as a whole, and, in part, a manifestation of deep-seated resentment of some men at women's expanded role in the armed forces. The closer women [have gotten] to combat units and missions, the greater has been the resistance" (1992, p. 11).

Almost all participants in the discussion of women's role in the military and the combat exclusion rules agree that women's presence will change the military. Of course, the discussants differ widely in their assessments of whether the changes brought about by women's presence in the military will be positive or negative. There is ample evidence that increasing participation by females in the control of military force will change the way that force is used. The difficulty lies in predicting the extent and exact nature of the changes.

Women's Use of Military Force and the New World Order

Women's role in implementing and commanding the use of military force has certainly increased during the last decade. At the same time, society as a whole and the world political situation have changed in a way that we feel exaggerates the effect of women's participation in military organizations.

First, the modern definition of male is less dependent on the ability to use physical violence. The heroes of the 1980s were the pirates of the boardroom who made vast fortunes by clever manipulations of the stock market. While these male role models still proved their masculinity by preying on the weak, they did not employ physical violence to do so. The bomber pilot heroes of the Gulf War did not rely on direct physical combat with the Iraqi air force to earn their hero status. Sports figures still engage in symbolic conflict, but it is considered a tragedy when real physical injury occurs. Thus, society as a whole seems to require less use of physical violence in order to define a hero and a leader.

A tragic exception to this redefinition of masculinity lies in the inner cities, where status can depend on a male's ability to deal in violence. A solution to the problems of the inner cities will require convincing citizens that while real masculinity may involve the wielding of power, it does not demand the direct application of lethal force.

As the definition of masculinity in terms of force has changed, so has the definition of femininity. Women are treated more as partners and less as objects to grace a home. New dating patterns involve groups of mixed-sex friends, rather than the mystique of a dating couple. This companionship model of pairing may make it more logical that females should participate in the use of force. Certainly in the inner cities, young women have increasingly joined their male counterparts in acts of violent domination.

Second, just as maleness in our society is being redefined in terms of power that does not involve the direct application of lethal force, so the global power structure has evolved toward a new paradigm in the use of military force as an instrument of foreign policy.

Historically the global status of nations has been defined in terms of military power. For the last fifty years, superpower status has meant the possession of nuclear warheads mounted on the ultimate twentieth-century phallic symbol, the intercontinental ballistic missile. Nations seeking superpower status or even regional dominance have scrambled to obtain both warheads and missiles.

The sudden collapse of the Soviet Union has forced a redefinition of global power and of the role of military force in foreign policy. In this new world order, a nation's power is increasingly defined by its economic strength. Nations that most efficiently produce goods and services in the largest quantities are considered superpowers. Gross domestic products and trade surpluses define modern power more clearly than numbers of missiles and warheads. The structure of society is still patriarchal, but the metric of power is economic rather than military.

Nations can no longer afford to maintain huge nuclear arsenals in order to prove their power by threatening a holocaust. Militaries around the world are being restructured and downsized. Nuclear weapons are being destroyed, and the role of war itself is being redefined.

The primary purpose of war remains the defense of the homeland. Thus, it seems unlikely that any nation will completely disarm in the near future, because the vast majority of women and men agree that the use of force is justified in the case of a direct attack against the homeland. This logic also justifies the maintenance of a limited nuclear arsenal as the ultimate deterrent against military invasion. Modern militaries will unquestionably be structured to protect the integrity of the homeland against all foreseeable threats.

Beyond the unquestioned role of defending the home, military force has two roles in the new world order. First, it may be used to protect economic assets around the globe or to improve a climate for economic growth. Because trade involves resources and goods produced around the world, revolutions and regional conflicts increasingly threaten national status. Military intervention can be an effective tool in promoting global economic interests. Linked economic concerns mean that more than one nation may be involved in a given military action.

The second use of military force is to protect the innocent in domestic and regional conflicts. In domestic civil wars, such as that in the former Yugoslavia or in Somalia, civilians suffer terrible casualties. Many view the use of military force as a moral duty of other nations to mitigate the suffering of the innocent by protecting aid shipments or guarding refugee camps. In many ways, the legal and moral problems of this second use for the military are those faced by police who intervene in domestic disturbances. Both the nation and the home are considered very private, and the rights of individuals in their homes are to be respected. However, the military or the police intervene to prevent lethal violence against the helpless. Such actions are frequently taken by coalitions of nations so that the action is sponsored by a world-governing system, which at present means the United Nations.

The Gulf War clearly involved both reasons for using military force. Moreover, it was conducted by a coalition of nations under the auspices of the United Nations, which also appears to be a pattern in the modern use of military force. Iraq's invasion of Kuwait and the implied threat to Saudi Arabia threatened the oil supplies of industrialized nations. The military intervention in the Gulf protected petroleum, an essential economic import for most of the industrialized world. Second, the invasion protected the Kurds of northern Iraq and, to some extent, the Shiites of southern Iraq. The protection of these people has been less successful than the operation to secure economic assets. Protecting the innocent and using United Nations inspection teams to monitor renewed threats illustrates the difficulties in applying military force to protect innocent people.

We are thus faced with a paradox. While the military structure and the political system that orders the use of military force remain male-dominated and follow masculine values and styles of organization, the world has changed so that the reasons for applying military force are those promulgated by women: the protection of homes, the defense of a means for earning a living, and the protection of the innocent. Increasing the number of women in power positions within the military and the policy elite may actually assist the United States in adapting to the more female approach to foreign policy required by the new world order.

References

Aberbach, J. D. (1991). The President and the executive branch. In C. Campbell, S.J. Rockman, and B. A. Rockman (Eds.), *The Bush Presidency; First Appraisals*. Chatham, NJ: Chatham House.

Accad, E. (1990). *Sexuality and War: Literary Masks of the Middle East*. New York: New York Univ. Press.

Acosta-Belen, E., and Bose, C. E. (1990). From structural subordination to empowerment: Women and development in third world context. *Gender and Society* (April 3), 299–320.

Adams, J. (1984). Women at West Point: A three-year perspective. *Sex Roles, 11*(5/6), 525–541.

Adler, D. A. (1984). *Our Golda*. New York: Viking.

Alarcon, N. (1990). The theoretical subject(s) of *This Bridge Called My Back and Anglo-American Feminism*. In G. Anzaldua (Ed.), *Making Face, Making Soul, Haciendo Caras: Creative and Critical Perspectives by Women of Color*, pp. 356–369. San Francisco: Aunt Lute Foundation Books.

Aldrich, J. H., Sullivan, J., and Borgida, E. (1989). Foreign affairs and issue voting: Do presidential candidates "Waltz before a blind audience"? *American Political Science Review, 83*(1), 123–141.

Allen, W. H. (1911). *Women's Part in Government: Whether She Votes or Not*. New York: Dodd Mead.

Almond, G. (1950). *The American People and Foreign Policy*. New York: Harcourt, Brace.

Amakosikazi, M. (1975). Women in the political struggle. In H. Bertstein (Ed.), *For Their Triumphs and for Their Tears: Conditions and Resistance of Women in Apartheid South Africa*, pp. 40-49. London: International Defense and Aid Fund.

Anzaldua, G. (Ed.). (1990). *Making Face, Making Soul, Haciendo Caras: Creative and Critical Perspectives by Women of Color*. San Francisco: Aunt Lute Foundation Books.

Arkin, W., and Dobrofsky, L. R. (1978). Military socialization and masculinity. *Journal of Social Issues, 34*, 151–168.

Artna-Cohen, A., Gove, N. B., and Martin, J. (In press). Katharine Way (1903–). In L. S. Grinstein (Ed.), *Women in Physics and Chemistry: A Biobibliographic Sourcebook*. Westport, CT: Greenwood Press.

L'Avispa. (Febrero/Marzo 1991). Borrador de anteproyecto deprincipios y programa politico del FSLN, 29–41.

Bales, J. (1988). Sexual aggression. *APA Monitor, 19*, 26.

Balkin, S. (1979). Victimization rate, safety, and fear of crime. *Social Problems, 26*, 343–358.

Ball-Rokeach, S. (1980). Normative and deviant violence from a conflict perspective. *Social Problems, 28*, 45–62.

Bardes, B., and Oldenick, R. (1978). Beyond internationalism: A case for multiple dimensions in the structure of foreign policy attitudes. *Social Science Quarterly, 59*(3), 496–508.

Barricada International. (March 1992). Diverse, yes . . . but united? 27–29.

Basow, S. A. (1986). *Gender Stereotypes: Traditions and Alternatives,* (2nd ed.). Pacific Grove, CA: Brooks/Cole.

Battersby, J. (1992). Articles in *The Christian Science Monitor,* April 9, p. 4; April 13, p. 3; April 14, p. 5.

Baxter, C., Malik, Y. K., Kennedy, C. H., and Oberst, R. C. (1987). *Government and Politics in South Asia.* Boulder, CO: Westview Press.

Baxter, S., and Lansing, M. (1983). *Women and Politics* (Rev. Ed.). Ann Arbor: Univ. of Michigan Press.

Beauvoir, S. de. (1968). *The Second Sex.* New York: Bantam Books.

Bensen, J. (1982). The polls: U.S. military intervention. *Public Opinion Quarterly, 46*(4), 592–598.

Benson, S. P. (1978). "The Clerking Sisterhood?": Rationalization and the work culture of saleswomen in American department stores, 1890–1960. *Radical America, 12,* 36–53.

Berkowitz, L. (1974). Some determinants of impulsive aggression: Role of mediated associations with reinforcements for aggression. *Psychological Review, 81,* 165–176.

Bernstein, H. (1975). *For Their Triumphs and for Their Tears: Conditions and Resistance of Women in Apartheid South Africa.* London: International Defense and Aid Fund.

Bingham, M. W., and Gross, S. H. (1987). *Women in Japan.* St. Louis Park, MN: Glennhurst.

Blake v. City of Los Angeles, 15 FED 76 (D. Cal 1977).

Bloch, P., Anderson, D., and Gervais, P. (1973). *Policewomen on Patrol.* Washington, DC: The Police Foundation.

Bloch, P., and Anderson, D. (1974). *Policewoman on Patrol: Final Report.* Washington, DC: The Police Foundation.

Blumberg, M. (1989). Controlling police use of deadly force: Assessing two decades of progress. In R. Dunham and G. Alpert (Eds.), *Critical Issues in Policing,* pp. 442–464. Prospect Heights, IL: Waveland Press.

Borchert, S. D. (1989). Masculinity and the Vietnam war. *Men's Studies Review, 6*(3), 1, 10–15, 21.

Boulding, E. (1977). *Women in the Twentieth Century World.* New York: Halstead/Sage.

————. (1988). *Building a Global Civic Culture.* New York: Teachers College Press.

Bourque, S. C., and Divine, D. R. (1985). *Women Living Change.* Philadelphia: Temple Univ. Press.

Branscombe, N. R., and Smith, E. R. (1990). Gender and racial stereotypes in impression formation and social decision-making processes. *Sex Roles, 22,* 627–647.

Branscombe, N. R., Crosby, P., and Weir, J. A. (Forthcoming). *Aggressive Behavior.*

Branscombe, N. R., and Owen, S. (1991). Influence of gun ownership on social inferences about women and men. *Journal of Applied Social Psychology, 21,* 1567–1589.

Branscombe, N. R., Weir, J. A., and Crosby, P. (1991). A three-factor scale of attitudes towards guns. *Aggressive Behavior, 17,* 261–273.

Branscombe, N. R., and Weir, J. A. (1992). Resistance as stereotype-inconsistency: judgments of rape victims. *Journal of Social and Clinical Psychology 11*, 80–102.

Brenner, C. (1974). *An Elementary Textbook of Psychoanalysis*, (2nd ed.). Garden City, NY: Anchor Books.

Brock-Utne, B. (1985). *Educating for Peace: A Feminist Perspective*. New York: Pergamon Press.

———. (1989). *Feminist Perspectives on Peace and Peace Education*. New York: Pergamon Press.

Brown, A. C., and MacDonald, C. B. (1977). *The Secret History of the Atomic Bomb*. New York: Dial Press/James Wade.

Brush, S. G. (1985). Women in physical science: From drudges to discoverers. *The Physics Teacher* (January), 11–19.

Bunch, C. (1987). *Passionate Politics: Feminist Theory in Action*. New York: St. Martin's.

Burch, M. (1983, Autumn). Mrs. Thatcher's approach to leadership in government. *Parliamentary Affairs, 36*, 414.

Bussey, G., and Tims, M. (1980). *Pioneers for Peace*. London: WILPF.

Buttari, J. J. (1979). *Employment and Labor Force in Latin America: A Review at National and Regional Levels*. Santiago: Organization of American States.

Bystydzienski, J. M. (1987). Women in politics in Norway. *Women and Politics, 8*(3/4), 73–95.

———. (March 1989a). *Women's political culture as a source of peace*. Paper presented at International Conference on Women and Peace. Univ. of Illinois at Urbana-Champaign.

———. (1989b). Women and socialism: A comparative study of women in Poland and the U.S.S.R. *Signs, 14*(3), 668–684.

———. (Ed.). (1992a). *Women Transforming Politics: Worldwide Strategies For Empowerment*. Bloomington: Indiana Univ. Press.

———. (1992b). Influence of women's culture on public politics in Norway. Ibid.

Caldecott, L. (1983). At the foot of the mountain: the Shibokusa women of Kitas Fuji. In L. Jones (Ed.), *Keeping the Peace*. London: The Women's Press.

Campbell, C. (1991). The White House and presidency under the 'Let's deal' president. In C. Campbell, S. J. Rockman, and B. A. Rockman (Eds.), *The Bush Presidency: First Appraisals*. Chatham, NJ: Chatham House.

Campbell, D. (1984). *Women at War with America: Private Lives in a Patriotic Era*. Cambridge, MA: Harvard Univ. Press.

Campus, K. F., and Johnson, L. K. (Eds.). (1988). *Decisions of the Highest Order: Perspectives on the National Security Council*. Pacific Grove, CA: Brooks/Cole Publishing.

Carras, M. C. (1979). *Indira Gandhi: In the Crucible of Leadership*. Boston: Beacon Press.

Carroll, B. (1976). *Liberating Women's History: Theoretical and Critical Essays*. Urbana: Univ. of Illinois Press.

———. (1987). Feminism and pacifism: Historical and theoretical connections. In R. Pierson (Ed.), *Women and Peace: Theoretical, Historical, and Practical Perspectives*. London: Croom Helm.

Carroll, S. J. (1992). Women state legislators, women's organizations, and the representation of women's culture in the United States. In J. M. Bystydzienski (Ed.), *Women Transforming Politics*. Bloomington: Indiana Univ. Press.

Cattell, R. B., and Lawson, E. D. (1962). Sex differences in small group performance. *The Journal of Social Psychology, 58,* 141–145.

CBS News Poll, conducted February 25, 1991, reported in *The Polling Report,* 7/5 (March 4, 1991), p. 1.

Chambers, G., and Tombs, J. (1984). *The British Crime Survey.* Edinburgh: HMSO.

Chase, S. E. (November 1987). *Social science for women: A reading of studies of women's work.* Paper presented at the annual meeting of the Association for Humanist Sociology, Lexington, KY.

Chesney-Lind, M. (1987). Female offenders: Paternalism reexamined. In L. L. Crites and W. L. Hepperle (Eds.), *Women, Courts, and Equality,* pp. 114–139. Newbury Park, CA: Sage.

Chinchilla, N. S. (1977). Mobilizing women: Revolution in the revolution. *Latin American Perspectives, 4,* 83–102.

———. (1982). *Women in revolutionary movements: The case of Nicaragua.* Paper presented at the annual meeting of the American Sociological Society, San Francisco.

———. (1990). Revolutionary popular feminism in Nicaragua: Articulating class, gender, and national sovereignty. *Gender and Society, 4/3,* 354–369.

Christian, B. (1988). The race for theory. *Feminist Studies, 14* (1, Spring). Reprinted in G. Anzaldua (1990), pp. 335–345.

Cihon, P. J., and Wesman, E. C. (November 1987). *Comparative worth: The U.S.-Canadian experience.* Paper presented at the biannual meeting of the Association for Canadian Studies in the U.S., Montreal, Canada.

Clark, S. M., and Corcoran, M. (1986). Perspectives on the professional socialization of women faculty: A case of accumulative disadvantage? *Journal of Higher Education, 57,* 20–43.

Clary, E. G., and Tesser, A. (1983). Reactions to unexpected events: The naive scientist and interpretive activity. *Personality and Social Psychology Bulletin, 4,* 609–620.

Cohn, C. (1989). Emasculating America's linguistic deterrent. In M. Harris and Y. King Y. (Eds.), *Rocking the Ship of State: Toward a Feminist Peace Politics,* pp. 153–170. Boulder, CO: Westview Press.

Collins, P. (1990). *Black Feminist Thought.* London and Cambridge, MA: Unwin Hyman.

Collins, R. (1974). Three faces of cruelty: Towards a comparative sociology of violence. *Theory and Society, 1,* 415–440.

Collinson, H. (Ed.). (1990). *Women and Revolution in Nicaragua.* London: Zed Books.

Congressional Yellow Book. (Winter 1992). Washington, DC: Monitor Publishing.

Connell, B. (1992). Masculinity, violence and war. In M. S. Kimmel and M. A. Messner (Eds.), *Men's Lives* (2nd ed.), pp. 176–183. New York: Macmillan.

Conover, P. J. (1988). Feminists and the gender gap. *Journal of Politics, 50*(4), 985–1010.

Constantini, E., and Craik, K. H. (1972). Women as politicians: The social background, personality, and political careers of female party leaders. *Journal of Social Issues, 28,* 217–236.

Conway, J. K., Bourque, S. C., and Scott, J. W. (Eds.). (1992). *Learning About Women: Gender, Politics and Power.* Ann Arbor: Univ. of Michigan Press.

Cook, A., and Kirk, G. (1983). *Greenham Women Everywhere.* Boston: South

End Press.

Cook, B. B. (1987). Women judges in the opportunity structure. In L. L. Crites and W. L. Hepperle (Eds.), *Women, the Courts, and Equality*, pp. 143–174. Newbury Park CA: Sage.

Cook, E., and Wilcox, C. (1991). Feminism and the gender gap: A second look. *Journal of Politics, 53*(4), 1111–1122.

Costello, C. B. (1985). We are worth it! Work culture and conflict at the Wisconsin Education Association Insurance Trust. *Feminist Studies, 11*, 487–500.

Costrich, N., Feinstein, J., Kidder, L., Marecek, J., and Pascale, L. (1975). When stereotypes hurt: Three studies of penalties for sex-role reversals. *Journal of Personality and Social Psychology, 40*, 520–530.

Cox, D. (1974). *Women in Law Enforcement: Police Work.* Master's thesis in Sociology. Long Beach, CA: California State Univ.

Crozier, M. (1965). *The World of the Office Worker.* Chicago: Univ. of Chicago Press.

Dash, J. (1973). *A Life of One's Own: Three Gifted Women and the Men They Married.* New York: Harper and Row.

Davies, M. (1983). Women in struggle: An overview. *Third World Quarterly, 5*, 886–913.

Davis, A. (1990). *Women, Culture and Politics.* New York: Random House (Vintage).

Davis, J. A., Lauby, J., and Sheatsley, P. B. (1983). *Americans View the Military: Public Opinion in 1982.* NORC Report 131. Chicago: National Opinion Research Center, Univ. of Chicago.

Deibel, T. L. (Fall 1991). Bush's foreign policy: Mastery and inaction. *Foreign Policy, 84*, 3–23.

Diamond, I., and Orenstein, G. (Eds.). (1990). *Reweaving the World: The Emergence of Ecofeminism.* San Francisco: Sierra Club.

Diener, E., and Kerber, K. W. (1979). Personality characteristics of American gun owners. *Journal of Social Psychology, 107*, 227–238.

Dietch, C. (1988). Sex differences in support for government spending. In C. Mueller (Ed.). *The Politics of the Gender Gap.* Newbury Park CA: Sage.

Diskin, C. (1985). Attitudes and fitness achievement levels of female law enforcement officers. *Police Chief, 52*, 32–34.

Donovan, J. (1986). *Feminist Theory: The Intellectual Traditions of American Feminism.* New York: Ungar.

Dowd, M. (May 21, 1991). Women at White House find it's still a man's world. *Detroit Free Press*, 1A, 4A.

Dragnich, A. N., Rasmussen, J. S., and Moses, J. C. (1991). *Major European Governments* (8th ed.). Pacific Grove, CA: Brooks/Cole..

DuBois, E. C. (1989). Comment on Karen Offen's "Defining Feminism?" *Signs, 5*(1), 195–201.

Dubrow, F. (1979). *Reactions to Crime: A Critical Review of the Literature.* Washington, DC: U.S. Government Printing Office.

Eagly, A. H., and Steffen, V. J. (1986). Gender and aggressive behavior: A meta-analytic review of the social psychological literature. *Psychological Bulletin, 100*, 309–330.

Eck, J., and Spelman, W. (1987). *Problem Solving: Problem-Oriented Policing in Newport News.* Washington, DC: PERF.

Edwards, S. (1984). *Women on Trial.* Manchester, England: Manchester Univ. Press.

Eder, D. (1987). The significance of cheer-leading for adolescent females. *Women's Studies in Indiana Newsletter, 12*(4), 1.

Eisler, R. (1987). *The Chalice and the Blade*. San Francisco: Harper and Row.

Eitelberg, M. J. (1991). *A Preliminary Assessment of Population Representation in Operations Desert Shield and Desert Storm*. Paper presented at the Biennial Conference of the Inter-University Seminar on Armed Forces and Society, Baltimore, MD.

Elshtain, J. B. (1987). *Women and War*. New York: Basic Books.

Enloe, C. (1983). *Does Khaki Become You? The Militarization of Women's Lives*. Boston: South End Press.

———. (1990). *Bananas, Beaches, and Bases: Making Feminist Sense of International Politics*. Berkeley: Univ. of California Press.

Enríquez Callejas, M. (3 de agosto, 1990). Hablemos de las mujeres. *Barricada.*

Envio. (June 1991). Women in Nicaragua: The revolution on hold, *10,* 30–41 (Published by the Institute of Human Relations, Loyola Univ., New Orleans).

Epstein, C. (1983). *Women in Law*. New York: Anchor/Doubleday.

Ewell, J. (1987). Barely in the inner circle: Jeane Kirkpatrick. In E. P. Crapol (Ed.), *Women and American Foreign Policy: Lobbyists, Critics, and Insiders*. Westport, CT: Greenwood Press.

Faludi, S. (1991). *Backlash: The Undeclared War Against American Women*. New York: Crown.

Federal Bureau of Investigation. (1981, 1988). *Uniform Crime Reports*. Washington, DC: U.S. Government Printing Office.

Federal Civilian Workforce Statistics: Employment Trends as of March 1991. (1991). Washington, DC: Office of Personnel Management.

Federal Yellow Book. (Winter 1992). Washington, DC: Monitor Publishing.

Feld, M. D. (1978). Arms and the woman: Some general considerations. *Armed Forces and Society, 4,* 557–568.

Feminist Majority Report. (March 1991). Global feminization of power, *3*(2), 1, 8.

Ferguson, K. E. (1984). *The Feminist Case Against Bureaucracy*. Philadelphia: Temple Univ. Press.

Fermi, L. (1954). *Atoms in the Family*. Chicago: Univ. of Chicago Press.

Ferree, M. M. (1987). She works hard for a living: gender and class on the job. In B. B. Hess and M. M. Ferree (Eds.), *Analyzing Gender: A Handbook of Social Science Research*. Newbury Park, CA: Sage.

FIDEG (Fundación Internacional Para el Desafío Económico Global). (4 marzo, 1991). *El impacto de las políticas de adjusto sobre la mujer en Nicaragua: Reflexiones de un estudio de caso.*

Finkelhor, D., and Yllo, K. (1985). *License to Rape: Sexual Abuse of Wives*. New York: Holt, Rinehart, and Winston.

Fishman, P. M. (1978). Interaction: The work women do. *Social Problems, 25,* 397–406.

Fisher, M. (August 10–16, 1992). Ossis are Ossis and Wessis are Wessis. *Washington Post National Weekly Edition, 9,* 23.

Fiske, S. T. (1982). Schema-triggered affect: Applications to social perception. In M. S. Clark and S. T. Fiske (Eds.). *Attitudes and Cognition: The 17th Annual Carnegie Symposium on Cognition,* pp. 55–78. Hillsdale, NJ: Erlbaum.

Fite, D., Genest, M., and Wilcox, C. (1990). Gender differences in foreign policy attitudes. *American Politics, 18*(4), 492–513.

Flora, C. B. (Spring 1984). Socialist feminism in Latin America. *Women and Politics, 4*, 69–93.

Forde, B. F., and Hernes, H. M. (1988). Gender equality in Norway. *Canadian Woman Studies, 9*(2), 27–30.

Frank, H. H. (1977). *Women in the Organization.* Philadelphia: Univ. of Pennsylvania Press.

Frankovic, K. (1982). Sex and politics—new alignments, old issues. *P.S., 15*, 439–448.

Fraser, A. (1989). *The Warrior Queens.* New York: Knopf.

Freeman, J. (1979). The women's liberation movement: Its origins, organizations, activities and ideas. In J. Freeman (Ed.), *Women: A Feminist Perspective.* Berkeley, CA: Mayfield.

French, M. (1985). *Beyond Power: On Women, Men, and Morals.* New York: Ballantine.

Frente Sandinista de Liberación Nacional. (1987). National Directorate. *Women and the Sandinista Revolution.* La Vanguardia.

Frye, M. (1983). *The Politics of Reality.* Trumansberg, NY: Crossing Press.

Gal, R. (1986). *A Portrait of the Israeli Soldier.* Westport, CT: Greenwood Press.

Gallup Poll Monthly (December 1983), p. 18.

Gallup Poll Monthly (January 1990), p. 17.

Gallup Poll Monthly (May 1990), p. 10.

Gallup Poll Monthly (November 1990), p. 16.

Gallup Poll Monthly (January 1991), p. 14.

Gandhi, I. (1980). *My Truth.* New York: Grove Press.

Garrison, C., Grant, N., and McCormick, K. (1988). Utilization of police women. *Police Chief, 55*, 32–35.

Gelb, L. H. (1988). Why not the State Department? In K. F. Campus and L. K. Johnson (Eds.), *Decisions of the Highest Order: Perspectives on the National Security Council.* Pacific Grove, CA: Brooks/Cole.

Gelles, R. J., and Strauss, M. A. (1988). *Intimate Violence.* New York: Simon and Schuster.

Gibbs, N. (1988). When women take up arms. *Time, 131*, 63.

Gilligan, C. (1982). *In a Different Voice: Psychological Theories of Women's Development.* Cambridge: Harvard Univ. Press.

Ginsberg, R. (1990). The Paradoxes of violence, moral violence and nonviolence. In V. J. Kool (Ed.), *Perspectives on nonviolence,* pp. 161–167. New York: Springer-Verlag.

Gluck, S. B. (1987). *Rosie the Riveter Revisited: Women, the War, and Social Change.* Boston: Twayne.

Goetz, A. (1991). Feminism and the claim to know: contradictions in feminist approaches to women in development. In R. Grant and K. Newland (Eds.), *Gender and International Relations,* pp. 133–157. Bloomington: Indiana Univ. Press.

Goldman, N. L. (Ed.). (1982). *Female Soldiers—Combatants or Noncombatants?: Historical and Contemporary Perspectives.* Westport, CT: Greenwood Press.

Goldstein, H. (1990). *Problem-Oriented Policing.* New York: McGraw-Hill.

Goode, W. (1971). Force and violence in the family. *Journal of Marriage and the Family, 33*, 624–636.

———. (1972). The place of force in human society. *American Sociological Review, 37*, 507–519.

Goodwin, I. (September 1991). Happer walks into the caldron of DOE's top research position. *Physics Today*, 65–66.

Gottfredson, M. (1984). *Victims of Crime: The Dimensions of Risk.* London: HMSO.

Grant, R., and Newland, K. (Eds.). (1991). *Gender and International Relations.* Bloomington: Indiana Univ. Press.

Green, J., and Mastrofski, S. (1988). *Community Policing: Rhetoric or Reality?* New York: Praeger.

Grennan, S. (1987). Findings on the role of officer gender in violent encounters with citizens. *Journal of Police Science and Administration, 15,* 78–85.

Hamilton, S., Knox, T., Keilin, G., and Chavez, E. (1987). In the eye of the beholder: Accounting for variability in attitudes and cognitive/affective reactions toward the threat of nuclear war. *Journal of Applied Social Psychology, 17*(11), 927–952.

Hardesty, N. (1984). *Women Called to Witness.* Nashville: Abington.

Harding, S. (1991). *Whose Science? Whose Knowledge?* Ithaca, NY: Cornell Univ. Press.

Hardy v. Stampt, 37 Cal App 3rd 958, 112 Cal Reptr 739 (1974).

Harless v. Duck, 619 F. 2nd 611 (1980).

Harris, A., and King, Y. (Eds.). (1989). *Rocking the Ship of State: Toward a Feminist Peace Politics.* Boulder, CO: Westview Press.

Harris, L. (December 7, 1990). The gender gulf. *The New York Times,* p. A35.

Harris, M. (1974). Mediation between frustration and aggression in a field experiment. *Journal of Experimental and Social Psychology, 10,* 561–571.

Hart, P. and Teeter, R. (1991). Survey done on January 23, 1991, by the polling organizations of Peter Hart and Robert Teeter for NBC News and *The Wall Street Journal. The Polling Report, 7/3* (February 4, 1991), 2.

Harwood, G. H. (1991). *Peacing It Together: Recruitment, Motivation and Social Critiques of Peace Activist Women in the U.S. in the 1980's.* Denver: Ph.D diss., Iliff School of Theology, Denver Univ.

Havemann, R. (May 12, 1990). State Dept. sex-bias case reopened. *Washington Post,* A14.

Hawkins, D. (1961). *Manhattan District History, Project Y, the Los Alamos Project: Vol. 1. Inception until August 1945.* Los Alamos, NM: Los Alamos Scientific Laboratory, LAMS–2532.

Hearing before the Subcommittee of the Civil Service of the Committee on Post Office and Civil Service, House of Representatives. (September 22, 1989). Washington, DC: U.S. Government Printing Office.

Heffner, P. (1979). *Impact of Policewomen on Patrol: Contributions of Sex Role Stereotypes to Behavior in an Astereotypic Setting.* Ph.D. diss.: Univ. of Michigan.

Helgesen, S. (1990). *The Female Advantage: Women's Ways of Leadership.* New York: Doubleday.

Hellmans, A., and Bunch, B. (1988). *The Timetables of Science.* New York: Simon and Schuster.

Henley, N. (1973). The politics of touch. In P. Brown (Ed.), *Radical Psychology,* pp. 421–433. New York: Harper and Row.

Henriksen, P. W. (June 25, 1986). Interview with Lilli Hornig, OH-128.

Herzog, C. (1975). *The War of Atonement: October, 1973.* Boston: Little, Brown.

Hindelang, M., Gottfredson, M., and Garofalo, J. (1978). *The Victims of Personal Crime.* Cambridge, MA: Ballinger.

Hochschild, A. R. (1975). Inside the clockwork of male careers. In F. Howe

(Ed.), *Women and the Power to Change.* New York: McGraw-Hill.

Hofstadter, R. (1970). America as a gun culture. *American Heritage, 21,* 4–11, 82–86.

Hokanson, J., and Edelman, R. (1966). Effects of three social responses on vascular processes. *Journal of Personality and Social Psychology, 3,* 442–447.

Holm, J. (1982). *Women in the Military: An Unfinished Revolution.* Novato, CA: Presidio Press.

Holm, J. M. (1992). Tailhook: A defining event for reform. *Aviation Week and Space Technology, 137*(6), 11.

Holsti, O. R., and Rosenau, J. N. (1981). The foreign policy beliefs of women in leadership positions. *Journal of Politics, 43,* 326–347.

————. (1984). *American Leadership in World Affairs.* Boston: Allen and Unwin.

————. (June 1988). The domestic and foreign policy beliefs of American leaders. *Journal of Conflict Resolution, 32*(2), 248–294.

Hooker, R. D. (1988). Affirmative action and combat exclusion: Gender roles in the U.S. army. *Parameters, 19,* 36–50.

Hooks, B. (1984). *Feminist Theory: From Margin to Center.* Boston: South End Press.

Horne, P. (1980). *Women in Law Enforcement.* Springfield, IL: Charles C. Thomas Press.

Horner, M. (1972). Toward an understanding of achievement-related conflicts in women. *Journal of Social Issues, 28,* 157–175.

Hough, M., and Mayhew, P. (1983). *The British Crime Survey.* London: HMSO.

Howes, R. H. (In press). Leona Marshall Woods Libby (1919–1986). In L. S. Grinstein, G.K. Rose, and M. H. Rafailovitch (Eds.), *Women in Physics and Chemistry: A Biobibliographic Sourcebook.* Westport, CT: Greenwood Press.

————. (in press). Chien-Shiung Wu (1912–). Ibid.

Hunt, J. (1992). The logic of sexism among police. *Women and Criminal Justice, 1,* 3–30.

Hunter, A. E. (Ed.). (1991). *On Peace, War, and Gender: A Challenge to Genetic Explanations.* New York: Feminist Press.

Hurwitz, J., and Peffley, M. (1987). How are foreign policy attitudes structured? A hierarchical model. *American Political Science Review, 81*(4), 1099–1120.

Hutzel, E. (1933). *The Policewoman's Handbook.* New York: Columbia Univ. Press.

Hyman, S. (1954). *The American Presidency.* New York: Harper and Brothers.

Insight Team of the *London Sunday Times.* (1974). *The Yom Kippur War.* New York: Doubleday.

Isaksson, E. (Ed.). (1988). *Women and the Military System.* New York: St. Martin's.

Jaggar, A. M., and Rothenberg, P. S. (1984). *Feminist Frameworks: Alternative Theoretical Accounts of the Relationship Between Women and Men* (2nd ed.). New York: McGraw-Hill.

James, W. G. (1987). *The State of Apartheid.* Boulder, CO: Lynne Rienner.

Jaquette, J. (May 1973). Women in revolutionary movements in Latin America. *Journal of Marriage and the Family, 35,* 344–354.

Jenkins, S. (March 31, 1983). *The Times,* 14.

Jensen, M. (1987). Gender, sex roles and attitudes toward nuclear weapons. *Sex Roles, 17*(5/6), 253–267.

Jones, C. (1987). *Predicting the Effectiveness of Police Officers.* Master's thesis.

San Diego: San Diego State Univ.

Jones, V. C. (1985). *United States Army in World War II—Special Studies—Manhattan: The Army and the Atomic Bomb.* Washington, DC: Center of Military History, United States Army.

Julian, M. M. (1990). Women in crystallography. In G. Kass-Simon, P. Farnes, and D. Nash (Eds.), *Women of Science: Righting the Record.* Bloomington: Indiana Univ. Press.

Kanter, R. M. (1977). *Men and Women of the Corporation.* New York: Basic Books.

———. (1981). Women and the structure of organizations. In O. Grusky and G. A. Miller (Eds.), *The Sociology of Organizations* (2nd ed.). New York: Free Press/Macmillan.

Kates, D. B., and Engberg, N. J. (1983). Deadly force self-defense against rape. In W. Garrison (Ed.), *Women's View on Guns and Self-Defense.* Washington, DC: Second Amendment Foundation.

Kaufman, D. R. (1984). Professional women: How real are the recent gains? In J. Freeman (Ed.), *Women: A Feminist Perspective.* Palo Alto, CA: Mayfield.

Kegley, C. W., and Wittkopf, E. R. (1987, 1991). *American Foreign Policy: Pattern and Process* (3rd. and 4th eds.). New York: St. Martin's.

Kelling, G. (1988). Police and communities: The quiet revolution. *Perspectives on Policing, 1.* Washington, DC: U.S. Government Printing Office.

Kelley, H. H., and Schmidt, G. (1989). The "aggressive male" syndrome: Its possible relevance for international conflict. In P.C. Stern, R. Axelrod, R. Jervis, and R. Radner (Eds.), *Perspectives on Deterrence.* New York: Oxford Univ. Press.

Kelly, J. A., Kern, J. M., Kirkley, B. G., Patterson, J. N., and Keane, T. M. (1980). Reactions to assertive versus unassertive behavior: differential effects for males and females and implications for assertiveness training. *Behavioral Therapy, 11,* 670–682.

Kempe, F. (May 14, 1982). *Wall Street Journal,* 94.

Kennedy, M. (1989). Seven hypotheses on male and female principles in architecture. *Heresies: A Feminist Publication on Art and Politics, 3*(3), 12–13.

King, A. (1985). *The British Prime Minister* (2nd ed.). Durham, NC: Duke Univ. Press.

Kirkpatrick, J. (1974). *Political Woman.* New York: Basic Books.

Kleck, G., and Bordua, D. J. (1983). The factual foundation for certain key assumptions about gun control. *Law and Policy Quarterly, 5,* 271–298.

Koenig, L. W. (1986). *The Chief Executive.* New York: Harcourt, Brace, Jovanovich.

Kollock, P., Blumstein, P., and Schwartz, P. (1985). Sex and power in interaction: conversational privileges and duties. *American Sociological Review, 50*(1), 34–46.

Koss, M. P., Gidycz, C., and Wisniewski, N. (1987). The scope of rape: Sexual aggression and victimization among a national sample of students in higher education. *Journal of Consulting and Clinical Psychology, 55,* 172–170.

Kramarae, C. (1980). *The Voice and Words of Men and Women.* Oxford: Pergamon Press.

———, Treichler, P., with Russo, A. (1985). *A Feminist Dictionary.* Boston and London: Pandora Press (Routledge and Kegan Paul).

Kubo, K. (June 1990). *Japanese women's participation in politics.* Paper presented at the Fourth International Interdisciplinary Congress on Women, Hunter College, New York.

Lafave, W., and Scott, A. (1972). *Handbook on Criminal Law*. St. Paul, MN: West.

LaFollette, S. (1973 [1926]). Concerning women. In A. Rossi (Ed.), *The Feminist Papers: From Adams to de Beauvoir*, pp. 541–565. Boston: Northeastern Univ. Press.

Lamont, L. (1965). *Day of Trinity*. New York: Atheneum.

Lancaster, J. (June 19–July 5, 1992). Eight years in the navy and 'treated like trash.' *Washington Post National Weekly Edition*, *9*, 32.

———. (July 20–26, 1992). A war over women in combat: Tailhook sends the controversy to the front lines. *Washington Post National Weekly Edition*, *9*, 34.

Lapchick, R. E. and Urdang, S. (1982). *Oppression and Resistance: The Struggle of Women in Southern Africa*. Westport, CT: Greenwood Press.

Laqueur, W. (1974). *Confrontation: The Middle East and World Politics*. New York: New York Times Book Co.

Lewis, R. (1975). *Margaret Thatcher*. London: Routledge and Kegan Paul.

Libby, L. M. (1979). *The Uranium People*. New York: Crane Russak and Scribner's.

Light, J. (February 5, 1992). Women's confab turnout elates Managua feminists. *Guardian*, 18.

Ling, Y., and Matsuno, A. (1992). Women's struggle for empowerment in Japan. In J. M. Bystydzienski (Ed.), *Women Transforming Politics: Worldwide Strategies for Empowerment*. Bloomington: Indiana Univ. Press.

Lipman, B. (1984). *We Make Freedom: Women in South Africa*. London: Pandora Press.

Lizotte, A. J., and Bordua, D. J. (1980). Firearms ownership for sport and protection: Two divergent models. *American Sociological Review*, *45*, 229–244.

Loáisiga M. (21 de marzo, 1992). Las universidades: Un presupuesto confiscado? *Barricada*, 3.

Lobao, L. (1990). Women in revolutionary movements: Changing patterns of Latin American guerrilla struggle. Forthcoming in G. West and R. L. Blumberg (Eds.), *Women and Social Protest*. London: Oxford Univ. Press.

Lodge, T., and Nasson, B. (1991). *All, Here, and Now: Black Politics in South Africa in the 1980s*. New York: Ford Foundation.

Lorber, J. (1984). *Women Physicians: Careers, Status, and Power*. New York: Tavistock.

Lubkin, G. (1971). Chien-Shiung Wu, the First Lady of physics research. *Smithsonian*, *1*, 52–57.

Lundman, R. J. (1980). *Police and Policing: An Introduction*. New York: Holt, Rinehart and Winston.

Lunneborg, P. W. (1989). *Women Police Officers Current Career Profile*. Springfield, IL: Charles C. Thomas Press.

Malespin Jirón, A. (1991). Para entrar: a sacar mantecas (UCA). *Barricada*.

Manley, K. E. B. (April 1990). Women of Los Alamos during World War II: Some of their views. *New Mexico Historical Review*, *65*, 251–266.

Marin, L. (1991). Speaking out together: Testimonials of Latin American women. *Latin American Perspectives*, *18*(3), 51–68.

Marinetti, F. T. (1991). The Founding and manifesto of futurism. In *Let's Murder the Moonshine: Selected Writings*. Los Angeles: Sun and Moon

Press.

Martin, S. (1980). *Breaking and Entering: Policewomen on Patrol.* Berkeley: Univ. of California Press.

Maxfield, M. (1984). The limits of vulnerability in explaining fear of crime: A comparative neighborhood analysis. *Research in Crime and Delinquency, 21*, 233–250.

McAllister, P. (1991). *This River of Courage.* Philadelphia: New Society.

McGlen, N. E., and Sarkees, M. R. (1993). *Women in Foreign Policy: The Insiders.* New York: Routledge, Chapman and Hall.

McIntosh, J. L., and Santos, J. F. (1982). Changing patterns in methods of suicide by race and sex. *Suicide and Life-Threatening Behavior, 12*, 221–233.

Megaree, E. I. (1969). Influence of sex roles on the manifestation of leadership. *Journal of Applied Psychology, 53*, 377–382.

Meir, G. (1975). *My Life.* New York: Putnam.

Melosh, B. (1982). *"The Physician's Hand": Work Culture and Conflict in American Nursing.* Philadelphia: Temple Univ. Press.

Mendiola, B. (1992). We have more serious problems. *Barricada International* (March), 25–26.

Metropolis, N., and Nelson, E. C. (1982). Early computing at Los Alamos. *Annals of the History of Computing, 4*(4), 348–357.

Mill, J. S. (1973). The subjection of women. In A. Rossi, *The Feminist Papers: From Adams to de Beauvoir* pp. 196–239. Boston: Northeastern Univ. Press.

Miller, W. (1973). *Cops and Bobbies: Police Authority in New York and London, 1830–1870.* Chicago: Univ. of Chicago Press.

Milton, C. (1972). *Women in Policing.* Washington, DC: Police Foundation.

———. (1974). *Women in Policing: A Manual.* Washington, DC: Police Foundation.

Ministry of Consumer Affairs and Government Administration. (1985). *The Norwegian Equal Status Act with Comments.* Oslo: Norwegian Central Information Service.

Mitchell, B. (1989). *Weak Link: The Feminization of the American Military.* Washington, DC: Regnery Gateway.

Mohanty, C., Torres, L., and Russo, A. (Eds.). (1991). *Third World Women and the Politics of Feminism.* Bloomington: Indiana Univ. Press.

Molyneux, M. (1981). Women in socialist societies. In K. Young, et al. (Eds.), *Of Marriage and the Market Women's Subordination.* London: CSE Books.

———. (1985). Mobilization without emancipation: Women's interests, the state and revolution in Nicaragua. *Feminist Studies, 11*, 227–254.

Moore, M. (September 24, 25, 26, 1989). Women in the military. *Washington Post.*

Moraes, D. (1980). *Indira Gandhi.* Boston: Little, Brown.

Morgan, M. K. (1986). Conflict and confusion: What rape prevention experts are telling women. *Sexual Coercion and Assault, 1*, 160–168.

Morgan, R. (Ed.). (1970). *Sisterhood Is Powerful.* New York: Random House (Vintage).

———. (1984). *Sisterhood Is Global: The International Women's Movement Anthology.* New York: Anchor Press.

———. (1989). *The Demon Lover: On the Sexuality of Terrorism.* Garden City, NY: Doubleday (Anchor).

Morgenthau, H. (1990). Another "Great Debate": The national interest of the United States. In John A. Vasquez (Ed.), *Classics of International Relations* (2nd ed.). Englewood Cliffs, NJ: Prentice-Hall.

Moskos, C. (August 1990). Army women. *Atlantic Monthly*, 71–78.

Mueller, C. (1988). The empowerment of women: Polling and the women's voting block. In C. Mueller (Ed.), *The Politics of the Gender Gap*, pp. 16–36. Newbury Park, CA: Sage.

Mueller, J. (1973). *War, President and Public Opinion*. New York: Wiley.

The New York Times. (November 22, 1991), A4.

Nicaragua Network. (April 7, 1992). *Update*. New York.

Nicholls, J. (February 1978). Profile—Hoylande D. Young Failey. *Women Chemists Committee Newsletter*. Washington, DC: American Chemical Society.

Nieva, V., and Gutek, B. (1981). *Women and Work*. New York: Praeger.

O'Ballance, E. (1978). *No Victor, No Vanquished: The Yom Kippur War*. San Rafael: Presidio Press.

O'Barr, J. (1985). Introductory essay. In Muthoni Likimani, *Passbook Number F.47927: Women and Mau Mau in Kenya*. London: Macmillan.

O'Connor, P. A. (Ed.). *The Middle East: U.S. Policy, Israel, Oil and the Arabs* (4th ed.). Washington, DC: Congressional Quarterly.

Offen, K. (1988). Defining feminism: A comparative historical approach. *Signs*, 14(1), 119–157.

———. (1989). Reply to DuBois. *Signs*, 15(1), 198–202.

Office of Equal Employment and Civil Rights. (1988). *Update of the Affirmative Action Plan and Annual Accomplishment Report of Equal Employment Activities for Fiscal Year 1987*. Washington, DC: Department of State.

Officers for Justice v. *Civil Service Commission*, City of San Francisco, 395 F. Supp 378 (N.D. Cal, 1975).

O'Neill, L. D. (1979). *The Women's Book of World Records and Achievements*. New York: Da Capo Press.

Opinion Roundup (April/May 1982). Women and men: Is a realignment underway? *Public Opinion*, 21, 27–32.

Oskamp, S. (1977). *Attitudes and Opinions*. Englewood Cliffs, NJ: Prentice-Hall.

Overholser, G. (June 15, 1987). Would women govern differently? *The New York Times*, A17.

Page, B., and Shapiro, R. (1983). Effects of public opinion on policy. *American Political Science Review*, 77(1), 175–190.

Palmer, Alison et al. v. *Baker as Secretary of State*, 815 F.2D 84 (D.C. Cir 1987).

Parisi, N. (1982). Are females treated differently? A review of the theories and evidence on sentencing and parole decisions. In N. H. Rafter and E. A. Stanko (Eds.), *Judge, Lawyer, Victim, Thief: Women, Gender Roles and Criminal Justice*, pp. 205–220. Boston: Northeastern Univ. Press.

Perlmutter, A. (1978). *Politics and the Military in Israel, 1967–1977*. London: Frank Cass.

Perloff, L. (1983). Perceptions of vulnerability to victimization. *Journal of Social Issues*, 39, 41–61.

Pharr, S. J. (1981). *Political Women in Japan*. Berkeley: Univ. of California Press.

Pitkin, H. (1967). *The Concept of Representation*. Berkeley: Univ. of California Press.

Poole, K., and Zeigler, L. H. (1985). *Women, Public Opinion and Politics*. New York: Longman.

Powell, G. N. (1988). *Women and Men in Management*. Newbury Park, CA:

Sage.

Price, R. M. (1991). *The Apartheid State in Crisis: Political Transformation in South Africa, 1975–1990.* New York: Oxford Univ. Press.

Prior, J. (1986). *A Balance of Power.* London: Hamis Hamilton.

Pyszczynski, T. A., and Greenberg, J. (1981). Role of disconfirmed expectancies and the instigation of attribution processing. *Journal of Personality and Social Psychology, 40,* 31–38.

Quester, G. (1982). The problem. In N. L. Goldman (Ed.), *Female Soldiers— Combatants or Noncombatants?: Historical and Contemporary Perspectives,* pp. 217–235. Westport, CT: Greenwood Press.

Quigley, P. (1989). *Armed and female.* New York: Dutton.

Randall, M. (1978). *Doris Tijerino: Inside the Nicaraguan Revolution.* Vancouver: New Star Books.

———. (1981). *Sandino's Daughters: Testimonies of Nicaraguan Women in Struggle.* L. Yang (Ed.). Vancouver: New Star Books.

Rapoport, R. (1971). *The Great American Bomb Machine.* New York: Ballantine Books.

Reardon, B. (1985). *Sexism and the War System.* New York: Teachers College Press.

Regulska, J. (1992). Women and power in Poland: Hopes or reality? In J. M. Bystydzienski (Ed.), *Women Transforming Politics: Worldwide Strategies For Empowerment.* Bloomington: Indiana Univ. Press.

Reif, L. L. (1986). Women in Latin American guerrilla movements: A comparative perspective. *Comparative Politics, 18*(2), 147–169.

Reith, C. (1943). *British Police and the Democratic Ideal.* London: Oxford Univ. Press.

———. (1980). *A New Study of Police History.* Edinburgh: Oliver and Boyd.

Remmington, P. W. (1983). Women in the police: Integration or separation? *Qualitative Sociology, 6,* 118–135.

Reskin, B. F. (1978). Sex differentiation and the social organization of science. *Sociological Inquiry, 48*(3/4), 3–19.

Rhodes, R. (1988). *The Making of the Atomic Bomb,* pp. 230–232. New York: Simon and Schuster.

Richardson, L. W. (1981). *The Dynamics of Sex and Gender.* Boston: Houghton Mifflin.

Ridd, R., and Callaway, H. (1987). *Women and Political Conflict: Portraits of Struggle in Times of Crisis.* New York: New York Univ. Press.

Riddell, P. (1989). *The Thatcher Decade.* Worcester: Billing and Sons.

Rigor, S., and Gordon, M. (1981). The fear of rape: A study in social control. *Journal of Social Issues, 37,* 71–92.

Rix, S. E. (Ed.). (1990). *The American Woman 1990–1991: A Status Report.* New York: Norton.

Roach, C. (1991). Feminist peace researchers, culture and communication. *Media Development, 28*(2).

Roberts, R. (March 15, 1991). The silence of the diplomat. *Washington Post,* C1, C6.

Robertson, I. (1989). *Society: A Brief Introduction.* New York: Worth.

Robins-Mowry, D. (1983). *The Hidden Sun: Women of Modern Japan.* Boulder, CO: Westview Press.

Robinson, P., and Hayden, P. (1970). A historical and critical essay for black women in the cities. In T. Cade, *The Black Woman.* New York: Signet.

Rockman, B. A. (1991). The leadership style of George Bush. In C.

Campbell, S. J. Rockman, and B. A. Rockman (Eds.), *The Bush Presidency: First Appraisals.* Chatham, NJ: Chatham House.

Rodriguez, N. M. (1988). Transcending bureaucracy: Feminist politics at a shelter for battered women. *Gender and Society, 2*(2), 214–227.

Rogers, D. L. (1991). *The force drawdown and its impact on women in the military.* Paper presented at the Biennial Conference of the Inter-University Seminar on Armed Forces and Society, Baltimore, MD.

Rose, R. (Winter 1977). The President: A chief but not an executive. *Presidential Studies Quarterly, 9.*

———. (1991). *The Postmodern President: George Bush Meets the World* (2nd ed.). Chatham, NJ: Chatham House.

Rossiter, C. (1960). *The American Presidency.* New York: Harcourt, Brace.

Rowbotham, S. (1974). *Women, Resistance and Revolution: A History of Women and Revolution in the Modern World.* New York: Random House.

Royal Norwegian Embassy. (November, 1990). New Labor Government resumes course towards EC-EFTA agreement. *News of Norway, 65,* 65–66.

Ruddick., S. (1989). *Maternal Thinking: Toward a Politics of Peace.* Boston: Beacon Press.

Rummell, R. J. (1963). Dimensions of conflict behavior within and between nations. *General Systems Yearbook, 8,* 1–50.

———. (1964). Testing some possible predictions of conflict behavior within and between nations. *Peace Research Society (International) Papers,* 79–111.

Russell, D. (1982). *Rape in Marriage.* New York: Macmillan.

Russell, D. (Ed.). (1989). *Exposing Nuclear Phallacies.* New York: Pergamon Press.

Russell, D. E. H. (1989). *Lines of Courage: Women for a New South Africa.* New York: Basic Books.

Sachar, H. (1987). *A History of Israel, Vol. 2: From the Aftermath of the Yom Kippur War.* New York: Oxford Univ. Press.

Sachs, R. G. (undated). Maria Goeppert Mayer. In National Academy of Sciences of the United States of America. *Biographical Memoirs,* Vol. 50, pp. 310–328. Washington, DC: National Academy Press.

Safa, H. I. (1990). Women's social movements in Latin America. *Gender and Society, 4*(3), 354–369.

Safran, N. (January 1974). The war and the future of the Arab-Israeli conflict. *Foreign Affairs, 53,* 216.

Sahgal, N. (1982). *Indira Gandhi: Her Road to Power.* New York: Ungar.

Schaffer, K. F. (1981). *Sex Roles and Human Behavior.* Cambridge, MA: Winthrop.

Schlafly, P. (1991). Feminist falsehoods, follies, and funding. *The Phyllis Schlafly Report, 24*(12, section 1, July).

Schreiber, E. M. (1979). Enduring effects of military service? Opinion differences between U.S. veterans and non-veterans. *Social Forces, 57*(3), 824–839.

Sciolino, E. (November 11, 1989). Friends as ambassadors: How many is too many? *The New York Times,* A1, A8.

Segal, D. R., and Segal, M. W. (1989). Female combatants in Canada: An update. *Defense Analysis, 5,* 372–373.

Segal, M. W. (1982). The argument for female combatants. In N. L. Goldman (Ed.), *Female Soldiers —Combatants or Noncombatants? Historical and Contemporary Perspectives,* pp. 267–290. Westport, CT: Greenwood Press.

————. (1992). Toward a theory of women in the armed forces. Paper presented at a meeting of the American Sociological Association, Cincinnati, OH.

Segal, M. W., and Segal, D. R. (1983). Social change and the participation of women in the American military. In L. Kriesberg (Ed.), *Research in Social Movements, Conflicts and Change*, Vol. 5, pp. 235–258. Greenwich: JAI Press.

————, and Hansen, A. F. (1992). Value rationales in policy debates on women in the military: A content analysis of congressional testimony 1841–1985. *Social Sciences Quarterly*, 73(2), 296–309.

————, Li, X., and Segal, D. R. (1992). The role of women in the Chinese People's Liberation Army. In E. Sandschneider and J. Kuhlmann (Eds.), *Armed Forces in the USSR and the People's Republic of China*. Vol. 14, Munich: Forum International.

Seitz, B. (1991). Songs, identity and women's liberation in Nicaragua, *Latin American Music Review*, 12 (Spring/Summer), 21–42.

————. (January/February 1992). Report on a trip to Nicaragua, August 3–31, 1991. *Against the Current*, 9–12.

Sella, A. (1981). *Soviet Political and Military Conduct in the Middle East*. New York: St. Martin's.

————, and Yishai, Y. (1986). *Israel: The Peaceful Belligerent, 1967–1979*. New York: St. Martin's.

Sen, G., and Grown, K. (1987). *Development, Crises, and Alternative Visions: Third World Women's Perspectives*. Prepared for the project Development Alternatives with Women for a New Era (DAWN). New York: Monthly Review Press.

Shapiro, R., and Mahajan, H. (1986). Gender differences in policy preferences: A summary of trends from the 1960s to the 1980s. *Public Opinion Quarterly*, 50(1), 42–61.

Sharp, G. (1971). *Exploring Non-Violent Alternatives*. Boston: Porter Sargent.

Sherman, L. (1975). Evaluation of policewomen on patrol in a suburban police department. *Journal of Police Science Administration*, 3, 434–438.

Shlaim, A. (1976). Failures in national intelligence estimates: The case of the Yom Kippur War. *World Politics*, 28, 380.

Sichel, J., Friedman, L., Quint, J., and Smith, M. (1977). *Women on Patrol: A Pilot Study of Police Performance in New York City*. New York: Vera Institute of Justice.

Sikula, A. (1973). The uniqueness of secretaries as employees. *Journal of Business Education*, 48, 203–205.

Sinclair, B. (1991). Governing unheroically (and sometimes unappetizingly): Bush and the 101st Congress. In C. Campbell, S. J. Rockman, and B. A. Rockman (Eds.), *The Bush Presidency: First Appraisals*. Chatham, NJ: Chatham House.

Sisco, R. (1992). One year later: For some women, there's no going back. *The Minnesota Women's Press*, 7(22). St. Paul: Minnesota Women's Press.

Skogan, W., and Maxfield, M. (1981). *Coping with Crime*. Newbury Park, CA: Sage.

Smith v. City of East Cleveland, 363 F. Supp. 1131 (N.D. Ohio, 1973).

Smith, D. A., and Uchida, C. D. (1988). The organization of self-help: A study of defensive weapon ownership. *American Sociological Review*, 53, 94–102.

Smith, H. (1982). *Reason's Disciples: Seventeenth Century English Feminists*.

Urbana: Univ. of Illinois Press.

Smith, T. (1984). The polls: Gender and attitudes toward violence. *Public Opinion Quarterly, 48*(1), 384–396.

Smity v. *Troyan*, 520 F22 492 (6th Cir. 1975).

Smolowe, J. (1992). An officer, not a gentleman. *Time* (July 13), 36.

Snitow, A. (1989). A gender diary. In M. Harris and Y. King (Eds.), *Rocking the Ship of State: Toward a Feminist Peace Politics*, pp. 35–74. Boulder, CO: Westview Press.

South, J. S., Bongean, C. W., Markham, W. T., and Corder, J. (1982). Social structure and group interaction: Men and women of the federal bureaucracy. *American Sociological Review, 47*, 587–599.

Spangler, E., Gordon, M. A., and Pipkin, R. M. (1978). Token women: an empirical test of Kanter's hypothesis. *American Journal of Sociology, 84*, 160–170.

Spender, D. (1980). *Man-Made Language*. London: Routledge and Kegan Paul.

Stanko, E. A. (1987). Typical violence, normal precaution: Men, women and interpersonal violence in England, Wales, Scotland and the USA. In J. Hanmer and M. Maynard (Eds.), *Women, Violence and Social Control*, pp. 122–134. London: Macmillan.

Stanley, S. C., and Segal, M. W. (1988). Military women in NATO: An update. *Armed Forces and Society, 14*, 559–585.

———. (1992). Women in the armed forces. *International Military and Defense Encyclopedia*. Washington, DC: Pergamon-Brassey's.

Stanton, E. C. (1975). On the politics of woman suffrage. In A. F. Scott and A. M. Scott (Eds.), *One Half the People*. Urbana: Univ. of Illinois Press.

State Department: Minorities and Women are Underrepresented in the Foreign Service. (1989). Washington, DC: General Accounting Office.

Steel, B., and Lovrich, N. (1987). Equality and efficiency tradeoffs in affirmative action—real or imagined? The case of women in policing. *Social Science Journal, 24*, 53–70.

Stiehm, J. H. (1984). The man question. In J. H. Stiehm (Ed.), *Women's Views of the Political World of Men*, pp. 207–223. Dobbs Ferry, NY: Transnational Publishers.

———. (1989). *Arms and the Enlisted Woman*. Philadelphia: Temple Univ. Press.

Stoper, E., and Johnson, R. A. (1977). The weaker sex and the better half: The idea of women's moral superiority. *Polity, 10*(2), 192–217.

Switzer, T. (1992). Making "men," making war. *Changing Men, 24*, 48–49.

Sylves, R. T. (1987). *The nuclear oracles: A political history of the General Advisory Committee of the Atomic Energy Commission, 1947–1977*. Ames: Iowa State Univ. Press.

Tatalovich, R., and Daynes, B. W. (1984). *Presidential Power*. Pacific Grove: Brooks/Cole.

Tavris, C. (1991). The mismeasure of woman. In J. D. Goodchilds, *Psychological Perspectives on Human Diversity in America*. Washington, DC: American Psychological Association.

Taylor, S., and Epstein, S. (1967). Aggression as a function of the sex of the aggressor and the sex of the victim. *Journal of Personality, 35*, 473–486.

Tharoor, S. (1982). *Reasons of State: Political Development and India's Foreign Policy Under Indira Gandhi 1966–1977*. New Delhi: Vikas.

Thorne, B., and Luria, Z. (1986). Sexuality and gender in children's daily worlds. *Social Problems*, *33*(3), 176–190.

Tobias, S. (1990). Shifting heroisms: The uses of military service in politics. In J. B. Elshtain and S. Tobias (Eds.), *Women, Militarism and War*. Savage, MD: Rowman and Littlefield.

Tong, R. (1989). *Feminist Thought: A Comprehensive Introduction*. Boulder, CO: Westview Press.

Treadwell, M. (1954). *The Women's Army Corps*. Washington, DC: Office of the Chief of Military History.

Truslow, E. C., and Smith, R. C. (1961). *Manhattan District History: Project Y, the Los Alamos Project. LAMS-2532 Volume 11, August 1945 through December 1946*. Los Alamos, NM: Los Alamos Scientific Laboratory.

Tuten, J. M. (1982). The argument against female combatants. In N. L. Goldman (Ed.), *Female Soldiers—Combatants or Noncombatants?: Historical and Contemporary Perspectives*, pp. 237–265. Westport, CT: Greenwood Press.

Tyler, T. (1980). Impact of directly and indirectly experienced events: The origin of crime-related judgments and behaviors. *Journal of Personality and Social Psychology, 39*, 3–28.

Unterhalter, E. (1983). Women in struggle: South Africa. *Third World Quarterly, 5*(4), 886–913.

U.S. Bureau of the Census. (1979). *Statistical abstracts of the United States— 1979*. Washington, DC: U.S. Government Printing Office.

U.S. Department of Energy. (1982). *40th anniversary: The first reactor*. Washington, DC: U.S. Department of Energy.

U.S. Department of Labor. (1991). *A Report on the Glass Ceiling Initiative*. Washington, DC: U.S. Government Printing Office.

U.S. Department of State. (April 1991). *Multi-Year Affirmative Action Plan, FY 1990/1992*. Washington, DC: U.S. Department of State.

U.S. Government Manual. (1988/1989). Washington, DC: U.S. Government Printing Office.

Vallance, E. (1979). *Women in the House*. London: Athlone Press.

Van Arsdol, T. (1958) Radiation was novel, weird job experience. Part of a series of articles on "The City That Shook the World," published in the *Columbia Basin News*.

Walker, C. (1982). *Women and Resistance in South Africa*. London: Onyx Press.

Walker, S. (1977). *A Critical History of Police Reform: The Emergence of Professionalism*. Lexington, MA: Lexington Books.

———. (1992). *The Police in America*. New York: McGraw-Hill.

Waltz, K. (1979). *Theory of International Politics*. New York: Random House.

Waring, M. (1988). *If Women Counted: A New Feminist Economics*. San Francisco: Harper and Row.

Washburn P., and Gribbon, R. (1985). *Peacemaking Without Division*. Washington, DC: Alban Institute.

Washburn, P. (November 1990). No money for Gulf war. *Witness Magazine*.

Webb, J. (November 1979). Women can't fight. *Washingtonian*, 144–148, 273, 275, 278, 280, 282.

Weissberg, R. (1976). *Public Opinion and Popular Government*. Englewood Cliffs, NJ: Prentice-Hall.

Welch, S., and Thomas, S. (1988). Explaining the gender gap in British public opinion. *Women and Politics, 8*(3/4), 25–44.

Welch, S. (1990). *A Feminist Ethic of Risk*. Minneapolis: Fortress.

West, G., and Blumberg, R. L. (Eds.). (1990). *Women and Social Protest*. New

York: Oxford Univ. Press.

West, N. (1976). *Leadership with a Feminine Cast.* San Francisco: R and E Research Associates.

Westkott, M. (1979). Feminist criticism of the social sciences. *Harvard Educational Review, 49,* 421–439.

Westwood, S. (1984). *All Day, Every Day: Factory and Family in the Making of Women's Lives.* Urbana: Univ. of Illinois Press.

Wexler, J., and Logan, D. (1983). Sources of stress among women police officers. *Journal of Police Science and Administration, 11,* 46–53.

Whetton, L. L. (1974). *The Canal War: Four-Power Conflict in the Middle East.* Cambridge: MIT Press.

White v. Nassau County Police Department, 15 FED 261 (D. NY 1977).

White, C. (1870). *Ecce Femina: An Attempt to Solve the Woman Question.* Hanover, NH: Boston, Lee and Shepard.

White, T., and Bloch, P. (1975). *Police Officer Height and Selected Aspects of Performance.* Washington, DC: The Police Foundation.

WIIS (Women in International Security) Panel. (October 1991). *Women in the military: Experiences from the Gulf and Panama.* Washington, DC.

Williams, H., and Murphy, P. (1990). *The Evolving Strategy of Police: A Minority View.* Washington DC: U.S. Department of Justice.

Williams, J. S., Marolla, J. A., and McGrath, J. H. (1981). Firearms and urban American women. In M. Q. Warren (Ed.), *Comparing Female and Male Offenders.* Newbury Park, CA: Sage.

Williams, R. (1981). Legitimate and illegitimate uses of violence. In W. Gaylin, R. Macklin and T. Powledge (Eds.), *Violence and the Politics of Research,* pp. 23–45. New York: Plenum Press.

Wilson, J. S., and Serber, S. (Eds.). (1988). *Standing By and Making Do: Women of Wartime Los Alamos.* Los Alamos, NM: The Los Alamos Historical Society.

Wintersmith, R. (1974). *Police and the Black Community.* Lexington, MA: Lexington Press.

Wittkopf, E., and Maggiotto, M. (1983). Elites and masses: a comparative analysis of attitudes toward America's world role. *Journal of Politics, 45*(2), 303–333.

Wittkopf, E. (1987). Elites and masses: Another look at attitudes toward America's world role. *International Studies Quarterly, 31*(2), 153.

Wright, J. D., Rossi, P. H., and Daly, K. (1983). *Under the Gun: Weapons, Crime and Violence in America.* New York: Aldine de Gruyter.

Yeager, M. G. (1976). *How well does the handgun protect you and your family?* Washington, DC: U.S. Conference of Mayors.

Yoder, J. D., Crumpton, P. L., and Zipp, J. F. (1989). The power of numbers in influencing hiring decisions. *Gender and Society, 3*(2), 269–276.

Yost, E. (1959). Chien-Shiung Wu. In *Women of Modern Science,* pp. 80–93. New York: Dodd Mead.

Young, H. (1989). *The Iron Lady.* New York: Farrar, Straus and Giroux.

Younghusband, P. (September 24, 1983). Black women battle police near Cape Town. *The Globe and Mail,* 15.

Zimmer, L. (1987). How women reshape the prison guard role. *Gender and Society, 1*(4), 415–431.

Zimmerman, D. H., and West, C. (1975). Sex roles, interruptions, silences in conversation. In B. Thorne and N. Henley (Eds.), *Language and Sex.* Rowley, MA: Newbury House.

About the Authors

Nyla R. Branscombe is assistant professor of social psychology at the University of Kansas. Her research has focused on the influence of gender and racial stereotypes on attribution and other types of social judgments, particularly those centered on aggression and violence.

Frances G. Burwell is the acting executive director of the Center for International Security Studies at the University of Maryland, where she previously served as executive director of Women in International Security Studies. She holds an M.Phil. in international relations from Oxford University and is pursuing her Ph.D. in government and politics.

Jill M. Bystydzienski is associate professor of sociology at Franklin College of Indiana. She is the author of numerous articles on women in politics and in cross-cultural perspective. She has edited a book, *Women Transforming Politics: Worldwide Strategies for Empowerment,* and currently is working on a book about women and politics in Norway.

Berenice Carroll is professor of political science and director of the Women's Studies Program at Purdue University. She has published several books on women's studies and peace studies. She was a founding editor of *Peace and Change: A Journal of Peace Research* and a cofounder and former chairperson of the Consortium on Peace Research, Education, and Development.

Barbara Carson is assistant professor of sociology and corrections at Mankato State University. Her research is focused on how society legitimates violence and how this, in turn, perpetuates violence in society, particularly against women and children.

Nancy W. Gallagher is assistant professor of government at Wesleyan University, where she teaches courses on international relations and U.S. foreign policy. She is the author of several articles about South Asian security cooperation and is writing a book on the politics of arms control verification.

Barbara Welling Hall is associate professor of politics at Earlham College in Richmond, Indiana, where she teaches international relations with the former Soviet Union and feminist political theory.

Caroline L. Herzenberg is a physicist on the staff of Argonne National Laboratory, where she has worked on programs in fossil energy and nuclear reactor safety. She is the author of *Women Scientists from Antiquity to the Present* and past president of the Association for Women in Science. She is a fellow of the American Physical Society and the American Association for the Advancement of Science.

Ruth H. Howes is George and Frances Ball Distinguished Professor of Physics and Astronomy and director of the Center for Global Security Studies at Ball State University. Her research interests lie in the application of physics to such problems as arms control verification and energy policy.

Linda M. Lobao is associate professor of rural sociology at Ohio State University, where her areas of research are the sociology of economic change and political sociology. Her research on Latin America centers on women's political mobilization, and she is author of the recent book *Locality and Inequality*.

Patricia T. Morris is assistant professor of political science at Purdue University. Her research interests include women in development, women in international relations, international political economy, and the foreign policy of developing states.

Susan Owen is a doctoral candidate in social psychology at the University of Kansas. Her research concerns how stereotypes are activated in memory and their consequences for social judgment.

Jo A. Richardson is assistant professor of political science at Louisiana Tech University at Ruston, Louisiana. Her research interests include international relations and comparative politics, focusing particularly on Asia.

Meredith Reid Sarkees is associate professor of political science at Niagra University. She studies international relations and U.S. foreign policy and is coauthor of the forthcoming book *Women in Foreign Policy: The Insiders.*

Mady Wechsler Segal is professor of sociology and associate dean for undergraduate studies at the University of Maryland. She has published widely on military women and military families. She has also served as a member and chair of panels and committees in her area of research, including the Scientific Advisory Committee for the U.S. Army Research Institute's Army Family Research Program and the National Academy of Sciences Committee on the Performance of Military Personnel.

Barbara Seitz holds a Ph.D. in folklore and ethnomusicology from Indiana University. Her research area is the folklore and ethnomusicology of the women of Latin America, particularly women and identity as expressed in song and folklore. She has published numerous articles and several book chapters based on her fieldwork in western Nicaragua and among the Quicha-speaking indigenous women in the Ecuadorian Oriente.

Michael R. Stevenson is associate professor of psychological science at Ball State University, where he previously served as director of Women and Gender Studies. He is interested in the psychology of gender and the application of research findings to social problems.

Ellen Treadway is a doctoral student in curriculum studies with an emphasis in multicultural education at Indiana University. She holds an M.A. in Latin American Studies and has been active in the sister cities program in Nicaragua.

Patricia Washburn currently serves as program staff for the American Friends Service Committee in Denver and is an adjunct faculty member in justice and peace studies at Iliff School of Theology. Her professional career includes four years as public education staff for the National Peace Academy Campaign, director of the

Justice and Peace Program at the Earlham School of Religion, and cochair of the Consortium on Peace Research, Education and Development.

Participants in the Workshops

In addition to the authors of the chapters of this volume, the project has benefited from the input of the following participants in the workshops:

Steering Committee Members
    Gale Mattox, U.S. Naval Academy
    Marian Rice, Midwest Consortium for International Security
        Studies

Participants
    Stacy Bergstrom, University of Chicago
    Sandra Jones, Ohio State University
    Cynthia Watson, Loyola University
    Deborah Yarsike, University of Michigan
    Phyllis Zimmerman, Ball State University

Index

About the Book

With the active participation of women in the Gulf War, their role in mandating and implementing the use of military force has become a subject of heated debate. Clearly that role has changed—and expanded—greatly in the last decades. The policymaking establishment, though, continues to be predominantly male. And the obvious question remains: is there a fundamental difference in the way women and men utilize force and view its utilization on the international scale?

Responding to this question, the authors examine the theoretical approaches, particularly feminist approaches, to women's use of physical force and present data on the role women actually play in the use of force—in the uniformed military, in revolutionary struggles, in the policymaking establishment, in the development of nuclear weapons, and in shaping the peace movement. The editors conclude by assessing the likely effect of increasing numbers of women decisionmakers on U.S. national security policy.